DEDICATION

This book is dedicated to anyone who is searching for spiritual fulfillment. I sincerely hope you find it.

How to Choose a Church or Synagogue A Twenty-One Pew Adventure. Copyright 2006 by Ruth Laker. Manufactured in the United States of America. All rights reserved. No part of this book may be reproduced in any form or by any electronic or mechanical means including information storage and retrieval systems without permission in writing from the publisher, except by a reviewer, who may quote brief passages in a review. Published by Seven Stars Press P.O. Box 744, Kimberton, PA 19442. 1-610-917-3021. First Edition.

Visit sevenstarspress.com for more information about this book, the author and other products.

Laker, Ruth
    How to Choose a Church or Synagogue A Twenty-One Pew Adventure/ Ruth Laker–1st edition.
    ISBN 0-9772846-0-3
      1. Religious humor 2. Religious satire

    LCCN 2005909837

Edited by Gina Newman
Designed and Illustrated by Ruth Laker
Cover by Anne Fera
Printed by Alcom Printing Group, Inc.

How to Choose A Church or Synagogue:
A Twenty-One Pew Adventure

I. **Introduction**..	3
II. **Assembly of God**:	
Just Saying No to Sex With Animals.................................	8
III. **Conservative Jew**:	
Stoning Their Own.	24
IV. **Christian Scientist**:	
Waiting For Word From the Mother Ship.........................	39
V. **Roman Catholic**:	
Recruitment! Recruitment! Recruitment!.........................	55
VI. **Independent Baptist**:	
Taking the Name of Vegetables in Vain............................	67
VII. **Mennonite**:	
Praying for Relief From Constipation..............................	83
VIII. **Jehovah's Witnesses**:	
Speaking English?..	96
IX. **Quaker**:	
Oh So Very Quiet..	109
X. **African Methodist Episcopal**:	
Sacred Scatting..	115
XI. **Presbyterian**:	
Polishing Silver for God...	130
XII. **Church of the Nazarene**:	
Rearranging Deck Chairs on the Titanic...........................	143
XIII. **Methodist**:	
Talking Erotica at Eighty..	154
XIV. **Reformed Jewish**:	
Toras and Fashionistas...	173
XV. **Evangelical Lutheran**:	
Getting Radical When You Least Expect It.......................	185
XVI. **Mormon**:	
"Elders" with Pimples...	201
XVII. **Bible Fellowship**:	
Dreading the Apocalypse and President Hillary...............	220
XVIII. **Unitarian Universalist**:	
Dedicated to Avoiding the "G" Word................................	235
XIX. **Episcopalian**:	
Deacons and Sextons and Rectors, Oh My!	253

XX. **moviechurch.com:**
Worshiptainment for Short Attention Spans.................... 268
XXI. **United Church of Christ:**
Theatre *Is* Dead in Some Places.. 284
XXII. **The Chapel on the Hill:**
Shakin' It For Jesus.. 294

XXIII. **Conclusion:** 305

How To Choose a Church or Synagogue:
A Twenty-One Pew Adventure

Americans like church. We like it a lot. About a third of us attend church regularly, while many more are dabblers. We're nothing like those Godless French.

How do we come to pick a church or synagogue? We usually just choose the faiths in which we were raised.

Gandhi would see nothing wrong with this approach. His view: God is God and it doesn't really matter where you worship. Although many people in the world have tremendous respect for Gandhi and know of his great wisdom and kindness, what they generally *don't* know is that Gandhi had been suffering from a near-permanent loincloth wedgie which could occasionally cut off his circulation and impair his thinking.

Why on earth would you just walk into a house of worship because it's got the same name on the front sign as where your parents took you?! When you do this, you are committing what two cognitive researchers, Kitchener and King, call "pre-reflective thinking." In other words, you aren't thinking. I hate to be bursting bubbles, but some of our parents weren't always so bright.

Each generation, collectively, should get smarter than the one before them. In some ways we are: young people don't smoke in numbers like their grandparents or do drugs in numbers like their parents. We let women and minorities do things like vote, go to college and have radio talk shows. We monitor products and recall things that are dangerous. We've built handicapped ramps and put baby-locks on our cabinets and most of us slather on the sunscreen.

But in many ways we are not getting smarter: we are a fat nation, sucking on "Big Gulps," and "super-sizing" ourselves into obesity; we still hit our kids in the grocery store; we sexualize images of girls and women as the norm; we drive big vehicles that consume natural resources at an alarming rate and ensure that the Greenhouse Effect is no longer a theory; we allowed disco and polyester to come back a second time; and we take no time in selecting our religious practices–blindly doing what our parents and grandparents did before us.

Americans recognize the need for religion and for that we deserve kudos. People who belong to religious groups and believe in a loving God are both healthier and happier than those who do not. Churches and synagogues will always hold the promise of comfort in a chaotic world.

But Americans do not recognize the need, as adults, to look around for a place of worship. You wouldn't just buy the first house you look at, would you? No–you'd want to see what kind of special features each has, what the neighbors and neighborhood is like, compare prices and think about if it will fit with your current needs and lifestyle.

It should be the same with your house of worship.

This book offers an example of what that process of shopping around is like. You, the reader, are about to embark on a journey with one person as she demonstrates the kind of critical consuming, the savvy shopping, the quizzical questions one must ask as they look for a spiritual home.

Here is a very simple and effective action plan for selecting a church: 1) Go to as many churches as possible before settling on any one. Plan to take at least six months, if not a year, and 2) rate the church or synagogue on twelve simple questions after each visit.

In order to make this selection process as complete as possible, you must try your hardest to set aside biases and prejudices and go to as many different places as possible. Go everywhere you can–that means *everywhere*. Don't pass by the places with weird names, the buildings that are suspect, the groups you always heard your aunt condemning, or the places that seem like private country clubs. Roll up your sleeves and get in there. Boldly go where you never thought you'd go before!

On this journey, you will experience Judeo-Christian places of worship, because that is a big enough realm for your guide. Some of you may choose to broaden your search with an even wider scope: you may go Hindu, Muslim and Buddhist, too. That's great! If you feel moved to explore as far as you can go to find the place that's right for you, do it!

No church or synagogue is above some basic assessment. These assessments will be those of your author, and yours will be yours. And of course, not all churches of one denomination will be the same across this great nation of ours. Each church will differ as much as the individual people within it. There is no absolute right or wrong in this approach. It's about finding out what's right or wrong for *you*. There's only one way that you can mess this up, and that is to just keep doing what you've always done without spending some time seeing what your options are and thinking for yourself.

If you already have a church, or you don't have the time to go to lots of different places, here's your chance to see what really goes on inside other churches and synagogues—without even having to get out of your pajamas.

In this book, you will taste a Whitman's Sampler of actual churches and synagogues. Although all identifying names of people and places have been changed, everything else is entirely true down to the smallest detail.

How To Use the Rating Scale

After you've visited each place, you will rate a dozen different questions on a scale of 1-10, one being the lowest rating you can give, and ten being the highest. You will develop your own twelve questions, based on what is important to you. For example, it might be important to you that the place where you worship is aesthetically pleasing, so you would include as one of your twelve items: "How beautiful is the worship space?" Then you'd rate each church or synagogue on that dimension, on a scale of one to ten. If you thought a particular place was a vile, festering, hell hole, you would give it a one. If it's magnificence took your breath away and left you grasping for the back of pews to steady yourself, you'd give it a ten.

Here are the twelve items which will be used by your guide and author, based on what is important to her in a church experience:

1) Is parking close and convenient?
2) How beautiful is the worship space?
3) How comfortable is the seating?
4) How welcoming and friendly is the congregation?
5) How enjoyable and uplifting are the musical aspects of the worship?
6) Does the leader have a pleasant speaking voice and does he/she make sense to me?
7) How clean are the bathrooms?
8) Are the people in the pews interesting to stare at?
9) How tolerant to many ways of seeing and doing things does this group appear to be?
10) Would I feel good about how these people would spend my money?
11) How close did I feel to God in this place?
12) Did I smile more than once during the experience?

Again, you should come up with your own twelve items based on what is important to you. You might be interested in "spreading the good news," doing things for others, or meeting new people. It's totally up to you.

The most important aspect of your rating system is that it be standardized, in other words, the same for all places you visit. So figure out your items and stick with them.

Make a copy of the rating form below and take it with you to each place.

Let's jump in!

	Dimension of Church Experience	Rating
1)		
2)		
3)		
4)		
5)		
6)		
7)		
8)		
9)		
10)		
11)		
12)		
	Total	

Assembly of God

Although one should plan to go into each church or temple with a clean slate, I will admit that, for me, it is a bit difficult to put aside all preconceived notions when it comes to the Assembly of God.

A Hungarian cousin of mine, a young lad of seventeen, just finished an exchange program in the United States so that he could learn English and eventually take over the family business. His first choices of places to live in the U.S. were California and New York City–you know–fun, happenin' spots where seventeen-year-old boys want to be.

He was assigned to a family in Shrevesport, Louisiana.

Tomika had no idea what he was getting into, poor guy, and he ended up spending nine months in a state of semi-bondage with a very religious family, having to attend Assembly of God services and Bible study three times a week, and being routinely harassed by his host mother to try to speak in tongues. He was barely getting a grasp on English and she was introducing a competing, non-Latin-based language.

Other things from his host family could ultimately be tolerated: their continual berating of his customs and behaviors; blocking the refrigerator so he couldn't get ketchup to put on his pizza; stealing his credit card and charging porn website use to it. But this continual pressure to speak in tongues seemed a bit over the top.

When we picked Tomika up at the airport after his nine months of confinement, he was wearing an over-sized T-shirt hanging to his knees, with the words "I AM A MESSENGER OF THE GOSPEL OF JESUS CHRIST" boldly proclaimed on the front. A normally inquisitive and hearty young man, Tomika looked battered and weary. He was going to spend a week with my family before going back to Hungary, but after what he had been through, we were amazed he hadn't swam back to Budapest months before.

Still, it is critical to remain open to all churches, and so on a beautiful, late spring morning in June, I head into the Cattaragus Assembly of God Church in western New York state. A simple wooden building resembling a large, one-room schoolhouse, this church does not suffer from "keeping up with the Catholics," when it comes to their building and adornments.

A few young couples are gathering in the entrance hall, which leads directly to a pair of basic wood doors with small windows in each. Presumably, the sanctuary is just beyond those doors. There is a literature table in the hallway to peruse. My eyes scan the offerings: *Following Jesus: A 30-Day Bible Reading Guide from The Gospel of Mark; New Believer Classes; The Importance of Prayer in Jewish Life and Worship*....odd, about the Jewish part...here is one that simply must be read: *The Assemblies of God-Our Distinctive Doctrine*.

I am about to go in, find a seat and do a little reading before the service, when a young man and woman stop and introduce themselves. They are very friendly and make me feel as though I am the most fascinating person they have ever laid eyes on.

I tell them I am a visitor, and have relatives in Cattaragus.

They are so glad I came.

"You can come and sit with us," the young woman, Theresa, offers. She says it so innocently and openly...as though we were all third-graders heading to the lunch tables and I am the new kid on my first day.

"Oh, I usually look for that one spot that feels just right, but I thank you."

I feel kind of bad afterward, but I know I'll have to talk to them, and I want to be more of a participant-observer than an outright member of the fold.

In the sanctuary, an adult Sunday school class is still going on. Only about a dozen people are scattered about the room, while a man who is the spitting image of Ned Flanders of the Simpsons--*spitting*, in voice, hair, glasses and bushy moustache-- carries on enthusiastically about Christian child-rearing, despite his small audience. His Hawaiian shirt bespeaks a certain casual approach to both his parenting practices and his role as a Christian moderator.

Ned, as I'll call him, is sharing stories about his own frustration with the messes his son makes around his wood shop, and his students chuckle appreciatively.

A stout African-American man raises his hand.

"Yes, Ron?" Ned calls on him.

"When I think of parenting, I think of REP. The "R" is gettin' em' ready for life, the "E" is equipin' the child for life, and the "P" is preparin' 'em for life...an everythin'..."

Ned nods readily. "Yeah–in athletic training, you're doing "reps"...that's beautiful! "

Not being one to pump iron regularly, I'm losing interest in this discussion and start to take in the room.

It's rather grim, I have to say.

The walls are half-paneled and the chairs, arranged in a semi-circle, are bright red. Under all of this lies a brown carpet. The effect on the space is dark on the bottom, lighter on top, like a cherry meringue pie hugged by a graham cracker crust. There really is no altar or pulpit to speak of; the front of the room is more like a...front of a room. "Mighty, Awesome, Wonderful God" surrounds a small, projected image of clouds on the upper part of the wall. Underneath are some big, blue foil stars, like what you might see at an elementary school tribute to our great nation. Floral balloon valences sit atop each slender window, which look almost like rectangular portholes amidst the wooden planks of the original ark.

I'm relieved to realize that this isn't the real service, but only the pre-show activities.

The literature beckons.

One pamphlet, about the Cattaragus Church itself, has this message: "If you would like to be a member or be baptized in water or any other questions that you might have, stop by and see our Pastor, Jim Duncan."

Hmm. Someone forgot to consult their Strunk and White, *Essentials of Grammar,* before they composed that sentence.

And what else would one be baptized in if not water? Jello?

The information on the perspectives of the Assemblies of God Church needs to be read, in order for me to make the most informed decision about where to worship. They have views on just about everything from suicide to genetic alteration, and it seems that they are particularly unhappy about pornography and abortion. I'm not in major serious disagreement with anything I'm reading, but I do become a bit confounded by the following: "...yet in some infrequent cases saving the life of the child or the mother might mean the death of the other...if after prayer for God's intervention, the problem is not resolved, consultation with attending pro-life physicians and your pastor will help in arriving at the proper conclusion."

Reading this, for some reason, brings to mind my friend Maria's intensely pro-life Italian grandfather, whom I once saw pouring scalding water from a tea kettle onto an ant hill in his back yard.

I like the sentiments against genetic alteration and cloning, because quite frankly, that stuff scares the hell out of me. But--and maybe this is just me-- their rationale might come up a bit short: *"Job declared that God gave life and He ended it (Job 1:21)."*

And that's that, I guess.

This is what they have to say on the mixing of animal and human cells: *"Exodus 22:19, Leviticus 18:23 and 20:15, 16 and Deuteronomy*

27:21 order death as the penalty for humans and animals that engage in mutual sexual intercourse."

Doesn't "mutual" mean, like, "consensual?" When, and perhaps more importantly, *how* would an animal give their consent for sexual intercourse?

There's more: *"The thought is repulsive and the death penalty could have been ordered because of the social stigma. But God may also have forbidden the practice because of genetic complications that could have resulted."*

Now there's a slippery slope: God *may* have meant this....or He *may* have meant that... Only the truly ballsy will go out on a limb to say what God *may* have meant.

I'm about to dive into the section on "AIDS/HIV: Is It God's Judgment?" when someone walks into the back of the room and calls out a full-bodied "HALLELUIA!"

I turn and look. It's a very handsome man, maybe in his late thirties, with a blond buzzcut, pearly white, straight teeth and a nicely sculpted body, as though he did his "REPS" all the time. He is wearing tightish pants and a khaki shirt with the sleeves rolled up part way. On his feet are caramel-colored cowboy boots. He radiates something from the moment he bounds into the room, although I don't have a handle yet on what that something exactly is.

He shakes hands with people behind me, and then he is beside me in a flash.

"Hi, welcome! It's nice to meet you, I'm Pastor Jim!"

My response sounds so flat next to his zestfulness. "Ruth Laker...I'm visiting relatives in the area."

"Glad to have you," he says jauntily, then moves on.

Pastor Jim starts shaking hands liberally and slapping backs. He bounces up and down entertainingly on the balls of his feet. Then it becomes clear as to what his aura is all about: "It's show time, folks!" Pastor Jim is on.

With one arm, Pastor J. straps on a guitar, while his other arm is reaching over to a laptop computer and typing in some commands.

A circle of people pray in the front, holding hands. Pastor Jim joins them. Then they break ranks and each goes to a musical instrument or grabs a big, bulky microphone. There is a drummer, bass guitarist, Pastor Jim on lead guitar, and four singers: two women and two men. The two women are at center stage and definitely seem to be more into working the crowd than the two men who stand off to the side, shyly clutching their mics close to their chest.

Everyone stands as Pastor Jim begins to strum his guitar energetically. By this time, the room has come alive with bodies, and more than a hundred people have made their way into the sanctuary. Lyrics appear, projected on to the wall in front by some Divine Force it would seem. Everyone starts to sing:

> *River of God flow through me*
> *Fire of God consume me*
> *Holy Spirit fill me, fill me*
> *River of God flow through me*
> *Fire of God consume me*
> *Holy Spirit come....*

Now this part I really like. I love music and everyone seems so relaxed...we're all just singin...singin in the church...

Some people lift their arms up toward the ceiling, and I'm presuming they mean to connect with Something even beyond that. Some people only lift one arm. I decide to try it out, it looks very inviting. I try the one arm first, very awkwardly and self-consciously, I'm sure. Even despite my awkwardness, something doesn't feel right. I try lifting both arms up...yes....yes...this is much better. Of course, you are a little exposed and vulnerable in the posture--and you certainly want to be sure you used your speed stick--but it feels much more balanced doing it with two hands. When you only have the one hand up, it's like you're only getting partial reception.

In between songs, the music doesn't really end. Pastor Jim keeps strumming, and the women keep singing, but all of a sudden, they've broken up as a unit, and everyone is just kind of free-associating for a few minutes. All around me, I hear people hissing. It starts to give me the creeps until I realize that they're just saying, "yesssss......yessssss, Jesussss." But it's everywhere, this hissing: "yesssss......yesssss.......yessssss..."

As we move through a few more songs, I get to experience a really fun feature of Assembly of God worship: a lot of the songs have neat little hand motions that go with the words, so we get to do them altogether, like on Miss Sally's Romper Room. When we sing, "Shout to the north and the south, sing to the east and the west," everyone points in those four directions, respectively. Then we swing our arms back and forth in the air as we finish: "Jesus is Savior to all, Lord of heaven and earth."

There are other really cool features of the music: men and women sing their own parts, we echo each other, we actually shout when we sing the word "shout."

As the music winds down, the clapping gears up. Everyone is hissing again and the clapping intensifies. There's a lot of electricity and excitement in the air, and I look around just in case some really important deceased religious figure might walk through the back doors.

Pastor Jim yells, "IT IS SO GREAT TO BE IN THE HOUSE OF THE LORD!"

The crowd yells, "AMEN!"

Pastor Jim pulls off his guitar and grabs his microphone. He walks toward the crowd. "WHO DESERVES THE HONOR?!"

"JESUS!"

"WHO DESERVES THE PRAISE?!"

"JESUS!"

"WHO DESERVES THE GLORY?!"

"JESUS!"

As this dialogue is unfolding, I happen to glance at the woman next to me. She is looking in a lipstick mirror—you know, those narrow, lip-shaped little mirrors—as she mumbles her "Jesus," "Jesus," "Jesus," her lips moving fish-like as she speaks. I'm not sure if she's studying something about her lips, or using the mirror to repeal evil, or what.

"We worship you, we worship you, we worship you, we worship you..."

Pastor Jim is into that whole repetition thing.

"Everybody grab hands...grab the hand of your neighbor...let's pray together!"

I take the hand of the lip woman to my left. I'm by the aisle, so I figure I'm off the hook with my other hand, but then I notice that everyone has joined all hands, creating a snakelike chain throughout the room. I turn behind me and see a woman standing next to a mentally disabled man in a wheelchair. She smiles at me and I reach out my hand to her.

As we start to pray, I relax into the feeling of all this hand-holding. It's not bad. No, not bad at all. I actually like it.

"Lift your hands up into the air!"

Oh, dear. Now this part I'm not liking as much. It's okay for the first fifteen seconds, but Pastor Jim is a loquacious fellow and my arms are tiring quickly, not being one to do reps and all. The prayer just keeps going on and on. Through squinted eyes, I see a few others in the sanctuary dropping their arms. Senior citizens, most of them. I can't drop my arms now...I have to wait until at least one other middle-aged person drops them first.

Thankfully, the young woman next to me tires and drops hers. I start to let my right arm fall slightly, sort of a little signal to the woman behind me, but she doesn't drop. She's holding on tight...a real stalwart in this prayer business. By the time the prayer ends, she's been holding up her arm and mine too. She gives my hand two good pumps of encouragement before letting go.

"HUG YOUR NEIGHBOR!! Tell them, 'I LOVE you!'"

Oh Jeez. Wasn't the hand holding enough?

I turn awkwardly to Ms. Fishlips. We embrace stiffly. She mutters, "I love you."

I try to say "I love you," but it doesn't come out. Instead I say, "Good morning."

"Good morning?" This poor woman musters up the courage to tell me that she loves me, and I respond with *"Good morning?"*

Why didn't I just say, "Stocks were trading high when the market closed," or "Please step away from my body."

"The children have a special presentation to make for Father's Day!" Pastor Jim tells us. "Trudy, you wanna call those kids up here?"

A heavy set woman wearing a long, bright floral skirt, wobbles toward the front of the sanctuary and motions for the children. "I don't know if it's a 'presentation,' but we'll git up here and do somethin'...I'm not sure just what!" Trudy shakes her head, at herself it seems.

A group of a dozen or so young people from ages three to eighteen assemble in front of the congregation. Trudy conducts them with a one-two-three.

"Happy Father's Day," they say, rather subdued.

The room is quiet. Trudy turns toward us. "That's it," she declares.

A few people in the room laugh, but most of us aren't sure what to do.

Trudy laughs, again, seemingly to herself. "Just kidding!" She turns to the group and gives them a one-two-three again.

The group begins to sing:

> *Jesus loves me this I know,*
> *For the Bible tells me so,*
> *Little ones to Him belong,*
> *They are weak but He is strong.*
> *Yes, Jesus loves me,*

Yes, Jesus loves me,
Yes, Jesus loves me,
The Bible tells me so.

I know we're supposed to be touched by the display, but I have to admit that when you've heard a song nearly as much as you've heard "Hotel California," it's hard to be moved by the tune. It's also questionable how extensive or even present the music program is at this particular church.

"Who wants to say something to their Dad?" Pastor Jim urges the group. He bounds to the music stand where there's a microphone and brings it to the group. He waves the mic in front of them, trying to entice them, not unlike the Child Catcher with his big lollipop in *"Chitty Chitty Bang Bang."*

Finally, one teenage boy, about seventeen or so, takes the microphone. The congregation claps enthusiastically, whooping and cheering.

When the crowd settles down, the lad speaks quietly, looking directly toward one man, sitting off to the side. "I'd like to thank you Dad, for everything you do for me...for getting up and going to work everyday...for always being there for me." There is a second of hushed reverence and I feel a tear well up in me.

"LET'S GIVE HIM A HAND!!" Pastor Jim yells, shattering the hush.

After the clapping dies down, our shepherd asks: "Who's got a testimonial?!"

I squirm slightly. This wasn't going to be one of those kind of places where I get pushed to the front of the room by a half-crazed crowd, cheering and clapping for me to tell them about how I found Jesus in the bottom of my toilet while I was hung over the bowl throwing up from another night of binge drinking...was it?

Lots of hands fly into the air, mostly those of men. Pastor Jim calls on a man standing in the back of the room, right near the double doors. He has a very pronounced belly, perfectly shaped like a large bowling ball hanging in a sack. "Earl?"

"Yeah. I was drivin' home the other night...I've been pullin' a lot of twelve hour shifts lately...and I'm goin' around this curve where there's this big ditch and all of a sudden my car is off the road and I see this telephone pole comin' right at the side of my car."

Gasps come from the room.

"I holler 'Help me Jesus!'....and my car bounces right out of the ditch and back on to the road." Earl says this last part with an understated, matter-of-fact quality in his voice.

People in the room "oh" and "ah." Many shake their heads and marvel that Earl warded off such an evil, and with a mere cry to Jesus for help.

"I mean I've been drivin' that road my whole life, and I've never gone in that ditch before. After he helped me, I heard Jesus say, 'I helped you, now what are you gonna do for me?' And I mean to tell you, if it weren't for Jesus, I'm not sure I'd be standin' here right now."

"Let's bestow our blessings on Earl, everyone." All the people turn in their seats toward the back of the room, and all hands reach out toward Earl, as though he's Hitler and we're all "Heiling" him. Pastor Jim goes on. "Heavenly Father, we thank you for keeping Brother Earl safe from harm and for delivering him to us here today. We ask that you continue to bless him and keep him safe in your care. Amen."

Another man shares how he miraculously caught the bus to church.

Then Pastor Jim calls on a man in the second row, and the crowd, collectively, goes "oh-oh." That can't be a good sign.

This man was already legendary to me as the guy who yelled the loudest in response to the preacher's exhortations and comments. In fact, one could even say he was competing with the good Pastor for the part of "Chief Charismatic." When Pastor Jim declared, "HE'S ALWAYS THERE TO TAKE CARE OF YOU!!" this man yelled out *"ALL THE TIME!!"* When Pastor Jim called on Jesus to save us, this man yelled even louder, *"SAVE US! SAVE US!"*

The man, who was identified as "Chuck," turned toward the group with great aplomb, and said, "Okay" as though he was settling in for a long-winded tale, only for us, it was going to be a long winter's nap, you could tell already.

Chuck starts to deliver a mini-sermon/story about a double date he went on and how they all ended up at a Korean prayer meeting. They didn't understand the Korean, but then the miraculous occurred: a woman who spoke both Korean *and* English came over and translated the basic message of the sermon to them–that "our hearts are a desert and only the living waters can satisfy it." I'm giving you the abridged version–the full length story went on for what felt like the time it would take to make passage *through a* desert.

In retrospect, I do see that the basic experience was kind of neat, but Chuck had that annoying habit of over-dramatizing his delivery, which generally causes an audience to tune out. I never quite understood why that was so until I had to sit, a captive on my big red cherry chair, listening to this histrionic man waving his hands about. But I figured it out. This is why the overly dramatic ultimately turn you away: it just takes too much energy to listen. And after awhile, you start to wonder if the speaker even needs you to be there in order to carry on.

I try to tune Chuck out by looking around and studying my fellow parishioners. I have to say that what comes to mind for me is Rudolph's Island of Misfit Toys. Never before have I seen such a motley crew assembled in a church: People Of The Odd Eye Contact; The Unusually Shapen; Those Who Are Not Fleet of Foot. One of the truly cool things about Jesus' ministry as I understand it is that Jesus was really about the poor and down and out. That is where he liked to hang and those are the people who are most holy in his eyes. If that is true, than there is more Jesus in this room than anywhere I can imagine.

Back at the ranch, Chuck is still going on. "...you know, Koreans are a *conservative* bunch..." He chuckles and the one person who is still listening chuckles also. "They don't get excited like we do...but after the sermon, the Holy Spirit *really* showed up ...they got excited, completely....praising the Lord in *tongues* ....and then things went from ear-deafening to silence! Just like that. And what was really amazing was that a woman came up and said she was interested in learning more about our congregation, so it was by divine appointment that we ended up there."

If this had been a lecture hall, or a PTA meeting, or even a conversation around the kitchen table with a neighbor's new boyfriend, I would have had to have asked any number of questions of Chuck, like: Is the Holy Spirit around only if you're jumping and clapping hysterically? And, how can you tell when a group of people who speak Korean are speaking in tongues? Or, is it more God's will that those Korean people switch over to your church, than remain in their own?

I opt not to raise my hand and get into it with Chuck. He's just so full of it (the Holy Spirit, that is) that I'd rather not tread there.

FIN-ally, Chuck is finished!

Another man with an ample belly like Earl's starts to walk forward from the back of the church. The pastor again, says "Oh-oh. Here's another one I've got to try to hold down!"

Great. I mean I want to give every church a fair shake, and I know we haven't even gotten to the sermon, but I've already been sitting here for ninety minutes at this point, and if this guy is anything like Chuck, I may just have to exit, or run the risk that I'll jump up from my chair and start screaming "GET TO THE POINT! GET TO THE POINT, FOR *GOD'S SAKE* MAN!!"

And that wouldn't be polite.

Burt, as he is called, expertly takes the microphone from the minister and asks his wife to come forward and join him. I have to stifle a smile at the way this regular Joe comes forward and pushes the minister right out of the way.

A tiny Asian-American woman with a small but sincere smile comes forward and stands by Burt. I'm thinking Korean war bride, but then what do I know. Burt puts his arm around her. "This lady and I celebrated our 47-year anniversary last night...47 years!"

Everyone claps and calls out their congratulations.

"I want to tell you that everything I am I am because of her...I wouldn't be nothin' without her...she gave me five kids, fourteen grandkids and seven great-grandchildren...and I just want to say how happy I am to have been with her all these years...and I'd like to ask Pastor to pray for us."

Pastor Jim lays his hands on the couple and says some words of tribute. It's all very touching. It would have been nice to hear what she had to say, but no one stopped to ask her and she didn't reach for the microphone like her good husband. I took the smile on her face to mean that it had all been pretty nice for her too. And if Burt was a wife-beating alcoholic who sodomized sheep, no one ever would have guessed by that little Mona Lisa curl in her lips.

These moments with the people are really kind of nice, for the most part. Folksy. That's how I would describe the Assembly of God experience so far.

We hear two more testimonials and I notice that the woman with the fishlips sitting next to me has had her hand up for some time now. Pastor Jim seems to keep passing her by, kind of like a teacher who just doesn't want to deal with a troublesome student. Finally, there are no more hands raised and he calls on her. "Yes, Tina?"

Tina stands up and I get a chance to see her fully. She's very unique looking: wide and ruddy-faced, her bleached yellow hair is clipped up loosely to the back of her head and the ends stick out, bringing to mind a pineapple. Her upper body is slight but it opens out to a very rotund mid-section which is accentuated by the tight, long T-shirt she is wearing over a cream-colored jean skirt. Her naked legs bow out from the knees and on her feet are some old, well-worn simple white sneakers with no socks. She speaks but makes eye contact with no one. Her words are lisped and she sounds slightly drugged. "I just want to say a prayer for the fathers who are not here...like my father...he's somewhere in Florida right now...I don't know where...but I know he's still in recovery...but I remember some good times with him...they weren't all bad...yep...some of them weren't so bad....I wish he were at my doorstep right now..."

"That's a very good point indeed–let's remember the fathers who aren't here," Pastor Jim interjects quickly. Tina sits down as bluntly as she first stood up.

"Everyone hold up your Bible!" Pastor Jim instructs.

Testimonial time must be over.

"Repeat after me: THIS IS MY BIBLE!"

"THIS IS MY BIBLE!"

"I *AM* WHAT IT SAYS I *AM*!"

"I AM WHAT IT SAYS I AM!"

"I *DO* WHAT IT SAYS I *DO!*"

"I DO WHAT IT SAYS I DO!"

"I *GO* WHERE IT SAYS I *GO!*"

"I GO WHERE IT SAYS I GO!"

I'm not able to participate in this part of the service because 1) I don't have a Bible, and 2) It scares me. Although I know I'm not a Bible scholar, I've read enough of it to be somewhat concerned about what Pastor Jim is asking me to say. I mean, the Bible indicates that God could, at any time, ask us to sacrifice our children, or that He might kill them off totally in a game with the Devil, or command us to extinguish entire populations of people so that our chosen group can move in.

At any rate, now I'm starting to squirm.

"I BOLDLY CONFESS HIS TRUTH!! MY MIND IS ALERT!! I'LL NEVER BE THE SAME! NEVER! NEVER! NEVER! IN JESUS NAME!!

One gets the feeling that Pastor Jim thinks that God is both deaf and slow to comprehend.

I try to imagine needing to yell like that when I was a professor and what kind of energy it would have taken to sustain that. A Human Development lecture could have exhausted me within minutes: "IN PREINDUSTRIAL SOCIETIES MOST CHILDREN WERE INTEGRATED DIRECTLY INTO MOST ADULT ACTIVITIES! UP UNTIL THE TWENTIETH CENTURY THERE WERE FEW DIFFERENCES IN LAWS FOR TEENS AND ADULTS!"

Pastor Jim now wheels a pulpit to the middle of the floor in the front of the room and attaches his microphone. He's very handy with the portable pulpit.

"I want to read you some emails that I received from some children this week." Now his mood is more subdued, but somewhat breezy, too. "God is like *Scotch-ed tape*...you can't see Him but He's still there..."

The crowd laughs, more than I think the joke warranted.

"God is like Coke—He's the *real thing!*"

They laugh *and* clap for that one.

"God is like VO5 Hairspray...gee, do they still have VO5...they do?....all right, well, God is like VO5 Hairspray—He holds together in all kinds of weather..."

How would children know about VO5 if it didn't still exist?

"God is like Dial soap—aren't you glad you have Him...don't you wish *everybody* did?"

They go nuts for that one.

"PICK UP YOUR BIBLES AGAIN! Turn to Malachi...Chapter 4....I want to talk right into the hearts of the fathers. Did you know that the Midwest states are being taken over by grasshoppers? Do you understand that God is trying to *get your attention*? It's Father's Day...we should have more fathers in church today than any other day...it's not a day to *'take off'*....shalia baliant cumia...HERE IS THE WORD IN MALACHI... *'And he shall turn the heart of the fathers to the children, and the heart of the children to their fathers, lest I come and smite the earth...with a **CURSE!**'"

Well, I'm figuring that we're into the sermon...finally. I glance at the clock on the back wall. I've been sitting here now for an hour and forty-five minutes. This sounds to be mighty entertaining, if not necessarily steeped in sound theology. And hey, I think I just heard my first official speaking of the tongues slipped in there by our good pastor.

Pastor Jim's voice gets very low and serious. He's very quixotic with his moods, this young man. "This generation is being raised in fatherless homes. We can have sex, do the 'fun thing,' and not be committed. Dad is not around ..doesn't want to take responsibility...she can get an abortion because it's the right thing to do...Well, God wants you to hear..."

He pounds the microphone against his chest, making a very dramatic beating sound.

"...the word of God. We in America allow the media to seduce us...it will all stop when fathers rise up and be men of God. It will stop when men get the heartbeat (again he pounds his mic against his chest) of the Father."

Well, I think I've heard enough. Pastor Jim's use of the Kansas grasshopper infestation as a curse from God for deadbeat dads is just too much of a stretch for me. Unless the Midwest is some type of hiding place that I didn't know about, where father's flee when they don't want to own up to their children, his reasoning is not particularly sound. More likely they're all down in Florida with Tina's Dad...I hear a lot of ne'er-do-wells go there because they don't have to pay for heat.

It's time for me to go. I need to leave this Assembly of God church. My daughter is at her grandparents sitting in front of the television and I'm starting to feel like a deadbeat mom.

The Assembly of God: entertaining, but is it the place for me? I guess I'll have to wait and see what else is out there.

Assembly of God

#	Dimension of Church Experience	Rating
1)	Is parking close and convenient?	8
2)	How beautiful is the worship space?	1
3)	How comfortable is the seating?	5
4)	How welcoming and friendly is the congregation?	5
5)	How enjoyable and uplifting are the musical aspects of the worship?	5
6)	Does the leader have a pleasant speaking voice and does he/she make sense to me?	1
7)	How clean are the bathrooms?	3
8)	Are the people in the pews interesting to stare at?	10
9)	How tolerant to many ways of seeing and doing things does this group appear to be?	1
10)	Would I feel good about how these people would spend my money?	1
11)	How close did I feel to God in this place?	2
12)	Did I smile during the experience?	4
	Total	46

KING DAVID'S KORNER BOUTIQUE

Conservative Jewish Synagogue

On the whole, Jewish people fascinate me. I guess you could call me a Jewish "wannabe" in some ways. They seem to be a very well-grounded people–they know who they are. Perhaps because they are always getting thrown out of places, they need to carry a strong sense of their culture with them.

Ever notice that you don't hear much about Jewish people when it comes to crime and the seedier aspects of human behavior? Have you come across any of these headlines lately: "NEW NIMH STUDY INDICATES THAT 80% OF DRUG ADDICTS ARE JEWISH." Or, "DOMESTIC VIOLENCE AND SPORTS RAGE HIGHEST AMONG JEWS." Or, "RADICAL JEWS LINKED TO BOMBINGS AT WOMEN'S CLINICS."

Chances are you haven't seen anything remotely like that. Sure, there are the occasional outliers, like the local Rabbi who had his wife killed so he could be with his stripper mistress, but on the whole, it's as if Jewish people are simply too sensible for lives of crime.

I check out the yellow pages to see what time the services start at the local synagogue. I would have called a Jewish friend to see when they started, but I realize that I have only one Jewish friend, locally, and she's not the synagogue type. She's more the I'm-going-to-hang-out-on-South-Street-all-night-with-my-latest-Latino-musician-boyfriend-who-is-great-in-bed-and-then-sleep-all-day type. That is something I need to amend, I tell myself. Not that I need a Latino boyfriend, but that I need to make more Jewish friends.

A flabby-sounding man's voice on the answering machine of the synagogue, indicates that they have a Friday night service at 8, and a Saturday morning service at 9:30. Oh yeah, everything holy happens early in the weekend if you're a Jew. If you're one of those types who like to get your religious stuff out of the way, it's choice.

I opt to go to the Saturday morning service, so at 9:15, I find myself meandering around B'Nai Brith, looking for a parking space. Already it's easy to feel inadequate; those who are parking their cars are dressed to the nines. I'm in a Goodwill summer skirt, a simple white blouse and open-toed sandals. My hair is frizzy except for the streaks where I haphazardly wet it down. Everyone else is wearing designer suits–men and women–and have perfectly coiffed hair. Few people are revealing their toes.

And can we talk cars? Without exception, every automobile looks as if it was just driven off the showroom floor and straight to the service. Brand new, spotlessly clean Passants, Jeeps and SUVs of every kind are lined up beside the synagogue. The Jewish car of choice appears to be the Acura, and many older couples are neatly removing seatbelts and craning themselves out of smooth leather seats, as I pull my fourteen-year-old Volvo station wagon with the broken hatch, no air conditioning and no radio into a space of shame on a side street.

Making my way to the front door, I pass a group of parishioners who look as though they are there for a wedding. The front doors are locked, so I stand waiting. The other worshipers come up the steps, also to wait, and snippets of their Jewish conversation wash over me:

"Have you been to the Crispy Cone restaurant? It's new. Adam Potashkin was there and I hear they've got great ice cream and good service."

"...we were in Israel this time last year...but I'm glad not to go back, not this year. It's too hot!"

"Were you there with your sister at the concert? Oh, it was lovely, wasn't it?"

"...here comes the Rabbi...he's got the key I think...Good Sabbath!"

The Rabbi is an older man, maybe in his late fifties, who has a bushy beard and a very nifty looking plaid yarmulke. He walks past the small group on the landing near the double doors.

"You could have entered through the side doors..." he mumbles, somewhat gruffly, it seems.

The building is totally modern and consists of a number of block-like structures that are connected in unpredictable ways, not unlike many museums of modern art. Entering through the glass door, I am struck with how clean–how minimalist things are. There is no clutter here–the woods are on the blonder side–light and uplifting. A hallway with a glass case and a few bulletin boards leads to an open area with doors that go to the offices and the sanctuary. I slow down to take in the displays.

On one bulletin board a sheet is thumb-tacked neatly in the corner, giving information on the current investment rates for State of Israel bonds. Beside this is a paper with three photographs on it and a caption overhead that reads: "Vandalism at Our Cemetery." The photographs show tire marks ripped through the grass and dirt thrown all over the sides of a building and on some tombstones.

Wow. I'm surprised to see this. Anti-Semitism even in our little neck of the woods. Our little redneck of the woods, it seems.

Next to the bulletin board is a glass case full of colorful goodies that one can purchase. Indeed, this synagogue appears to have a gift shop. You can buy brass menorahs for $20, children's books, like "The Purim Parade"...even a Fiddler on the Roof snow globe, with two men dancing in the middle of the glass ball, and a fiddler sitting atop an attached cottage. The price tag isn't visible on that one.

At first this seems kind of strange in the middle of a house of God, but then, many of these items are probably not carried in Wal Mart or even FAO Schwartz, so it makes sense that Jewish folk would want somewhere to purchase a nice gift for a loved one that speaks of the faith. Christians have "The Mustard Seed" and the "The Master's Mercantile"....stores that carry things like Amy Grant CDs and Veggie Tales videos and DVDs. It seems doubtful that the population exists to support a store like "Sons of Israel Stuff" or "King David's Korner."

No one is rushing into the sanctuary, so I meander around outside with a dozen people or so. Some are looking at a newspaper article attached to the other bulletin board across the hallway. I stand behind them and look over their shoulders. It's about an 85-year-old Jewish woman who still runs a grocery store in a local neighborhood. I listen to the people.

"She's a celebrity now, isn't she?" one woman says, smiling and reading over the tops of her glasses.

"Oh, she is a really wonderful woman, and a great citizen," a man responds.

Everyone is smiling and reading proudly, as though she is their very own grandmother. I like hearing the warmth and respect in their voices, and in general, it's easy to be taken with how kind and pleasant everyone is in their conversation.

After looking at the "tree of donors" on another wall, I've seen about all there is to see in the hallways of B'nai Brith, so it's time to go into the sanctuary.

It's a small room, shaped like a blunt fan, with windows up high on either side of the altar. There is a series of four stained glass windows along one side the room, which depict, in blues, whites and golds, scenes, presumably, from the Old Testament. It's surprising how high up all the windows are, in fact, the entire building is up high. One has to climb a full flight of stairs to get to the entrance doors. It's almost like a fortress, or a very fancy prison, with high windows like the kind that keep prisoners from climbing out. But in this case, I'm wondering if the architects of B'nai Brith designed things because they feared bricks or rocks flying in.

Only the Rabbi and two other men are chatting rapidly at the front of the room, and I feel a bit self-conscious walking into the place. In the lobby all the men are donning prayer shawls and little satin navy blue yarmulkes, and the women are attaching lace to the backs of their hair. I feel as though a sign might be on my back that says, "Not a Jew," or "Nosy Gentile," as I slink into the back pew, hoping that the Rabbi won't stare me down and ask, "Who are you?"

The Rabbi breaks away from the other two men and stands at the pulpit, slightly agitated. "I'm starting now! Good Sabbat! Good Sabbat! I'm starting the service! It's 9:30! Turn to page 65 in your prayer book."

It's only me in the room, and I dutifully grab a book and find page 65, lest he discover that I'm an infiltrator. The Rabbi starts chanting in Hebrew, and then stops and turns to one of the men, irritably. "What's with all the *noise?!*"

One of the men, a very short, old but muscular-looking man with solid white hair (who turns out to be one of two cantors, and the one with a voice to wake up the dead) walks to the back and makes an announcement to the group in the lobby: "The service has begun and we need for you to come in and stop talking!"

The people start to trickle in, smiling and continuing to talk, but now in very whispered, inaudible voices.

The Cantor on the left side of the altar is mumbling in a Hebraic frenzy. The Rabbi answers what must be prayers coming from the Cantor, with the following: "Men.....Men.....Men.....Men.....," I suppose as in "Amen," but abbreviated, for busy, short-tempered Rabbis who have things to do and want to keep it moving along.

The service starts moving forward at a break-neck pace, and the Cantor is doing everything. The Rabbi's singular task appears to be calling out the page numbers as we race through 50-some pages of a Jewish prayer book, all read in Hebrew by a manic Cantor rocking left and right with his back to the congregation. Periodically, the Rabbi says, "Stand, page 83" and then "Please be seated, page 84," but other than that, he just calls numbers out Bingo-style: "86" ... "92" ... "100."

What I notice about this congregation is that they are somehow respectful while still talking, socializing, *blowing kisses* and even forming mini-groups within the pews. Everyone talks from time to time, but in such a finely tuned whisper, you can't hear a thing. You can see that people are whispering, laughing and sharing things that I am guessing are not about the prayer book, but nothing is audible.

Amazing.

I start to relax into things and open up my bulletin....wait a minute...on the inside is an insert that says "Alan David Epstein's Bar Mitzvah."

Maybe this is why everyone is so dressed up. And this would explain the young lad who moved up front to sit behind the Rabbi in a chair, facing the congregation.

Good heavens. I'm an uninvited guest at a Bar Mitzvah! But this is the regular service time, according the message on the answering machine. What should I do? What if everyone is asked to do something, like go to the front of the room and say something about Alan....or go give him a hug and say something in Hebrew?

I guess I could make something up. I could just say, "Alan is about the most blond little Jewish boy I've ever known!"

I think about ducking out, but then I am intrigued. If they ever stop this incessant prattling in Hebrew, it might be kind of neat to hear what this young man has to say, on this most important of occasions in his life.

I opt to stay and just keep acting as Jewish as possible.

Now the Rabbi and a cantor are pulling the Torah out of what the bulletin calls the "ark" and start parading around the room with it. They come toward the back. Many people are touching their prayer books to these scrolls, instead of their hands, and then putting their prayer books to their lips. I decide to pass, kind of like when they come around with the dessert tray in the restaurant, and you smile but shake your hand in a small, polite manner.

Now it seems that the Cantor is out of center stage and different people are coming up to read from the scrolls, with help from the Rabbi. The voices of the people are so small, compared to the hearty, full-bodied Hebraic chanting and singing which is coming from the Rabbi's mouth.

Well, I guess that's what they're paying him for.

In the midst of these various "lay readers," the Rabbi announces: "It is our tradition to say a prayer for those who are ill--if you know of anyone after I have read my list, stand up and say their name."

The Rabbi goes back to singing in Hebrew, and every now and then a name is discernable....like "Sal Soloman," or "Judy Abramowitz." Others stand and offer names, including a few Gentile sounding names like "O'Grady" and "Manelli." It's very funny to hear this river of Hebrew, with the word "O'Grady" stuck in the middle of it like some blip in the screen.

I wish there were more for me to hold on to in this service, but it's just endless Hebrew. Endless, endless Hebrew. More Hebrew than you're likely to hear even in the heart of Israel. Will this Hebrew never stop, I ask God in slight desperation.

At that very second, a miraculous thing occurs: the Rabbi addresses us in English. "We are now at the danger point in the service where Adina is going to pass around some candy. This is to throw at Alan after he finishes his Torah reading, as a sign of the success we all wish for him...but this candy is a little hard–so just toss it–don't use it as a missile, please."

People chuckle.

A girl of about seven starts passing around candy. A few other lay people who are important to Alan (I have read in the bulletin) read the Torah in, yes, you guessed it, more Hebrew.

Now that candy is being unwrapped, the room is turned up a notch in terms of the buzz factor. In the very back of the room, there is a row of seven adolescent girls, who look at be all about thirteen or so, and behind them are six boys, also around thirteen. Friends of the Bar Mitzvah boy, one could reasonably guess. This group is not particularly tuned in to the reading and is engaged in a highly active, two-pew flurry of flirting and whispered joke-telling.

Finally it is Alan's turn. Everyone quiets down considerably as he launches into what will turn out to be another diatribe. Okay..maybe it's not a *diatribe*, but it might as well be to those of us who don't understand a blessed word of Hebrew.

People listen politely for quite some time, but after awhile, the two rows of teenagers start to get a bit too boisterous, and the boys even have one quick eruption of laughter, which they just as quickly suppress. Two or three adults are looking over at the group, but no one seems to feel any strong need to walk over and ask the young people to be quiet. Finally, the good Rabbi himself stands up from his chair near Alan, and stares the group down. A parent in front of them turns and puts a finger to his lips. They settle down and the Rabbi sits again, shaking his head just once, as a sign of his disapproval.

Alan's Torah reading is a bit subdued, but what it lacks in luster, it makes up for in steadiness. Suddenly, the stream of Martian-like vocalizations ends.

"Today I am a man....okay, a little man, but a man..."

Chuckles pass through the room.

"What I read today was very important because it can be considered one of the first feminist stories and an assertion of women's rights."

I sit up in my pew. Did this young lad...this little, blond, man-boy just use the "F" word?

"Every family had land, but in this one family, there was no male heir so they would not be given land. The father died and the mother and daughters were left with nothing. They went to Moses and said that they didn't think it was fair. He agreed and changed the law. So 3,500 years ago it was decided among the Jews that women could own land. It amazes me that there are still religions where women can't own land or property."

There is something so refreshing about hearing a thirteen-year-old boy talk about women's issues that I almost want to cry. It's hard enough to find a thirteen-year-old girl who is interested in the struggle of women, let alone a boy.

Alan talks about his interest in helping others, the volunteering he does in a reading program for younger children, he thanks his Hebrew teacher, Mrs. Spicer, and suggests that he may have been one of her biggest challenges. He also thanks the Rabbi, his parents and all his friends for coming to his Bar Mitzvah.

Without any warning, everyone starts throwing the candy at Alan. The boys in the back have totally disregarded the Rabbi's instruction that they not use the sweets as missiles. Some of the throws rival the speed of a Pete Sampras serve. One candy pings off the podium, another off Alan's head. Everyone is laughing, including Alan, as the congregation, from their collective cultural perspective, throws candy to signify wealth and success for Alan. To me, from my different cultural background, it appears as though the congregation is acting out the stoning of an adulterer or prostitute in old Jerusalem.

Alan's parents come to the podium. His father says how proud they are of him and thanks everyone who taught him. He concludes with "Yes Alan, today you are a man, but you must still go to Middle School."

A few members of the congregation present gifts to Alan: a certificate and a copy of the Torah. The Vice President of the congregation, a Dr. David Farbstein, says that for years he asked Alan what he had learned in Hebrew School and the response was always "nothing." He pointed out that today Alan had shown that this wasn't true.

Finally, the Rabbi stands to say a few words.

"I try not to say nice things about the kids in public because I don't want it to go to his head. Alan has just started and this isn't the end of something for him, just the beginning. Alan knows this--he's too smart not to."

Oh, come on Rabbi...throw him a bone or two.

"I was thinking this morning that this is a safe place to break a leg with all the medical personnel here. I hope Alan realizes the importance of his father's work. In Judaism nothing is more important than the work of a healer."

So *that's* why Jewish women always want to marry a doctor.

"Alan mentioned women–this reading is one of the most fascinating in all the Torah. It talks about one of the greatest revolutions that took place 3500 years ago, when women were basically commodities. Women were given by their fathers to other men to be their property. Life for women was extremely difficult and full of perils. If her husband didn't want her she was finished. She had no way to survive. It took America 150 years to give women the vote. It took the Jews three months in the desert to give women the right to own property. The women complained to Moses and he was taken aback. But, he said you've got a point...I'm going to see what God thinks...not what *I* think, but what *God* thinks. What he hears from God is simple: 'the women are right.'"

I'd like to use this strategy with my husband: "Hon, let me go talk to God and see what She has to say about this....guess what, She says I'm right."

"Nothing has changed in 3500 years among the Jews, but women's issues have not gone far beyond Judaism. There are still societies today who obviously didn't read that chapter in our Bible. There are still societies that say that women are a commodity. It's a shame that we don't speak more forcefully against these societies! I refuse to believe there is one woman out there who would turn down her rights if they were given to her. Of course they go along with the way it is–what other choice do they have? But give them their rights and you will see women empowered! They will never turn back!"

I'm stunned. Never before in my life have I heard a religious leader speak with such passion about the plight of women. Usually, if a minister brings it up, it's a one-liner thrown in as an aside.

"It is our responsibility to go to war VERBALLY when we see evil! And women having no rights is a form of evil!"

Right on, Rabbi! Take that evil-angle right out of the hands of Jimmy Swaggart! It's the people who *oppress* women, who expect them to "submit" themselves to their husbands and stay unempowered who are evil! Praise King David!!

We end with a few more prayers and a song. I feel exhilarated.

Everyone has been invited to stay for a luncheon provided by Alan's parents. I decide it probably wouldn't be good form to go to a meal not knowing the host family. Someone at my table would ask me how I know Alan, and I'd have to say, "I don't, I just walked in off the street. Could you pass the roast beef?"

The people meander back toward the congregational hall. I'd like to experience more of these progressive people–even with all that annoying Hebrew. So, I'll come back on a Friday night for the shorter service.

I head toward the Synagogue at 7:55 p.m. the next Friday and note that there is only one SUV in the parking lot. Cruising past the building, slooowly....there are lights on everywhere, including in the sanctuary.

Well, maybe they don't always have a Friday service, or the Rabbi is holding office hours. Pulling my old gray bucket of bolts in beside the nice, clean forest green Jeep, I've decided to "out" myself as far as my car is concerned. I ascend the stairs to the front doors, expecting that they will be locked.

They're open.

The hallway is empty as I tiptoe down and peer around the corner into the main office. The sounds of shuffled papers can be heard.

"Hell-ooo...." I call like a person who doesn't want to intrude.

The same Rabbi from the Saturday frenzy of Hebrew comes bouncing out of his office to the outer one in which I am standing.

"Hello, I'm Rabbi Feldman," he says pleasantly. It's hard for me to imagine that this is the same irritable man from the previous week, but I like him instantly. "Ruth Laker," I say as we shake hands.

"I don't think we're going to be having a service tonight," he laughs. "Someone in the congregation is having her 90th birthday party, and everyone wanted to go to that rather than come here." He is taking it very well.

I smile and nod my understanding.

"It's a little embarrassing for me as the Rabbi," he concedes, "but then, she's a really wonderful person so I can understand."

"Well, may I talk with you for a minute?" I ask.

"Sure!" he pulls out the chair at the secretaries desk and sits down. "I have all the time in the world now." We laugh.

33

"I have to tell you, I was at the service last Saturday and that was the first time I've ever heard a religious leader talk so much and so forcefully about women's rights."

"You're kidding," he says simply.

"No, I'm not.

"Well, now you have," he says, again, as though it's no big deal to him.

I try to gear up for my next question. "I'm not Jewish, but I'm wondering what the process of conversion involves." Then I chicken out. "My brother is in a relationship with a Jewish woman and if he wanted to convert, I'd like to help him figure out what to do. He lives in Buffalo. He's kind of shy, but very in love with his girlfriend."

Now, essentially, everything I just said is true. I do have a younger brother who has a Jewish girlfriend. He is in love with her. He is shy. He's just never indicated to me that they were planning to practice Judaism or that he would like me to do some field work on the conversion process for his sake. Still, I rationalize to myself that if the issue comes up, big Sis will be right there with the answers. Somehow, I don't feel comfortable about telling the Rabbi that it is I who am interested in the faith and whether or not I could be a part of it. I guess because I don't know if they would really want me.

"Well, I'd want to meet with the couple for the most part... a lot of times one person converts and then they end up knowing more about the faith than the person who was born into it." He laughs again. "And if they are going to have kids, they need to stick together with one faith, that is my feeling. It's too hard on children when parents try to raise them in homes with more than one religion. So they should pick Christian or Jewish...I would hope they'd pick Jewish, but as long as they choose the same one, that is the main thing. Do you know what her background is?" he asks me.

"Um...I think she's Reformed, if that's what you mean."

"Yeah, I mean she's not Orthodox, right?" The way this Rabbi says "Orthodox" it comes out "Orodox" and it's cute. He seems to have some kind of accent, but I don't know what it is.

"No, I don't think so."

"Well that's good," he says. "Cause those guys are a small percentage of the Jewish population and their lifestyles are kind of like extra-terrestrials."

I nod understandingly, even though I don't really. If those are the Jews that dress in severe black and have those little ringlets of hair along their faces, I can certainly see how they might be considered of another world.

"It all depends on the individual Rabbi, but there are three rituals he would have to go through to become Jewish...the first is called the mikveh, kind of like a Christian baptism, and then there is the Hatafat Dam Brit. Do you know if he is circumcised?"

He asked that with a straight face so I guess it would be rude to laugh out loud. "Um...no, I sure don't."

"Well, there would be a small blood-letting from the penis, just a drop....it's no big deal...believe me."

"I'm not sure if my brother would see it that way." I laugh kind of awkwardly.

"Oh, listen–they use a local anesthetic...." he motions down toward his own...manhood. "It's over in two seconds...you don't even know it." He waves his hand in true "no-big-whoop" fashion and smiles winningly.

I like this Rabbi's mannerisms-his twinkling eyes, the way he pulls his pants up high over his belly, his cute beige oxfords–so much, that if he wants to draw blood from my brother's penis, it's okay by me.

"Then there's a lot of study essentially...he would have to do a lot of reading. That's the biggest part. Afterward he would meet with three Rabbis and they would want to see if he is of sound mind because we don't want anyone converting who is mentally unstable, and if it really is his will to convert because we don't want him doing it if he doesn't really want to. So that's basically it!" He smiles again. He has cute, straight teeth that just appear in the middle of his beard in a Jewish nutcracker kind of way.

"Well let me ask you something, and please be honest with me," I say.

"I'm always honest. I'm nothing but honest," he says matter-of-factly.

"Do Jewish people born into the faith really accept the presence of others who don't come from this long lineage...you know, who don't come from the same ethnic–I guess you would call it, background....or well..."

"I don't understand the question," he snaps. "Ask it again. Make it simpler."

"I'm not sure I understand the question either....if you don't come from the original sons of Israel, would you ever really be considered a true Jew?"

"Of course you would," he looks at me incredulously. "Listen, no one cares about that. In fact, I don't think I've ever been asked this question before in my life. If you convert to the faith everyone accepts you as Jewish."

"But I don't think that most people raised Christian identify with the early Christians like Jews identify with those who were led by Moses to the promised land of the Old Testament. You are all one people with a long history."

"Well what you call the 'Old Testament,' I call the Jewish Bible, but that's no big deal. Yes, there is a long history of the people, but you will find that Jews are a very liberal people. They are interested in all kinds of people and it is about worshiping God together, in the end."

"What is the Jewish God like for you?"

"Theoretically, it's the same God as the Christian God. For most Jews, our God is a very personal one. We talk to Him all the time–just like Tevia in the 'Fiddler on the Roof,' we shake our fists at Him and expect Him to keep His end of a bargain...we share our worries and our joys with Him...like I said it's very personal."

We sit together quietly for a few seconds while I imagine shaking my fist at God and what would prompt me to do that. Maybe if I sent in one more rebate form and never got the money back.

"I like that idea of shaking your fist at God...you know, being genuine in your relationship with Him. It shows too, that you've got chutzpah. I used to have Jewish men interested in me all the time when I was single," I share with him. "I think it's because I have chutzpah."

"I think it's because you're not Jewish," he laughs.

"I like the way Jewish men treat their women," I continue, ignoring the little grin on his face. "Jewish women seem to be very strong within the family...there is a balance between men and women that is missing in so many cultures in the world."

He nods his agreement. "You are right. There is still a traditional division of labor in the minds of most Jews that the man will be the primary provider and the woman will be responsible for the upbringing and education of the children, but you see Jewish men taking care of children and Jewish women as successful professionals all the time. They don't stick to those roles in a rigid way. But, yes, there is a very strong bond between Jewish children and the mother, and a Jewish man can talk to God all day long if he wants to, but when he comes home, he better remember that his wife is God around the house. If he doesn't, he pays the price!" He chuckles.

I'm thinking that I should really let the man go. He has a nice opportunity here for an evening off, and I'm keeping him in the office.

"So what's the position on Israel in the congregation?" I ask. "Is everyone together on it, or do you have a variety of opinions?"

"You find that everyone supports Israel and for one primary reason–because before World War II there were eighteen million Jews in the world, and after that war we had lost a third of our population. We were down to twelve million. We are only now back up to fourteen million...there are very low birth rates among Jews. And we have vowed not to ever let that happen again." He makes direct eye contact with me on that one. "Israel is the most likely place where that kind of annihilation could occur again. There are six million Jews in Israel. There were six million Jews killed in World War II."

"Yeah, but because you don't want to keep losing Jewish lives, like the lives of the Israeli soldiers, does anyone argue that giving up some land would be the best way to prevent more bloodshed in the long run?"

"Unfortunately it's not about a tract of land here or there. The Middle East is a very macho place and there are large groups of people who want to see the State of Israel replaced entirely by a State of Palestine. I mean, it's written in their documents. And they bring religion into it, which makes it much more heated. There are some Palestinians who would, I'm sure, be satisfied with certain lands being given up, which eventually will happen, I think. But to many Israelis, it's not about giving up the West Bank it's about what happens the day *after* we give up the West Bank."

I nod thoughtfully and then stand up. He says, "Let me get my keys." He locks up the office and we start strolling down the hall together. I'm aware of how grounded and confidant this man is. How big of a presence he has in his 5'4" body.

I point to the photos of the vandalism in the cemetery. "I was surprised to see this."

"Oh, that happens in all the cemeteries near ours...the Catholic and the Protestant. Every spring kids rip around in the mud with their cars and it goes everywhere. It's not anti-Semitic vandalism. Just kids."

I shake the good Rabbi's hand and he tells me how nice it was to talk with me. I believe he means that. And it was nice to talk with him, too. Overall, it's been really neat to share time with these thoughtful and interesting people.

I spend a few days meditating on my time in the synagogue, in common prayer with American Jews. I know I can't possibly participate in this religion if most of it is shared in another language. I don't want to go to Hebrew School and no one can make me.

Maybe the Reformed Synagogue would be different.

It's worth one more try.

Conservative Jewish

#	Dimension of Church Experience	Rating
1)	Is parking close and convenient?	4
2)	How beautiful is the worship space?	6
3)	How comfortable is the seating?	7
4)	How welcoming and friendly is the congregation?	5
5)	How enjoyable and uplifting are the musical aspects of the worship?	3
6)	Does the leader have a pleasant speaking voice and does he/she make sense to me?	10
7)	How clean are the bathrooms?	10
8)	Are the people in the pews interesting to stare at?	8
9)	How tolerant to many ways of seeing and doing things does this group appear to be?	10
10)	Would I feel good about how these people would spend my money?	8
11)	How close did I feel to God in this place?	4
12)	Did I smile more than once during the experience?	6
	Total	80

Christian Scientist

Although the words "Christian" and "Scientist," separately, are both perfectly fine and useful, they are a strange combination. I wish I could say that I know more about the Christian Scientists other than 1) they publish an excellent newspaper, 2) people get mad at them for not taking their children to the doctor and 3) Tom Cruise and Nicole Kidman had something to do with the group and that it may have been a bone of contention in their marriage. In their case, I think that it probably wasn't about religion at all–I think that Tom Cruise needs continually to fall in love and that it won't be long before Katie Holmes will be ex-wife number three.

Isn't it great how celebrities have to offer up their lives to us so we can sit around and pass judgment on them without any hesitation? We all know what kind of money Tom Cruise makes. We have to be able to judge him–he owes us.

Oh...someone just told me that Tom and Nicole didn't belong to the Christian Scientists but rather the Church of Scientology.

Well, I digress.

It's a lovely summer day when I drive to the Christian Scientist church in our town. A small but tidy-looking place, the billboard announces the worship time and invites people to visit "spirituality.com." Parking is around the back. There is a sign near one of the doors that advertises the library and times to come use the reading room.

The front door is propped open. I walk in. A slender woman with nicely sculpted legs greets me from across the lobby. Another man is sorting bulletins on a table and also greets me.

"I guess I'm a little early," I say.

"Well, you're our first customer," the woman smiles. "If you'd like to look around in the reading room, feel free."

"Thanks."

I walk to the table where the man is laying things out. There are copies of the Christian Science Monitor, a Christian Science Journal and the Weekly Bible Lessons.

"That gives you the order of the service," he tells me. "Our services are run by people within the church. This is the program that comes from the Mother Church."

"Where is the 'Mother Church?'" I ask.

"In Boston."

I don't know why, but that expression, "Mother Church," just sounds kind of weird to me. It brings to mind "Mother Ship," as in aliens.

"Can you tell me where the 'Scientist' part comes from in the name of your church?" I ask him.

"I better have you talk to Nancy. She's the real expert. I've only been involved for three years."

Yeah, I guess 1,095 days aren't really enough time to get around to some of the more esoteric questions like: what does our name mean?

Just then a girl of about ten comes toward the man and slides under his arm.

"This is my granddaughter," he tells me.

"Hi, I'm Mrs.Laker, it's nice to meet you. I love the corn rows in your hair and that beautiful headband."

She smiles happily. "I got it done in the Virgin Islands."

"No kidding! I had it done when I was there a few years ago, but I looked silly. You look really good."

"You should have seen my brother–he looked *really* good."

Just then a blond boy of about eight comes bounding into the foyer and screeches to a halt, looking at the three of us curiously.

"This is my brother."

"Oh, so you had corn rows in your hair too? I bet you looked cool. You still have a very nice tan." The boy stares at me and gives a small smile, apparently unimpressed by his tanning ability. If he were one of the People of the Pasty Skin, like me and my husband, he wouldn't be so nonchalant about his pigment. When we were in the Virgin Islands, we spent ten days worshiping the sun: lying on the beach, walking around town in our bathing suits, swimming in the buff, only to receive this comment from our daughter when we returned: "Did you stay out of the sun because you were afraid of getting cancer?"

"Well...I'll just take some of this literature inside the sanctuary and look it over until Nancy comes."

The sanctuary of the Christian Scientists is minimalist, almost to the point of being austere. Still, there is more color and attention to aesthetics than one would find with the Quakers. The room is painted cream with Williamsburg blue trim on the doors and wainscoting. Two simple but elegant gold chandeliers hang from the ceiling. On the wall behind the altar, the words "God is Love," are stenciled in an old English font of gold. On one side wall, also in gold, are the words, "Divine love always has met and always will meet every human need-Mary Baker

Eddy." On the other wall are the words, "God is Love and he that dwelleth in love dwelleth in God and God in him–I. John. 4:15."

Hey...Mary Baker Eddy...as in a *woman?* A woman is being quoted on an entire wall of a church? Then I remember that somewhere in the remote recesses of my mind, I did once learn that the founder of the Christian Scientists was a woman.

The same slender woman who greeted me when I first came in, comes and sits down in the pew with me.

"I understand you had some questions?" she smiles.

"Yes, I have never been to a Christian Scientist Church and I was wondering where the word 'Scientist' comes from."

Nancy looks away thoughtfully. "Well, our leader said that science is based on laws, and that our church is based on God's laws, which are perfect and if applied correctly, like science, will always result in the same thing–perfect Love."

I nod. That makes sense...I guess. Prior to her explanation, I thought that "Christian Scientist" sounded much like an oxymoron–in the same camp as "military intelligence" or "jumbo shrimp."

"And the 'Christian' part comes from the fact that God's laws were brought to us most explicitly by Jesus Christ," she offers.

"Yes, I figured that part."

"Our worship is not led by clergy, we have two readers who are appointed for a three year term. The Mother Church in Boston determines what the readings are for each week, and they make up the sermon."

Again with the Mother Church...

"Now what is the thinking about not having clergy?" I ask.

"Well, our leader thought that no one person should be responsible for the church–that everything should be shared by the congregation and that everyone could share God's words."

"Your leader being Mary Baker Eddy?"

"Yes. She founded the church in Boston."

"Founded," or *"landed,"* I'm wondering to myself. I'm starting to see how it might have happened: the Mother Church-Ship landed in Boston, and a group of aliens walked down the ramp--Nancy's grandparents and many other well-groomed types among them. One spoke: "I am Mary Baker Eddy, the Leader of the Christian Scientists and Captain of the Mother Church. Take me to *your* Leader."

"It's amazing that a woman would be able to do that," I observe out loud. "Even today, I wouldn't expect people to follow a woman in a religious movement."

"Yes it was amazing. There are only two religions that were founded in America; Mormonism and the Christian Scientists. All the others came from other countries."

"She must have been one persuasive person."

"Yes. As a woman, she wasn't able to buy the land for the church in Boston, so she set up a Board of Directors with men and had them buy it. But she was very much in control. She believed that the traditionally feminine qualities of nurturance, humility and service were most Christ-like, but she herself had to demonstrate many more traditionally 'male' attributes, like assertiveness."

"That's very interesting. I'd like to read a biography of her."

"We have several in our library."

I decide to tread into some of the deeper waters. "It's funny, but people have so many stereotypes about Christian Scientists. You have that great newspaper, but then you seem to get a lot of negative press when it comes to the issues of children and whether or not to take them to the doctor."

"Yes, that is the thing that seems to put off most people."

"Do you have different views on it in the congregation?"

"Well, we have had people who have resorted to medical interventions, and we would never judge them for doing that. I've been fortunate that my children have always had quick healings. They are usually better after one day of the flu or a high fever. We meet every Wednesday night and share our healings and pray with each other. We've had really astounding healings in this congregation. Now that everyone is talking about the power of mind over body, we think Christian Scientists will grow in numbers. We see ourselves as being ahead of the times, when it comes to the issues of prayer and healing."

"How many people do you have in this church?"

"We're very small. We have ten to twelve regular members."

Ten to twelve? So what this woman is saying is that if I bought a baker's dozen bag of doughnuts, there would be more doughnuts in that bag than there are people in this church?

She must sense my surprise. "Believe it or not, we've been able to maintain this building, and there has been a worship service in this church every Sunday since 1919, except when there have been blizzards. And Christian Scientist services are pretty much the same way they were one hundred years ago."

Couldn't take a little snow, eh?

I'm imagining that there must have once been many more CS people, back in the old days, and I'm curious about why their numbers dwindled so.

Nancy leans back to talk with someone over her shoulder. Then she turns to me. "I've got to do something before the service starts...you're welcome to come to our Wednesday night meeting. That's when you see the more personal side of the group. The woman who is one of our readers is a retired lawyer and is also very knowledgeable about Christian Scientists if you want to talk with her after the service."

"Thanks so much for your time."

I look around and notice that fourteen people have taken a seat in the pews. Everyone is sitting in perfect silence.

An older man and woman, both appearing to be in their early sixties and very fit, stand at the pulpit, which is really more like a wide podium.

"The Scriptural Selection is from Acts..." the man begins. He reads flawlessly, with a very clear and pleasant voice. "Let us sing together Hymn number 198, which was written by our leader, Mary Baker Eddy... 'Shepherd show me how to go, o'er the hillside steep...how to gather, how to sow, how to feed thy sheep. I will listen for thy voice...lest my footsteps stray...I will follow and rejoice, all the rugged way.'"

Organ music begins to play the introduction to the song. I look up at the organ and notice that no one is playing, but sound is coming from the instrument. I rise slightly in my seat to see if the keys are going up and down like a player piano, or like the haunted house organ in *The Ghost and Mr. Chicken.* They're not.

Everyone stands and begins to sing. Although there are exactly eighteen people in the church, the sound from the group is strong and sincere. I reflect on the words. Mary could turn a phrase, that's for sure. And she did a nice job with the rhymes. I *will listen for thy voice/ lest my footsteps stray/ I will follow and rejoice/ all the rugged way.*

That is one of those double rhymes: voice-rejoice and stray-way. Nice. And I like that image: following and rejoicing all the "rugged way." I'm picturing the von Trapp family climbing over the Alps to freedom from the Nazis. My own father escaped the Communists in the same way–climbing over the mountains from Czechoslovakia into Germany. He has always seemed to rejoice on his rugged way.

"Let us pray together in silence, then say together the Lord's Prayer with its spiritual interpretation as given in the Christian Scientist textbook."

We sit quietly. I close my eyes to offer up prayers of gratitude to God. After a few minutes, the man's voice begins to lead us: "Our Father which art in heaven..."

The woman speaks: "Our Father-Mother God, all harmonious..."
The man: "Hallowed be Thy name..."
The woman: "Adorable One..."

What the heck? I look at my Bible lessons booklet. Inside the front flap the Lord's Prayer is printed out, with what both the man and woman are saying. Mary Baker Eddy is also quoted before the prayer. She writes: "Our Master said, 'After this manner therefore pray ye,' and then he gave that prayer which covers all human needs....Here let me give what I understand to be the spiritual sense of the Lord's Prayer:..."

This woman gave her own interpretation of the lines of the Lord's prayer? That's pretty darn bold. I have to admit, I like some of her lines better than those of Jesus.

JC: Thy kingdom come.
MBE: Thy kingdom *is* come; Thou art ever present.
JC: And forgive us our debts, as we forgive our debtors.
MBE: And Love is reflected in love.

So Mary thought she could expound upon the Lord's prayer. Why on earth wasn't she burned at the stake, I wonder?

"Let us now sing Hymn number 263. 'Only God can bring us gladness, only God can give us peace...Joys are vain that end in sadness, joy divine shall never cease...'"

He reads the entire first verse. I'm getting the impression that Christian Scientists' are a "word people." They like words. They pay attention to words. Especially those of God, Jesus and Mary Baker Eddy, but not necessarily in that order.

We rise and sing again. When it is over, we sit down in unison.

"Welcome to our worship service," the man begins, "this church is one of the many worldwide branches of the Mother Church, The First Church of Christ, Scientist, in Boston, Massachusetts."

I'm starting to wonder if Big Mother might be watching me.

"Our Sunday service is held at 10:30 AM. In addition to our Sunday service, we invite you to our Wednesday evening meetings held at 7:30 PM. At these meetings you will hear testimonies of healing brought about through the study and application of Christian Science. Membership in Christian Science is a blessing. If you would like to join, you may obtain a membership form."

This man is again, flawless in delivery, but he seems so stiff and wooden. His entire demeanor seems to say 1950's accountant, but with a frozen smile on his face that has been there since he first stood up. Maybe he's a cyborg, a remnant of that first group that landed with the Mother Church. I can tell that everything he is saying has been printed out, and he is not deviating from his script by even one word. I find myself longing for him to stop and say, "Oh heck....I'm tired of saying this over and over--you can read it in your bulletin." But a *cyborg* wouldn't do that....*would* they.....

He continues: "Next Sunday evening, The Philadelphia Christian Scientist Church will have a guest speaker, Lorraine Montgomery. The topic of her talk is, 'Who Are My Neighbors?' All are welcome."

I guess this tiny group has to wonder who their neighbors are since they don't seem to be coming into the church.

The man sits down while a young woman stands up beside the pulpit. The organ starts to play, this time being propelled by an actual flesh and blood person. The soloist starts to sing *The Stranger of Galilee:*

"And I felt I could love Him forever, so gracious and tender was He, I claimed Him that day as my Saviour, this Stranger of Galilee."

I notice that all the words to this solo are printed out on an insert to the "Weekly Bible Lessons." The young singer has her hair pulled back in a severe schoolmarm kind of way. Her voice is pleasant. Still, I'm not sure if she is really feeling what she is singing, she seems so tense and contained. Although I have found the trend of women putting stripper poles in their bedrooms to be rather sad, this is one young woman who might actually benefit from such an opportunity to loosen up a bit. She wouldn't need to take her clothes off, just swing around a bit and yell, "WEEEeee!!"

The man and woman stand back up when she is finished.

"Friends," he says, "we shall now read scripture from our textbook, page 18. Our subject is the Doctrine of Atonement."

Then the woman starts to read and we answer her responsively for a few lines. She moves into a series of sections from the Bible, starting with Romans, then switching to Mark and then John. Her voice is also flawless and even. There is something so precise and anal about the way that everyone delivers what they say. Either they are not a very relaxed group, or they feel a call to carry themselves with perfect reserve and dignity as children of God.

Or they are *cyborgs*...

Now it's his turn again. "I shall now read from the textbook as written by Mary Baker Eddy."

I don't know what kind of intellectual property rights Mary Baker Eddy worked out before she passed on, but her ancestors must be getting some good coin. That is, if there are more Christian Scientists out there. Maybe this "Mother Church" is all a ruse...a way to draw unsuspecting people into this sanctuary, which is really a pre-coordinated spatial vortex, before we are assimilated like Captain Jean-Luc Picard was with the Borg in *Star Trek: The Next Generation.*

Good Lord. I'd better keep one foot out in the aisle and one eye on the back door.

Now we're back to the woman reader and a list of scripture selections: Psalms, Chronicles, John, Matthew, John again. The man and woman go back and forth in this graceful ping-pong style for quite some time. I can tell by the "Order of Sunday Services" section that this will continue for some time longer. I start to look around again. The handful of people in the room all have their eyes closed and are apparently drinking in every word. Unfortunately, there is no new visual stimulation of any kind.

But wait. I have my copy of the latest *Christian Scientist Monitor* to peruse. I unfold it on the seat beside me, keeping it low as to try to respect the worship process. Nothing says "not really engaged in the sermon" like an open newspaper held high in front of one's face.

The headlines on the front page read: "Bush support softens," and "How anger over Florida recount still roils politics." Well I guess we know what their political leanings are. I imagine changing words and letters slightly, just for the fun of it: "Bush support stockings," or "Bush sports soft tennies," or "Bush stupor softens."

Another article on the search for weapons of mass destruction in Iraq suggests that on their own, Iraqis seem to have routinely sent banned chemicals to factories for disposal. Bush's new position is that it doesn't matter because Sadam himself is a weapon of mass destruction. Reading these articles, as with all media input about Iraq, leaves me feeling befuddled. I really don't know how to feel about this war. On the one hand, I don't think Iraq was a pressing, immediate threat, on the other hand, having relatives who had to live under Communist rule for 40 years with substantial oppression, I want to give the Iraqi people a chance for some political freedom. My cousins often tell me that they would have loved for another country to get involved and liberate them from the Communists. Though I'm not so sure that's how the majority of Iraqis feel.

I tune back in to the speakers for a second. "Revelations...."

Yeah, yeah, yeah.

More headlines aren't particularly Bush-friendly: "Concern over Iraq eats into Bush's poll numbers," and "Taliban's grip still strong."

There is a neat article about a woman from Yemen, Amat al-Aleem Alsoswa, who was named the country's first Minister of Human Rights. She has risen to a level most women can't even imagine in that part of the world, and she is active in matters of women's rights. A glimmer of hope in a world where women can't drive, expose their limbs, vote, run for office or go out without a male escort. It's better here, except for the rape, harassment, domestic violence, sexual abuse of about one-sixth of our girl children, glass ceiling and wage discrimination, lack of support for child rearing, sexualization of females and devaluation of women as they age.

"Luke..." says the woman.

I listen because Luke is a really good one.

"And he spoke this parable unto them, saying, what man of you, having a hundred sheep, if he lose one of them, does not leave the ninety-nine in the wilderness, and go after that which is lost, until he find it? And when he has found it, he layeth it on his shoulders, rejoicing."

Nice.

Back to my paper. Here's an interesting article: "Murderer, or just a man who made Mom happy?" It tells of an 81-year-old man who married the author's 75-year-old mother. The writer finds out after the marriage that the man had killed his first wife and mother-in-law, shooting them both after returning from China at the end of WWII. The man had been tortured in prison for some time, and seemed to have lost it, obviously. He spent 30 years in an institution for the criminally insane. After he got out, he eventually married the writer's mother and they ended up spending ten happy years together. She died first, after an illness, then he died a year later. The author was trying to reconcile what it had meant.

That brings to mind one of my favorite lines in *"Dead Man Walking,"* when Susan Sarandon says that Christ taught that every man was better than the sum of all his terrible deeds, or something to that effect. That is a truly wonderful thought; imagine being the most horrible person in the world, someone everyone hates and fears as a monster. But there is God, knowing who you are inside, loving you when no one else does.

I think we've moved to the last part of the man's bit. He says, "Now a reading from our textbook by Mary Baker Eddy."

When I was at the Jewish Synagogue, they took the Torah out of the "Ark" toward the end of the service and paraded it around the room. People touched it with their prayer books and then touched the books to their lips. I wouldn't be surprised if this group does something similar, only they'll bring out Mary Baker Eddy's mummified body and roll it around on a refrigerator dolly.

He reads for a few minutes and finishes with: 'Whoever learns the principles of Christian Science will be able to perform cures and healing, but this will only come by taking up the cross and following Jesus Christ. You will find yourself suddenly well–the ego will be absent from the body and present with Truth and His divine principles of Love."

I heard a similar presentation at an Amway meeting. As the leader went through his pitch, he ended with: "You too, can reach the 'Diamond Level' and success, riches and happiness beyond your wildest dreams will be yours."

Finally, the man and woman sit down.

The organ starts to play by itself again. I'm wondering what kind of organ it is that can do this. And where is this organ purchased? Does an organ salesman target tiny congregations and come around, giving them an opening pitch like, "We have this little beauty, a player organ...it will make you feel as though a real person is tickling these ivories...."

A man who had been sitting in the pews is now walking down the aisle for collection. There are so few people that I don't have time to get any money out before he is gone. I do see the collection plate for one split second: gold-rimmed with a red velvet sack inside. Very different and chic.

Here's the accountant again. "Let's sing together Hymn number 261. I'll read the third verse."

Oh please don't. Sitting through this hour, with all the canned reading, has been like chewing on stale bread.

We rise and they start to sing the last hymn. I have to slip out the back because I'm expected somewhere in fifteen minutes. But I will come back for the Wednesday night meeting. Nancy did say I'd get to see a more "personal side" to the group. Who knows? Maybe these Christian Scientists can really let their hair down.

Wednesday night I pull into the parking lot, half expecting that no one will be there. All the lights are on and at least four other cars are already parked. I want to make sure that it's not going to be just me and Nancy, because if it is, I'm going to feel so sorry for this woman who seems to be bravely carrying on as one of the last local disciples of Mary Baker Eddy, that I'm liable to sign myself up and start a campaign to try to get them more members.

Inside the door, three people are standing near the entrance to the library. They all look at me with as I walk toward them.

"Hi," I say.

"Hello," an attractive middle-aged woman greets me. We share names and shake hands. The elderly woman is her mother and the other person is a man who does not seem related to them.

"I just came by to see what your Wednesday night meetings are like. Nancy asked me to come by."

"Oh great!" the man says, as though it didn't occur to him that I was here to participate. Maybe he thought I was lost and just looking for directions.

"Are you from around here?" the woman asks.

I tell her that I live only a few miles away. Again, I'm getting the feeling that they don't get a lot of visitors to their church.

I glance over her shoulder into the library. It's a very impressive room, with beautiful furniture, a smooth long wooden counter and lots of books. It looks very inviting. "So that's the reading room," I say.

They all "um-hum" at the same time.

"Is this where we meet?" I ask them.

"No, it's in the sanctuary," they all tell me.

"Well, thanks." I head to the sanctuary, somewhat disappointed that we won't be sitting in that lovely library.

Oh no.

The accountant is up at the front of the church again, sitting in his wingback chair. The person-less organ is playing slow, lamenting hymns again, and there are only three people in the pews. I sit down not too close to the back, but not too close to the front either. A woman who was there Sunday and met me, says hello to me by name. Then the other three come in from the hallway. Now there is a grand total of seven of us in the pews, and the accountant up front.

Maybe we move into a cozy circle after a few prayers, and break open the cider and doughnuts.

The room is so still and everyone seems so intense and centered. I'm coming to the conclusion that this group is really very deeply spiritual. They truly believe in all this Christian Science stuff. During the three days since I attended Sunday worship, I read a biography of

Mary Baker Eddy. I'm not so sure that her "miracle cure"--when she supposedly broke her back and then just stood up the next day--was such a miracle. She could have staged the entire thing, but I have to give her credit for developing so much power and influence as a woman of her time. In fact, it seemed that as soon as she really became powerful, she had to spend the rest of her life, tirelessly fighting lawsuits brought against her by men who begrudged her that power and slandered her at every opportunity.

I also read an article in the Christian Science Journal before I came over, entitled: "Spiritual Healings at a Distance." These folks really do believe that if you start to feel sick, all you have to do is focus on the fact that Life is God, that all of us are inseparable from intelligence and goodness, and that one divine Mind is present everywhere at all times. You will immediately feel well. We do not live in matter, we live in God.

I decide to give it a try. What the hay. I've started having allergies from all the rain and jungle-like overgrowth on our property. Particularly annoying this evening, has been my itchy throat.

I close my eyes and breathe deeply several times. I imagine that I am not the body I live in, but rather a being of energy, connected directly to God. I am perfect and untouchable by any of the plagues of the material world. I work very hard to connect to this visualization and I *really* believe this. Almost immediately, my throat stops itching! I get very excited and start to lose my focus. I try to get back to that place again.

"Let us rise and sing hymn number 288, 'Our Beloved Shepherd.' I'll read the third verse."

Oh turds. I have to stand with our little band and sing another old hymn.

The next thirty minutes are a repeat of Sunday morning. The accountant welcomes us all, saying the same words he said on Sunday– making reference to "The Mother Church" and Mary Baker Eddy and to the talk in Philadelphia. It's almost absurd with only seven of us in the room. He's talking as though the church is packed with all sorts of people. There's something both brave and almost pathetic about it at the same time. Like when the handful of musicians kept playing on board the Titanic, even as the boat was halfway under water.

Finally, after many more agonizingly bland scripture readings, the man says, "we will now open the meeting for testimonies of healings that have been brought about through the study and application of Christian Science." He carefully takes off his glasses, and sets them down. Then he stares straight ahead, the same, unbroken smile on his face. His eyes are like lasers and the smile is so tight that his mouth almost disappears. I can't even look directly at him because I'm afraid we'll lock eyes and I'll turn to stone.

Everyone is quiet. For several minutes, no one speaks. Several loooong minutes. Oh dear, what happens if no one says anything? He must have some pre-written script for such a scenario.

Finally, Nancy stands up. She is looking very casual tonight in exercise clothing. "In my preschool class," she starts, "there is one little girl who can't sit still and won't sit on the floor like a pretzel. She has difficulty doing anything we ask of her, and she can't make even a simple art project."

Something about the way Nancy is talking is strange. Each word is said very evenly and without any inflection in her voice at all, but somewhat loudly, as though she is having to force herself to do this. "This-little-girls-parents-don't-seem-to-like-us-which-makes-it-hard-to-help-her." Nancy is in the front pew and standing only halfway toward us. She's looking at the side wall the entire time she talks. She shares how her calmness in the face of this child's unsettling behavior helps to bring about major changes, and that the little girl is able to produce an art project, which although not something to "hang in a museum," makes Nancy feel very happy for her. She finishes with, "I am grateful for what Christian Science has taught me about children," and sits down quickly with her back to the group.

The accountant, who has been peering at her with the same embalmed smile the entire time she has spoken, simply says, "thank you."

Now I'm sorry, but this just strikes me as odd. Everything this woman said was very thoughtful, and I felt, enlightening, too. She gave some very good guidance about how to manage a difficult child. But the way that this is being carried out is so formal and promotes no real warmth in the group. It's like: this is the way this was done in 1902, as led by Mary Baker Eddy, so this is how we are going to do it now one hundred years later. No wonder their numbers have dwindled. They've got some good stuff to offer–Mary Baker Eddy seems to have been one of the first serious practitioners of mind over body. But come on people-bring it into the 21st century! Not many people are going to feel gratified sitting in these stiff pews on a Wednesday night, looking up at the accountant and singing stodgy old hymns.

Two other women get up and give testimonies: one about how she got a friend to read Mary Baker Eddy's book–a motorcycle man with lots of tattoos; and the other, how the health care crisis in our country could be so easily dealt with by adopting the principles of Christian Science and prayer. Both seem seriously to study books about the topic.

There is no interaction in the group, except when the moderator says "thank you," and the women each thank him for "the readings." It's as if all interchanges must be followed within a strict set of guidelines. I hate to tell them this, but they might want to look around. Everyone in the room is 40 and up–I'm definitely the youngest. There is no next generation to carry on this ritual. At least not in this congregation.

I walk out as the last hymn is being sung. I decide not to stay because it would be disingenuous for me to act as though I have any further interest in this church. I don't. But I do have an interest in some of the teachings of Mary Baker Eddy and in developing my own mind-body-spirit connection more.

If I were to fill out a feedback form for this group, I'd suggest the following: make Christian Science accessible to others who did not grow up with these traditions. Get the word out that Mind-Body is happening right here in our town. Have some flea markets, carnivals and spaghetti dinners at the church. Get your heads out of the books and tell people why you're so into your faith. Tell people that you don't think using doctors is wrong, even if you try not to do it that much.

They seem like genuinely nice and deeply spiritual people. Just a bit too serious and regimented, from my perspective. And in their case, it's not helping to bring in the customers.

And for goodness sake, get rid of the "Scientist" part of the name.

It's just silly.

Christian Scientist

#	Dimension of Church Experience	Rating
1)	Is parking close and convenient?	10
2)	How beautiful is the worship space?	3
3)	How comfortable is the seating?	2
4)	How welcoming and friendly is the congregation?	6
5)	How enjoyable and uplifting are the musical aspects of the worship?	2
6)	Does the leader have a pleasant speaking voice and does he/she make sense to me?	4
7)	How clean are the bathrooms?	8
8)	Are the people in the pews interesting to stare at?	1
9)	How tolerant to many ways of seeing and doing things does this group appear to be?	5
10)	Would I feel good about how these people would spend my money?	2
11)	How close did I feel to God in this place?	2
12)	Did I smile more than once during the experience?	1
	Total	51

Roman Catholic

Catholicism has always been an enigma to me: I've known so many people who were raised Catholics and their adult views on that religion run all over the board. There are those who absolutely despise the Catholic Church and would never set foot in one again. Many have scary stories of abuse and terror to share about their time in the confessional or in the classroom of a Catholic school. One friend told me that he remembers a prune-faced nun staring his class of third-graders down with great intimidation, while telling them the following: "God gives you every breath you breathe, and He can *take it away* from you, *just–like–THAT!*" She snapped her fingers to show how quickly their little lungs could stop working.

I wonder if any studies have ever been done on early onset asthma, and whether or not it is higher among Catholic school children.

Dozens of other stories of priests and nuns have passed by me over the years: stories of priests who made children cry in the confessional; parents who left the church in a huff because their children were considered "bastard;" a nun who locked a teenage girl in a closet.

But I've met other adult Catholics who are very devoted to their church and their faith, who understand the limitations and the problems with the church, but see tremendous good in it as well. Like my friend Sheila, who grew up going to a Catholic school and said the nuns were the nicest people she ever knew. She said that they taught every child in the school to respect and love each other and that no one was ever bullied by anyone because of how important that philosophy was. Indeed, my own younger brother, when having difficulty with bullies in the public school, was sent to the Catholic school in our little village, where they nurtured him and shared their lunches whenever he forgot and left his sitting on the counter.

As a woman who has married two recovering Catholic men, I've smelled the remains of things Catholic that still linger on their flesh. Neither one has chosen to continue with their childhood faith as adults. As I was about to marry my first husband, I courted a Father O'Brien in an attempt to have him co-officiate at my wedding--a bid to please my future father-in-law in a way that only a youthful lass of 26 would have the zeal to do. He agreed, but only after I signed a paper saying that I would raise my children Catholic.

What *was* his last name? Tendershanks? Cockenfield? Father Brian...*Rumpelstilskin,* yeah...I believe that was it. I guess he figured if he was going to take the number two spot in the service, he'd have to get a little something in return.

Well, everything with fresh eyes, right?
It is a cloudy day when I visit the first of the Catholic churches I would attend. All Saints Catholic Church sits on a hill on the edge of a little town. I am running late and don't get in until things are rolling along. My husband agrees to accompany me and explain aspects of the service, since he was raised Catholic. He parks the car as I run up the handicapped ramp and through the glass doors.

I don't have time to study the entrance foyer and move through the second set of doors, straight into the sanctuary.

OH MY! It's FLORENCE! The architecture in this place is fabulous, and I find myself thinking, now *here's* a sanctuary that really seems to glorify God!

The ceiling alone is a sight to behold, and brings to mind the inside of Napoleon's Arch de Triumph in Paris. Little squares are decorated with ornate designs, in bold contrasting white, rust and black colors. The statuary and wall frescos are beautifully done and everything is gilded with gold.

There are two men standing at the back doors, bouncer-like, but neither has any handouts, which disappoints me. I need a bulletin in a church or temple...something to hold. It makes one feel secure because they can follow along and know just what is coming next.

The church is about three quarters full and I slide into a pew near the back.

"NOOOOOOO!" a little voice shrieks behind me. Oh great, I inadvertently sat in front of a screeching child. There is nothing more torturous than sitting in front of a crying child in church. Yes, we're all supposed to bear it good-naturedly, but can you imagine the same situation with an adult making all that noise? What if you were at the movies and an adult behind you was grabbing on the back of your chair, yelling, "STOP IT!" and "GET OOOOFF!"

I want to look around the place, but realize that the priest is somewhere in the middle of his sermon and that we're apparently more than a few minutes late. I try to focus on the man and his message. The priest is very old, seems to be leaning heavily into the pulpit, and sounds like a bored Howard Cossell.

"....and so....we must turn to the Holy Spirit...in matters of our...sex life....we must turn to the Holy Spirit...in matters of....our self esteem....and we must ask the Holy Spirit for help....with our family...and in all our concerns. Let the Holy Spirit work through you. Amen."

Bummer. I must have missed much of the sermon. For this last part, I imagined he was holding a little 3x5 index card with "Holy Spirit" written on the left-hand side, and arrows going to a list of words on the right: "sex life," "self esteem," "family." Probably his outline of the sermon--maybe he forgot the expanded version back in the rectory.

I notice that this priest really seems to be ailing. When he turns, he has to slide his hands along the walls to steady himself, and when he walks from place to place, he hangs on to the shoulder of the altar girl.

My husband slides in beside me with a pained look on his face. Parking, I figure.

We hear a thump behind us. "WHAAAAAUUUGGGH!" Someone whispers and tries to console the child, but you know it's one of those crying spells where that first outburst was only the beginning. They're merely inhaling before they really get going. Hopefully the parents will take the child out.

"WHAAAAUUUUUUGGGGGHHHH! WHAAAAAAUUUUUUUUUGGGGHHHH!!"

They don't. Apparently there is more than one little cherub behind me, because I keep hearing something being slammed against the pew, and then can feel it sliding across my shoulders....I think it's a rosary...at least it sounds and feels very beadlike in consistency.

"WHAAAAUUUUUGGGGGHHHH!! WHAUGH! WHAUGH!"

"You need to be quiet....ssshhhh....when we get home I can fix it for you but I can't right now." The Dad is trying to calm the beast. I'm relieved to hear him say "when we get home I'll fix it," as opposed to "when we get home I'm gonna beat the shit out of you if you don't shut up."

I notice everyone holding a thin book in front of them and I pull what appears to be worship guide out of the pew in front of me and take a look. Interesting...everything is dated and spelled out. Kinda cheap paper....like those books of crossword puzzles that you can buy at the dollar store.

We jump right into the sign of the peace, and communion.

"DOOOOON'T!" comes from behind us. It wouldn't help to move because there are squirming kids all over the place. Don't Catholics have a nursery, or some kind of kids program....a room with a trampoline even?

I look over at my husband who continues to have a pained look on his face.

"Do you want to move?" I whisper in his ear.

He seems to be coming back from some faraway place.

"Oh...that doesn't bother me."

How could it not? "Well, you seem to have a pained look on your face."

"This is making me very uncomfortable..." he says in a low tone.

"What....church?" I ask innocently.

"Yeah," he replies, his facial expression seeming to say, "what did you think, dummy."

I try to focus on the activities up front. Someone is jingling bells whenever the priest puts something in his mouth.

Just hear those sleigh bells jingling, ting-ting-tingling too...come on it's lovely weather for a sleigh ride together with you.

Oh great. Now I'll have that song in my head all day.

"See those pictures on the walls?" my husband has leaned into me.

I nod.

"Those are the fourteen stations of the cross. I remember as a kid, before Easter, I would have to walk around the church, visit each of the pictures and say prayers, really thinking about the experience Christ went through. To this day, if I even see that little station book at my mother's house, it makes me sick to my stomach. The experience was so gruesome that by the time I was finished, I felt as though *I* had been crucified."

I look at the stations on the wall. All of them are frescoes that stick out in three-D style. They are very gloomy in content, I have to admit, and the titles of the pictures aren't so uplifting either: *"Jesus is Condemned to Death," "Jesus Falls the Second Time," "Jesus is Stripped of His Garments," "Jesus is Nailed to the Cross," "Jesus Expires on the Cross."*

Looking at these pictures makes me remember how Pontius Pilate wasn't even going to have Jesus crucified, that it was never his intention until the mob insisted on it. That made me wonder about what the future of Christianity would have been if Jesus had only gotten a prison sentence, or had to do community service. Certainly, it would have taken some of the punch out of these stations. People would have to walk around meditating on: *"Jesus is Walked to His Jail Cell,"* or *"Jesus Sits on His Cot and Talks to a Little Mouse."*

I try to imagine my husband as a small boy, walking around the church with a prayer book, thinking about this beautiful man having his clothes ripped off and nails driven through his hands and feet. My husband is so sensitive that as a 45-year-old, he couldn't watch the animation in Disney's *Tarzan* where the Gorilla mom is being chased by the leopard.

Other images in the sanctuary are equally gruesome, like the full-size sculpture of Jesus on the cross, with the blood pronounced on his knees and feet and hands--but they exist alongside lovely busts of the Virgin Mary and paintings which show a happy mother and son.

Before you know it, we are standing and hearing words of benediction. I turn to comment to my husband that I guess I got the times of the service wrong, but he is already gone and near the exit. Most of the people appear to be stampeding toward the doors, not lingering even a little. No one stays to chat with other parishioners. Within minutes, the entire church has been emptied of bodies, and I, who have been trying to study more of the fantastic art, am the last to leave. Even the priest has vacated his post at the back door by the time I get there, and I realize that if I want to be Catholic, I am either going to have to learn how to move swiftly with the pack or always be taking up the rear.

My husband has the car running in front when I get there, and as I climb in, he has started to accelerate before the door is fully closed. I thank him for coming with me, and as either consolation or penance, I take him for a brunch of pancakes and greasy bacon. I make a mental note that the next time I will have to do this Catholic thing on my own.

I return to All Saint's the following Saturday–exercising my option to worship on what feels like a nontraditional religious day to me. I tell my husband that the place will probably be empty, given that it is a Saturday and the 4th of July weekend. He scoffs.

"It'll be packed."

"Why?" I ask.

"Cause people want to get it over with."

"What do you mean 'get it over with?' If they're so unhappy about going, why go at all?"

"Because you have to. It's a sin if you don't go to church every week. That's why they have so many services throughout the week. And for it to count you have to go after 5 on Saturday and then it counts for Sunday. And you have to get there before the Gospel reading, and stay through Communion."

I'm not sure I like the idea of having to punch in and punch out at church.

At any rate, I get there a few minutes early this time and have a chance to look at some of the literature in the front foyer. There is a flyer about the week's activities at All Saints. Their theme for an upcoming picnic is "Red White and Blue, USA Colors and Slovak Colors too!" This is followed by a thank you to those volunteers who helped fill cabbage on Friday.

There seems to be a fair amount of gambling going on at this parish: BINGO and 50/50 tickets figure prominently in this flyer. And the back is covered with ads–ads for everything from Funeral Homes to braces to real estate to a bakery.

The other flyers in the rack advertise that people should "Respect Life," and "Get Involved in Catholic Charities." An advertisement for the priesthood shows a variety of young men of all racial types, doing happy priest things: holding a wafer over a cup in a bright robe of crimson red; smiling ecstatically shoulder to shoulder; preaching from the pulpit in another lovely robe of chartreuse green with a striking gold trim; being surrounded adoringly by a group of women with their babies; joking around with a good 'ole Bishop. It's probably just an unfortunate oversight that this flyer which boldly proclaims on the front: "Follow me; Do not be afraid," is positioned right beside another flyer that advertises assistance to any one who as a minor has been sexually abused by a priest, deacon, teacher, employee or representative of the Archdiocese of Philadelphia.

Pondering this, I am reminded of a television documentary I had watched just a few nights before about Martin Luther and the Protestant Reformation. The Pope at the time, Leo, had a penchant for the flesh and at parties he threw (parties which exhausted the coffers of the Catholic Church which brought about the selling of indulgences to get into heaven), he had naked boys jump out of cakes.

Well, at least now they're offering assistance after the abuse.

I head on into the sanctuary and note that my husband is right: the place is packed. A different priest is in front, as old and unsteady on his feet as the first. The average age of the two of them is probably 88. As this priest moves around, I notice that they have installed some rehab-looking metal railings to help these senior men of God move up and down the few steps to the altar.

A woman is singing and people are all answering her in song, all of it coming straight from the worship guide. After the singing and a few

Bible readings recited stiffly by a muscular middle-aged man, the priest moves to the pulpit.

"Good evening everyone."

"Good evening, Father," the room of two hundred says in near perfect unison.

"I'm Father Jack Hannagin, visiting all of you from Philadelphia. I'm from a community of priests known as the 'Josephites.' How many of you out there have ever heard of the Josephites?...I see a few people raising their hands, but not too many. We aren't as big as the Jesuits or the Franciscans, there are only 109 of us, but we are the only sect to work only with Black people in the United States–we are American Missionaries."

Two skinny older women come up on my right and want to squeeze into the pew. They might as well turn around and leave, because they've come after the Gospel, and God, up there looking down, has just put an "x" in their attendance record for today.

"Our community was started in 1871 when priests were invited from England to come and work in Baltimore, Maryland, with Blacks who were former slaves and now wanted a better life....as many of you know, the schools that were available to Blacks in those times were segregated and offered an inferior education....and that's putting it nicely. If a Black family wanted an education for their child in the Catholic school, we accepted them gladly...and expected only the following: that they would have to attend Holy Mass every week. Yes, many of them would still go to their Baptist Churches, or their storefront churches after mass, but bit by bit we made converts."

Hmmm. He's saying all this so smoothly, as though it's the most natural thing in the world. But somehow this reminds me of the priest who said he'd officiate at my wedding but only if I'd sign a paper saying I'd raise my daughter Catholic. Is "extortion" too strong a word for the tactics of these genial-looking old men?

"I always thought I'd be a Midshipman at Annapolis, or a Cadet at West Point...you look like a million dollars in those uniforms and the girls would all chase you....but I've been a priest for 58 years and I absolutely love it. And I'm only 6 days younger than our dear Pope John Paul...and we were baptized on the very same day!"

Well, I'm relieved that the focus has moved off of the coercion of Blacks into the Catholic Church.

"....anyway....in the past 75 years, we've gone from having 250,000 Black Catholics to 2.5 million–and this has something to do with your prayers, I'm sure..."

I seriously doubt that the two teenage girls sitting in front of me in spandex bell bottoms have been praying fervently for the numbers of Black Catholics to rise.

"Still, we must note that 23% of Americans are Catholic, but only 4% of Blacks are Catholic. So we still have a lot of work to do..."

I don't know, call me selfish, but I'd rather work toward bettering my own soul, or helping those people in the pews who are here with me right at this moment, or to praying for world peace and the spread of harmony and love, than to focus on increasing market share, i.e., getting the number of Blacks Catholics into double-digits.

"Please pray with me that we will have more young men becoming priests and Josephites..."

We're back to the priest theme.

"...there are so little following in our footsteps and we worry about what will become of our order....there is a *terrible* shortage of priests....pray that more young men will knock on the doors of our seminaries and say, 'Let me in! I want to be a priest of the Josephites!'"

Listening to him reminded me that in the local news, they had just reported that a huge billboard had been erected along the Schuylkill Expressway leading into Philadelphia. It made reference to this shortage of priests and read: If You're Looking For a Sign, Here It Is: Ordain Women Priests."

Father Hannigan talked a bit more about the work of the priests and ended with a big pitch for money for their group. The collection baskets would be passed around twice, once for the parish, and once for the Josephites.

The collection process in Catholic Churches strikes me as a no-nonsense affair. Older men with somewhat crusty faces and the look of those who have toiled hard with their arms and hands, walk down the aisles, swiftly shoving a wicker basket on a stick in front of each and every parishioner.

We move on to the communion and I note that we are only offered the body of Christ and not his blood. This is disappointing because the consistency of wafers in this Catholic Church is like freeze-dried paper and you need a little something to try to help wash it down.

The priest moves slowly to the pulpit. "If no one has announcements, we will now end Mass." An organist moves right into "America the Beautiful," and it's clear that if one did have announcements, they would have had less than a nanosecond to jump in and make themselves heard.

Four males march out of the church: An altar boy carrying a cross, the man who did the readings who is holding a huge Bible up high in front of his face, the priest, and another altar boy who is doing nothing particular as far as I can tell. The woman who stood at the pulpit and sang doesn't march down the aisle with them–they probably asked her to and she told them to go on ahead without her.

Once again, I linger in the sanctuary and enjoy the beautiful art. I have to say that this is one of the most lovely American churches I have been in, and I am taken back to trips to Italy and Germany.

I make my way behind the final stream of worshipers, again, bringing up the rear. But this time I make sure I get there before the priest has taken leave. He stares straight at my breasts for at least two seconds, then looks up.

"Well, hello my dear," he says with a red-faced smile.

"Hello," I say. I assume my most non-threatening, chummy demeanor. "Do you think they'll ever ordain women priests?" I ask.

He looks slightly taken aback for a second, but he recoups quickly. "Oh....I don't know..." Then he seems to brighten. "It may come to pass..." He pats my arm.

Whoa! It's then that I get a whiff of strong booze and we're not talking that little sip of wine he had ten minutes ago.

"Do you think they should?" I follow-up.

He looks toward the sanctuary, perhaps lifting his eyes to the hills for some help. "Oh...I don't have a firm belief about it one way or the other...it's part of tradition, ya know...."

(I'm gonna take that as a "no.")

"But you have this 'terrible shortage of priests,' as you pointed out in your sermon."

"Oh, we've had that before," he says with a breezy, dismissive wave of his hand.

"You have?"

"Oh, I'm talking centuries ago..."

He says that as though it was only yesterday.

Just as I'm about to come in with my final and I think, most compelling question: Why *shouldn't* they be priests, a young woman interrupts us and asks me if the umbrella she is holding is one I left behind in the church.

"Thank you," I say.

"Oh! What an angel! Bless you my child!" Father Hannigan seems so elated about the umbrella that you would have thought it was not mine but his, and not originally his, but one that belonged to his great-grandmother, which she had given to him on the day he became ordained as a Josephite.

He takes advantage of this distraction and makes a move toward the sanctuary, while still smiling a frozen smile.

"Well, thanks for your time," I decide to let him go. He's probably fearful that I'll set my teeth into his leg like a pit bull and that he'll have to drag me down the center aisle.

Women.

He moves back toward me and shakes my hand once more, again patting my arm. "Okay Darling, *you be good.*"

I want to ask him what my "being good" would look like, from his perspective. Would I go home and pray for the percentage of Black Catholics to go from 4 to 6...or even 7? Would I stuff some cabbages? Or would I simply put this business about women being priests out of my head and get down to my callings in life: those of being a wife and mother? I certainly wouldn't mind the cabbage or the wife and mother thing, but I'd like to think that if I became a Catholic, that they'd invite me to do a reading, or collect the money, or stand at the back door, or process down the aisle, or that the potential existed for my daughter to be the spiritual leader in the service–yes, the priest herself.

Well, as the man said, "It may come to pass."

Like a kidney stone, probably.

I attend several other Catholic services in this quest for the right church for me. I think because I have heard so many negative things, and because I have so many concerns of my own, I am trying very hard to find things to like and embrace about this very quirky but extremely powerful religion.

If churches were restaurants, one could think of the Catholic Church as one big chain of McDonalds: serving up the same, basic, fast food in every single church across this nation of ours. Open nearly twenty-four hours. Getting it to you fast and moving you on your way.

In the end, I just don't think I can be a Catholic. It's not because of the many problems the church has which are so well known but somehow never resolved.

It's because in the five Catholic Churches I attended, where I sat for five hours, amidst over 1,000 Catholics—I never saw a single person smiling.

Roman Catholic

#	Dimension of Church Experience	Rating
1)	Is parking close and convenient?	1
2)	How beautiful is the worship space?	10
3)	How comfortable is the seating?	2
4)	How welcoming and friendly is the congregation?	1
5)	How enjoyable and uplifting are the musical aspects of the worship?	1
6)	Does the leader have a pleasant speaking voice and does he/she make sense to me?	1
7)	How clean are the bathrooms?	6
8)	Are the people in the pews interesting to stare at?	2
9)	How tolerant to many ways of seeing and doing things does this group appear to be?	1
10)	Would I feel good about how these people would spend my money?	1
11)	How close did I feel to God in this place?	1
12)	Did I smile more than once during the experience?	1
	Total	29

Independent Baptist

Years ago they came up with the term "Super Model," I suppose to describe those women whose height, exposure and pay had all soared through the ozone. They weren't just run-of-the-mill models, they were SUPER models–behemoths in their field, towering over all the other pretty faces.

Now, it seems, we are experiencing what we could call "Super Churches," churches that are so huge in size and scope, that they cannot be called a plain 'ole church. These mega-churches are being built to attract as many people as possible, and in the case of Mount Zion Baptist Temple, it seems to be working.

There are many kinds of Baptists. It would be a mistake to assume that they are all cut from the same bolt as some of the more famous, or perhaps infamous Baptists, like Jerry Falwell or Bill Clinton. There are American Baptists, Southern Baptists and, as in the case of Mount Zion, Independent Baptists.

This church is a mighty complex of attached buildings, sitting alongside a major, busy highway near our home. It's impossible to miss. The size alone makes it intriguing. Surely big things have to be happening in that temple–why else would they have made it so palatial?

On a hot Sunday in July, I head out to experience my first "Super Church." No sooner have I rounded the corner into the parking lot, when a young man in a white shirt and tie comes jogging up to my car, a walkie-talkie in his hand. I power down my window.

"Hi, first time with us?" he asks.

"Yes."

"Alright then, just pull your car over there and we'll be right with you."

Excellent! As a first time visitor, I get to park my car right in the front lot. Walking great distances from my car to any front door has always been one of my lazy points, and I make a mental note that if I continue to come to Mount Zion, I will have to try to pass myself off as a first-timer as much as I possibly can. In a church of this apparent size, it shouldn't be too hard.

There are many of these young men in dark pants and white shirts with walkie-talkies, positioned all over the parking areas. In their sunglasses, they look very young and hip-- a veritable force of secret service men working the grounds of the temple.

As I pull myself out of my car, I see that the young man who directed me is jogging toward another young man, who is also jogging toward him, and as they meet, he turns and points his arm toward me. The second man starts running over.

"Yo Dude," I want to call out, "no need to run! I'm not going anywhere..."

He comes up next to me as I start to walk toward the temple.

"Have I met you before?" he asks me.

"No, I'm Ruth Laker," I extend my hand. I want to say, "Buddy, do you think I'd be parking in the visitor's lot if I had been here before? What do you take me for? Some kind of person who would *lie* so she could keep parking up front?"

"I'm Don," he says simply. "Well...so this is your first time with us?"

"Yes, " I respond, aware that Don is moving me along at a steady clip and funneling me toward one of the front doors, amidst a gazillion other people.

"Well, I'll take you right in to our information desk–we always like to ask people, how did you find out about us?"

Hmmm. He's getting the marketing questions out there right in front. Don's breath is a bit choppy–obviously he's been covering a lot of ground this morning.

"Oh, since you're right on the highway, you're hard to miss."

Don is nodding his head in that way that people do when you know they're only half-listening and thinking about the next thing that they have to do.

Just inside the doors, an elderly man and woman greet me and hand me a bulletin. I smile and thank them. The space is immediately disorienting; I feel as though I am in the lobby of a grand, busy hotel. Don leads me toward an information desk, where if I don't catch myself, I am likely to ask for some towels or an extra pillow. A young man and woman, both in navy blue blazers with pins on that say "host" and "hostess," are working the desk.

I sense Don is about to give me another pre-packaged line, so I interrupt his schtick.

"What's with the walkie-talkie?" I ask.

Don smiles and sighs, sticking out his tongue as though he just finished running a marathon. "There are ten of us out there working the parking lot, if you can believe it! We use these to communicate!"

"How many people go to this church?"

Don lifts a bulletin off the front counter. On the back is a very large number printed in the corner. It reads, "Last week's attendance: 894." Don confirms this with the two people behind the desk.

The young woman smiles. "Well, right now it's summer, so a lot of people are away on vacation. But we usually have around 950."

I reel at the thought of so many people in one church building. The entire town I grew up in had only 2000; my high school graduating class, 200. My college had 750 women on a 350 acre campus, spread out over thirteen buildings.

I turn back to Don. "That's a whole lot 'a people," I observe.

"Yeah," Don concedes, "but everyone is so friendly...that's what made me want to come. Everyone *cares* here."

Well, I have to admit that what he is saying is consistent with their ad in the yellow pages. It did say: "We *Care* About You!"

"Well, this is where I leave you..." Don touches my arm lightly and turns on his heel. He jogs off to herd more of the flock to the caring people behind the huge mahogany...information desk.

The young woman moves swiftly. "Here is some information about the church...and here is a complimentary Bible...a *gift* from us....now, what was your name again?" She has an information card out and her pen poised. They are going to suck me right into the machinery, I can feel it.

The doors to the sanctuary are closing and I really just want to go in and sit down.

"Ruth....Laker....L-A-K-E-R.."

"Address?"

I give it.

"Phone number?"

I give a fake one.

"Are you married?"

"Yes."

"Do you have children?"

"Yes."

"Their names and ages?"

"You know, I just want to go inside, if you don't mind..."

"Oh, sure," she says. She writes something on the children line, hopefully not, "This woman indicated that she had children but would not cooperate and give me their names."

Inside, it is clear that this is *not* your grandmother's church.

The temple was obviously tailored to modern tastes: an auditorium style room which is carpeted and round in design, with comfy, padded chairs, so one feels they are on the set of a homey talk show rather than a stuffy old church with stiff pews. State-of-the-art technology exists: microphones are everywhere, lighting and sound can accommodate any needed mood, video cameras sit on tripods, ready to catch important moments.

The place is pretty packed, but I do see an empty seat right on the aisle, not too far from the front. It almost seems too good to be true that I should not have to climb over others or wedge myself between two hefty, all-you-care-to-eat buffet kind of folks. I move a Bible and hymnal out of my way and settle in. The crowd is hearing some announcements from a suited man, who then tells us that the choir would like to sing a song, "There is a Peace."

The size of the choir is impressive. It's the middle of the summer after all. In most churches, the choir, which might consist of twenty people on a good Sunday, takes the summer off. Here at Mount Zion, the diminished summer choir consists of about fifty people. They stand together in perfect unison and launch into a smartly polished version of the song.

I look around and notice the other members of the studio audience. They look like pretty nice folk. There is some racial diversity which is nice for a change. There are Asian-Americans, African-Americans, Hispanic-Americans....people of all ages. Then I look back up front at the leadership: five white men in suits. Come to think of it, all six ushers are young white men in suits, just like the force of men working the parking lot.

Suddenly, one of the suits is standing beside me.

"I had saved a seat for two of us–right there!" An irritated woman points a finger at me accusingly. The young man smiles at me, says "excuse me," and reaches behind me to pull out the woman's Bible. It's wedged between me and the man next to me, who looks like a former biker in his late 50s, who maybe cleaned himself up for his woman and for God. I look at my accuser apologetically, but she is not pacified. The young man moves her on and helps her find a seat. As he passes by me again, after completing his mission, he whispers to me, "it's all right," and smiles. Now that was certainly nice of him. He must have gone through Usher Sensitivity Training, or UST, as I believe it's called.

One of the men in suits is now at the microphone. I can see from my flyer that he is the head pastor: Lamar Atherton. On the back of the flyer is a picture of five other men in suits, sitting in a semi-circle–all of them "Associate Pastors." Each has an interesting name....kind of old English or Southern sounding–like "Reeves, Braystock, Hamilton and

Coulter." A "Martinez" or "Tyminski" would stick out like a sore thumb in this group.

"Pick up your course book!" the Chief Pastor instructs us. Lots of people are pulling out neat little three-ring binders, unzipping leather cases and pulling out their pens. "Ushers will pass out the study page for today. Our theme is 'Rejoice in the Lord', so we will sing it as they get your sheets to you!"

Not one organ, not two organs, but two organs and a grand piano start playing in unison. Everyone seems to know the song by heart. I feel ill-prepared for this church experience. My mom didn't take me to Staples to buy my folders and pens, or one of those nifty little satchels for carrying my Bible. And I don't have a course book, for heaven's sake! What am I going to do?

"Before we get started, we're going to have our morning collection," Lamar says with his winning smile. A young blond woman comes to the microphone and starts singing a song entitled, "I Call You To Grace."

I'm tempted at this point to call out, "Where's the fire?" I've never seen such a slick, highly orchestrated service unfold, and at such a breakneck pace. As with television and radio, apparently not even one or two seconds of dead air time can be allowed.

Six men pass around gold collection plates. The woman at the microphone has a magnificent voice, except when she hits the really high notes. Then she goes just a little flat. But her sound is rich and clear and the music keeps mounting. It's one of those songs that has a big flashy ending.

All who stand before him stand amazed,
Praaaaiiiiiiise Hiiiiim!
Praaaaiiiiiiise Hiiiiim,
All who stand before him stand amaaaaaaaaazed!

As she hits those highest notes, I feel the hairs on the back of my neck stand up.

I love when that happens.

Many people say "Amen," when she finishes. The pastor walks to the microphone and thanks her. He probably has her name written on a little slip of paper.

"Open your Bible to Psalm 138–verses 1-5. We're talking today about developing a heart for God!"

Everyone opens their Bibles and all pens are in position. I look at the little green study sheet we've been given. On it are a series of half-finished sentences with blanks to fill in, rating scales, things called a "spiritual check up".....I flip over to the other side expecting to see a word find or crossword puzzle.

Darn it! Everyone is scratching something on to their sheets. While I was putzing around looking at the back of the form, Pastor Lamar had already given the first answer. I hate when that happens! Now I'm going to have an empty blank. Man...

The sentence is this: "Developing a Heart for God begins with being_____."

I have absolutely no idea what the answer is because I wasn't paying attention. It's not in the Psalm either. One of those sneaky ones that's not in the book so you have to pay attention to the lecture.

I decide to try and figure it out on my own.

Developing a Heart for God begins with being... punctual? No, that's not it.

Developing a Heart for God begins with being... open? Nah---too psychobabble sounding.

Developing a Heart for God begins with being... humble? That sounds pretty Bibley and church-like.

It's going to drive me crazy that I've missed filling in the first blank and if I don't stop messing around here, I'm going to miss the next one. So I decide to do what any good Christian would do under the circumstances: copy off of someone else's paper.

Who's gonna see in a class this size?

I lean slightly to my left and try to look at the Bikerman's sheet. Aw, he's not even filling it out. He's just leaning into his wife or girlfriend, helping her fill out hers. They're probably so in love that they want to do everything together.

That's really cute, actually.

So I lean just a bit more and try to see hers. The man turns and sees me a mere inch from his shoulder. I smile up at him.

"I missed the first blank. Do you know what the answer is?" I whisper sweetly.

He pulls the sheet off his girlfriend's lap and holds it where we can both see it. "Born again," he whispers back.

Great. I pen in the words and thank him for his help. Phfew! Wait a minute... *"Born again?"*

I've never actually understood that expression, but it's always had a negative connotation in my mind. These people--all 950 of them--are *"Born Again Christians?"*

Someone once told me that the problem with many "Born Again Christians," is that they make you wish they had never been born the first time.

Well, these people seem all right so far.

The pastor is moving things along. Not one beat has been missed in this entire church experience so far. It's all one big, smooth production as far as I can see–and yet, with a homey feel. It's hard to tell that the room is holding roughly 600 people by my estimate, a third of whom are upstairs in the balcony.

"What do *you* have to praise God for today?" Lamar asks us.

I look on to my sheet to see where we are. Shoot! We're already at the rating part with the Likert Scale and I missed another blank!

I ease forward in my seat and try to look over the woman's shoulder in front of me. The Bikerman nudges me and shows me the page again. I smile–embarrassed.

The answer to the second blank is "Praise." "Begin with a Heart of Praise."

Now we all get to circle numbers between 1 and 5 and rate our praiseworthy items, such as health, money, friends, and something that reads "close walk" or "no walk." Well, on that last one, if they're talking about our parking spaces, I definitely got a "close walk." I'd like to know how I could get the "no walk" option.

Pastor Atherton tells us what he circled, all in a highly entertaining and engaging style. He is a "1" on health, and a "3" on money. He encourages us to see that even a "5" on health is all right because God may decide not to make us well, but He will bless us with his Grace, so it doesn't matter if we are sick or not.

The close-walk, no-walk dimension is about how close we are to God–not about parking spaces. So I don't want the "no-walk" option after all. I circle an honest 4 to 5 on that one, and then it scares me to realize that if I really want to have a close walk with God, I might just have to do what these guys are saying and be "Born Again," however that is done.

As if he read my mind, the Pastor has this to say: "You can only walk with God if you make a commitment to do it! God doesn't want you to have doubts! God is pursuing you today! You think that being here is a coincidence? That you came because a *friend* told you? NO!! God is *pushing* you to be here today! He is *pursuing* you!"

Good heavens. They've got a stalker God here.

Again, Lamar has read my thoughts: "But he will not force you! He will not." Lamar knocks on the podium three times. "He'll just do that." He knocks again. "He'll just wait for you to open the door." The good pastor smiles an all-knowing kind of smile.

"We need to sing songs of praise...to surround ourselves with beautiful, Christian music! Here are some real country song titles. I want to ask you, what would listening to these songs do to you? *I Went Back to My 4th Wife for the 3rd Time and Gave Her a 2nd Chance to Make a 1st Class Fool Out Of Me."*

Everyone laughs as the Pastor tries to sing the song.

"Here's a real spiritual one: *You're the Reason that Our Kids Are Ugly."*

People roar at that one.

"How about this one: *I'm Ashamed to Be Here, But Not Ashamed Enough to Leave."*

They gasp.

"Or how about, *If My Nose Was Blowing Money Honey, I'd Blow It All On You."*

This seems to be the all-time favorite of the studio audience, but I have to say, I liked: *If You Can't Live Without Me, Why Aren't You Dead?*

"Does the music that fills your car, home and work honor God? When you need to be healed....Christian music will do it for you." Lamar smiles again, and there are a rare few seconds of silence.

But it's time to move on again. We plow on through the study sheet, learning that we can maintain our heart with worship, particularly worship at Mount Zion Baptist Temple. We learn that we can strengthen our heart with God's word (i.e., the Bible). Lamar tells us that God exalts His Word above His Name. That is what God thinks of his Word.

Still, His Name is pretty gosh darn important too. So much so, the Lamar wants us to know that God's name is too special to use in vain.

"You can say, 'OH MY GOD!! I *LOVE* YOU!!"

Wow. He yelled that so loud and with so much feeling I thought he'd surely drop to his knees or start convulsing in a fit of rapture.

"But don't use God's name to express surprise...or disbelief...or annoyance. Oh, you may say, 'I know, but it's a habit....' CHANGE IT!"

Dozens of people yell their agreement from the audience. "AMEN!" "THAT'S RIGHT!"

"Say something else...say, 'Oh my word!' or 'Oh my goodness!' or 'Oh my tomatoes!' Say something other than God's name."

I look around again at the studio audience, and at the men on the podium with the pastor. Everyone in the place has a big smile on his or her face as they watch the pastor's performance. Everyone is having a great time here in the temple.

"But remember brothers and sisters, God's Word is exalted even above his name. How many here have read the Bible all the way through....I don't mean, 'Well, I got to Revelations and didn't quite finish that, but otherwise I did'...I MEAN: *ALL THE WAY THROUGH!* HOW MANY?!"

A significant number of people have their hand raised, mine not being among them.

"Look at your contract on the sheet friends. Make your decision and sign it now. Make a contract with God that you will read the Bible all the way through and not stop until you do!"

I look at my study sheet. It reads: "My Decisions about God's Word: I have read through the Bible completely. Yes or No. If not, I promise to read the Bible within the next 12 months."
Signed_____."

Oh my tomatoes. I've been so diligent about filling out my form, but now....now I may have to leave something blank.

This is where I always have difficulty with organized religion. This insistence that the Bible is THE word of God end of story, and not a group of works written by many different men in a time and context, many of which contradict each other.

I have read the Bible. Not all the way through, no. I've read it in dribs and drabs, in chunks and chunkets, over years and years and years. It has some beautiful writing in it, but it's not all beautiful.

I look back at this sheet. Should I read the bible all the way through? Cover to cover? Suddenly, I remember a women's retreat I had participated in at another church. I was in a small group with two other women, one in her late twenties, another nearly 90. We were talking about a story from the Old Testament, one of those ones where God seems quasi-sadistic. I decided to confess my feelings about the story to the two women. I told them I didn't like it, for the most part. They sat quietly for a few seconds.

Then the 90-year-old woman had a confession of her own: "You know, I remember going through this Bible class where we read every single word of the Bible and studied every little thing about it. By the time we were done, I was sick of that thing! The stories were so depressing! I couldn't wait for it to be over!"

I smiled in relief.

The younger woman also shared. "Yeah, I figure God has given me a brain for a reason. And my brain tells me that a lot of those stories don't make sense."

That was one of the most validating experiences I had ever had in a church.

So I take my green study sheet, and I circle "No" that I haven't read the Bible all the way through. Then I pen in two words of my own to the pledge: "I *do not* promise to read through the Bible within the next 12 months. Signed, Ruth Laker."

We're nearing the end of the two pages, which I assume means the sermon is almost over. Pastor Lamar ends with a request that we pray. As everyone bows their heads, the Pastor starts speaking very quickly, but again, with the easy flow of the master performer that he is. I don't bow my head, and I notice him hiking up the sleeve of his suit jacket and checking his watch, while speaking rapt words to God.

We are about to have a baptism, so Pastor Lamar invites one of the young men sitting behind him to lead the congregation in a hymn while he exits to prepare for the event.

The strapping young man with a winning smile comes to the microphone, the same one who has led us in two other hymns, and conducts us through three verses of "More About Jesus."

It's interesting how everything here is facilitated by someone: parking your car, walking into the building, finding a seat, singing a song...I'm almost afraid to go the bathroom.

The man yells out to us at the beginning of each verse, "On the first! On the second! We're on the thiiiiird!" The two organs and piano pound out the song and again, I'm feeling as though we are racing toward something, but who knows what that is.

No sooner have we sung the last note of the song, when the lights dim and a spotlight appears up in the sky. Under a large silver cross which appears to be suspended in the air by a wire of some kind, there is a little compartment of some sort. Kind of like a box seat at the opera. The Pastor walks down a small flight of stairs into the little cubby, and he is followed by a boy. They are wading right into a tub of water.

The pastor speaks. "This is Matt. He's been at our summer camp and he would like to be baptized. All those in favor of Matt being baptized signify with a hearty 'AMEN!'"

Everyone signifies it.

Matt is dunked into the water while the Pastor repeats some words befitting the occasion. I am amazed to be watching this. I mean, having been baptized as a baby, with one of those little trickles of water to the head, the same way we had our children baptized, I find it fascinating that people would set up these big bathtubs right in the church and actually dunk people under them.

There are so many questions I want to ask: Where does the water come from? What's the temperature? Is it heated? Do they use chemicals like chlorine to keep it bacteria-free? Do they have a "Pool Man," to come by and clean it from time to time? Where do they go after they've waded out? Where do they put their soaking wet clothes?

We've certainly come a long way from John the Baptist in the river Jordan, and it's kind of a shame. Personally, I'd like us to move beyond a lot of things from the past, but the idea of baptism in an actual river of water seems so...romantic, if you will. Why don't we just walk on down to the nearest creek and do it there? Why not spread out picnic blankets and make a church event of it? One of the associate pastors comes to the microphone to end the service in prayer. You can tell that he is pumped for his big moment at the podium. He jumps into the final prayer with gusto, and as he is praying, at least twenty to thirty people are getting up and leaving. That's not very nice. Perhaps since he's not the big star of the show, his message doesn't carry as much punch. Poor guy.

Out in the lobby, one is swept up in a sea of bodies and chatty, smiling people. The bulletin said that newcomers should come to the Hospitality Room, but I have no idea where that is and I can't seem to find it. I stumble into the nursery, a huge conference room with a long table and lots of maroon-colored chairs, the gift shop. I'm too overwhelmed to ask anyone–there are just so many people!

Finally, a middle-aged woman comes up to me. "I don't believe we've met. I'm Mary Knox," she says in a very friendly way.

It's impressive that she knows a newcomer. "I'm Ruth Laker."

"Is this your first time?"

"Yes, it is."

"Praise the Lord!"

"I'm not sure this is the right kind of place for me. It's just so big," I tell her honestly.

"Oh, keep coming," she winks at me. "You'd be surprised at how quickly you get to know everyone. We are one big family!"

It's tempting to say that there aren't too many families of 950. "Well, it was nice to meet you, Mary."

"Very nice to meet you. Hope to see you again."

I opt not to go the "Hospitality Room" today. I'm just feeling alone in the crowd, and I want to get home to my family, which consists of 5 people. That's 945 less than the Mount Zion Baptist family, but it's big enough for me.

I leave Mount Zion Baptist Church with a sense that it is probably not the place for me, but I am intrigued by the mega-church phenomenon, and put in a call to one of the pastors to ask a few questions. It takes three days for the call to be returned, but when it is, I hear the voice of a pastor, sounding very commanding in his masculine baritone.

"This is Pastor Don Reeves from Mount Zion Baptist Temple," he says.

"Ohhh, thanks for calling!" I say enthusiastically. I had forgotten about someone calling me back. "I was at your church on Sunday and I had some questions if you have a few minutes."

"Absolutely."

"Great. Well, I was wondering how you manage such a large church...my idea of a church is so different as far as size is concerned...that it is smaller and everyone is closer and knows everyone else well...how do you meet the needs of the people in a church that size and how big do you want to become?"

"We didn't start out as such a large church. Pastor Atherton had a small church when he began. But it is God's will that we grow and we will respond to God's will to meet the needs of God's people as best we can. We have attempted to keep up with the growth because it is God's design that we cannot question. We will accommodate as many of God's people as come to us, since that is His will."

That was the most God-dense sentiment I'd ever heard.

He continues. "We may eventually build some smaller sister churches which could accommodate others in the area, but for now, we have welcomed our growth because it is God's wish."

I'm wondering which came first: the mega-building, or the 950 people. Was it, "if you build it, they will come," or "they keep coming so we have to build it."

I move on to another fascinating aspect of Mount Zion.

"I noticed that all your pastors are men and I'm wondering, do Independent Baptists have women pastors? Would you ever have any at the church?"

"No...we take our model for church leadership directly from the Bible...specifically first Timothy, Chapter 3, and Titus, Chapter 2, that the pastors and the deacons are men, and that that is the way that God intends for it to be. It doesn't mean that the role of women is less important, it is just different. We see men in the 'headship' role and women in the 'helper' role."

Hmmm. How conveeeeeenient. I'm not sure if it's how *God* intends for it to be, but I'm certain it's how the men who wrote the Bible intended for it to be.

"Well, what if a woman wanted to be a leader in the church? What would you say to her?"

"Yes...we have many women in lay leadership roles within the church. My wife, for example, is in charge of the 'Moms Ministry,' reaching out to mothers with children...we have women who are in charge of Sunday School and the nursery...many women fill important roles of leadership within the church."

So it's okay for a women to be a leader in the domain of diapers and daycare because, what the heck, they're already doing that stuff.

"You know, I don't think you're the right church for me, and vice versa," I tell him honestly. "But I thank you for calling. And I'm wondering if you could pass a bit of feedback on to Pastor Atherton."

"Of course."

"Could you suggest to him that it might be nice if he referred to 'women' as 'women?' He made reference to the 'girls and men' at a college in China, and he often talked about the 'ladies'....I just think that language is very important and that concerned me."

"I agree with you completely. When did this happen?"

"This past Sunday."

"*Oh*. I wasn't there last week."

So if Don had been there, I guess he would have jumped up from his seat and exclaimed, 'Lamar! My tomatoes man! Stop demoting the women by referring to them as *'girls!'*"

"I hope you won't let that one unfortunate choice of words discolor your entire view of Mount Zion," he continues.

"Oh no. There are many other things that discolor it for me. Like your interpretations of the Bible and your certainty that you have it all figured out. But I thank you for calling and you have a nice day."

After hearing about their positions on women and leadership, I thought back to all those happy-looking women in the congregation at Mt. Zion: the young pregnant Asian-American woman who was snuggled up under her husband's arm; the middle-aged woman cozy with her former biker boyfriend; all the women in the choir with their perfect hair and make-up; the young moms in the latest fashions, chasing after their little tots; the older women clutching their Bibles and hanging on the arms of the young male ushers and deacons. How could these women all be content with positions that give them far less power, visibility and voice than the men of the church?

If our children, upon reaching the age of 21, wanted to be driven around by someone, to have someone else totally financially support them and pay all their bills, to have someone explain to them all about the meaning of life and tell them exactly what they could and couldn't do or believe, if they nervously declared that they couldn't possibly take on leadership roles or didn't want to speak in a position of authority about important matters in front of other adults, we'd think we failed as parents in raising them. Why don't we consider it a failure when full-grown, adult women assume that same dependent, needy attitude within a marriage or a church?

A week after chatting with His Headship, I found a pamphlet stuck in our door at home. On the cover was a very eerie picture of the moon emerging through parting clouds, with a cross in the lower right hand corner. My immediate association was with Count Dracula. On it was a handwritten note: "Just came to repay your visit to Mount Zion Baptist Temple. I'll call again. Lisa."

"Repay?"

No, Lisa...really, that's fine. It's yours to have and keep the change.

Independent Baptist

#	Dimension of Church Experience	Rating
1)	Is parking close and convenient?	2
2)	How beautiful is the worship space?	2
3)	How comfortable is the seating?	8
4)	How welcoming and friendly is the congregation?	5
5)	How enjoyable and uplifting are the musical aspects of the worship?	5
6)	Does the leader have a pleasant speaking voice and does he/she make sense to me?	4
7)	How clean are the bathrooms?	7
8)	Are the people in the pews interesting to stare at?	4
9)	How tolerant to many ways of seeing and doing things does this group appear to be?	1
10)	Would I feel good about how these people would spend my money?	1
11)	How close did I feel to God in this place?	1
12)	Did I smile more than once during the experience?	4
	Total	44

Mennonite

What I know about Mennonites is this: the women wear little white caps and they sell things like pies, honey and quilts at farmer's markets. I seem to remember something about persecution of Mennonites and their steadfast pacifism, and I know they share Pennsylvania Dutch roots with the Amish. I always imagined them as "Amish *Lite.*" Driving cars, wearing patterned fabric and taking in television, maybe even sneaking an occasional show like "Baywatch" or "Survivor."

There just so happens to be a Mennonite Church right down the road from my house, sitting pleasantly in the middle of a cornfield, so it wasn't necessary to break a sweat trying to get to the service, as I often do when I drive in my old car with the broken air conditioning.

I think we're all born with a sense for good and evil. Walking into Westover Mennonite Church for the first time, I immediately sense *good.* Pure, humble, warm, accessible *good.* It's as if not one negative thought has ever passed through anyone's mind in this space, as though no one within these walls had ever given another driver the finger, or stolen something or picked up a piece of pornography. It is goodness: plain and simple. As I stroll down the hallway toward the sanctuary, passing a little table with bright markers and pictures of children from other countries, and the bulletin board which displayed pictures of "God's Creatures," from bald eagles to bears, I feel elevated as a person. I feel that underneath all the complications of my life and my mind, which often makes things even more complicated, underneath I am a simple, good person too.

The lobby is abuzz with chatter as people are making their way toward the sanctuary. I check out a table piled high with homemade bags filled with something. Across from this table is another smaller one, with empty bags and instructions on how to turn them into "School kits" for needy children. What a nice idea. I notice that much of the fabric is of a vintage 1970s nature: obviously someone had been saving all their scraps from the heyday of polyester and paisley. Some look like they were made out of cotton with a pattern intended for men's underwear.

Inside, I find a nice spot on the edge of a pew in the middle of the room. This sanctuary is a modern, cozy, wide rectangle. It looks to be built for only a few hundred people. There is no fancy organ or choir loft. A simple, upright piano sits in one corner, being played by a skinny woman with thin blond hair and big bug-like glasses. Only one aspect of the church seems to put it in line with most modern Protestant churches: a huge screen is on the back wall of the sanctuary. There is no cross, or image of Jesus or Mary, nothing but a big, big screen. On an outer wall are two floral wreaths, one on each side of the screen, and that's about it.

I have to say that these screens and the projectors and overhead machines which always accompany them are in my mind, a rather distracting and disturbing trend and an ill-fitting substitution for religious images and symbols.

Talk about worshiping false gods.

No sooner have I settled down into my spot when a robust older woman with a commanding voice takes to the pulpit.

"Welcome! We are so glad to see you!! It's a bit humid, but, well...we've been through so much so far this summer...what's one more week. There's a few things I'd like you to be aware of....we're going to hold off elections until next week. Those of you who are working the craft fair need to get in touch with Ken....Liz....did you get a hold of him?....oh, all right....the rest of you need to meet with him briefly after the service. Tim has an announcement..."

A young man walks up to the pulpit. His voice seems relatively timid compared to the woman, who from the looks of it, is our worship leader–one, "Gloria Hunsberger."

Tim tells of a mission trip to Mississippi to help victims of a May tornado which destroyed 200 houses. The trip will involve lots of physical labor–shoveling, pounding nails, plastering, hauling, painting. He invites anyone who thinks it sounds like "an adventure" to please talk to him. I, who was totally passed over by the upper body strength fairy, think it sounds like hell on earth.

"Does anyone else have any announcements?" Gloria booms. She seems to be fumbling with papers and trying to sort some things out on the pulpit. There is a long period of silence while she figures out what she is supposed to say next. A really long period of silence. This is a refreshing contrast from the Mount Zion Baptist Temple, where silences or "dead air time" in their slick religious show, were simply not allowed to exist.

Finally Gloria gets it all straightened out. "Okay. Forgive me. I'm still adjusting to those medications. Jiminy Cricket! For call to worship, I'll read Psalm 10." Gloria reads with confidence and ease, like the Bible is really a close, personal friend of hers. She loses her place more than once, mutters "Oh Jeez," finds it again, and keeps on going.

A no-nonsense prayer is followed by the offering. The traditional gold plates of many Protestant churches are passed around while the piano plays a humble tune.

I glance at my bulletin. Every church is a little mini-culture, and Westover Mennonite is no exception. There's a heap 'o Pennsylvania Dutch all right. The names seem to say it all: Kolb, Yoder, Shenk, Hoffman, Guntz, Koontz, Fritz, Putz.

Okay....I just made up that last one.

Two men's first names stand out in the bulletin: Homer and Wilmer.

Looking around the room, I count exactly eleven women with the little sheer white caps on their heads. Most of them seem to be over 55. One catches my eye as I look at her and gives me an incredibly endearing smile and tiny wave, as though I'm a cute kitten or baby bunny and she can't wait to play with me after church.

I wave and smile in kind.

There are people of all ages in the group....good, salt of the earth looking folks. Directly in the pew in front of me, three little girls between the ages of five and eight, all with very bright blond hair, are frenetically engaged in some type of mobile arts and crafts session, which carries them from one end of the pew to the other and then back again. Scissors, markers and paper seem to be coming from everywhere. The really impressive thing is that they move while still sitting, just sliding their bottoms back and forth across the pew. If one needs to pass the other, she stays low and swings herself past. It's like they're stealth artists.

Gloria takes to the pulpit again. "Okay, we'd like to hear from you today...what good news has God offered you?...what concerns or testimony would you like to share?"

Oh goody! I love this kind of thing. When you hear directly from the people, it's all about authenticity. Nothing is rehearsed.

A beefy young man comes from the back of the room with a microphone and hands it to an older woman, who is waiting, arm outstretched.

She closes her eyes as she starts to speak. "Bear with me folks...my heart is giving me troubles. My sister Ellen was operated on...and wants to thank you...for the prayers and to Mabel... for showing her how to do quilts." She sighs and hands the microphone back.

Another woman reaches for the microphone. "Just an update on Mike's mom–we moved in while his sister was on vacation. They put her on Droxifin and that helps her eliminate. She lost 12 pounds in 4 days. Thank you for keeping her in your prayers."

I can see all these older, earnest Dutch women, hands clasped together as they knelt at the edge of their beds just nights before, homemade quilts pulled back...praying: "Dear Lord, please, *please* help Mike's mom to eliminate. She's blowing up like a balloon and if something doesn't happen fast...well...it won't be pretty, Lord."

A man's voice comes from the back of the room. "Remember my mom. Tomorrow she's having a total hip replacement at 50-years-old."

Another man speaks—it's Tornado Tim with the upper body strength. "My testimony today is...that in Christ we have our full being. And I'm so glad that we can look to Jesus and God for protection and safety. We don't need a government or military or guns or knives to have protection. We only have to look to God, and I am so grateful for that."

Gloria leans forward into her mic at the front of the sanctuary. "Thanks for saying that, Tim."

Ooohhh. Somebody just made what sounded like an anti-Iraq War, anti-Smith and Wesson statement. And it was seconded.

"An update on my neighbor Phil," a middle-aged woman with brown hair now has the mic. "The leukemia is very aggressive. He's having excruciating pain, especially in his hip. We really need to pray for his wife Nancy, who feels she has to do everything. We've all been very pushy, bossy and a pain in her butt. Last night we actually threw her out. Right now I'm so tired I could lay down right here and sleep."

"You go ahead," Gloria laughs. "Pastor won't mind if we don't wake you up for the sermon."

"Don't wake me up either!" the pastor calls out.

Everyone laughs.

"Jim wants to say something," Gloria says in her full-bodied way.

"Thank you," someone says in a strange voice from behind me.

I turn and see what looks like an older, mentally disabled gentleman, who is shaking his head back and forth rhythmically.

Gloria smiles. "We all had such a great time at your 50th birthday party Jim. We need to thank *you!*"

"Thank you," the man with the strange voice says again, exactly like the first time.

Gloria chuckles a little.

A man thanks God for all his blessings. A woman thanks the congregation for their prayers and says she is feeling better today.

Gloria looks around the room to see if anyone else has anything they'd like to say. "What do we hear about Kathy?" she inquires.

The pastor comes out of his seat, and I get the first good look at him. A huge man who looks to be near retirement in age but stands tall and robust, Pastor Walter Heinz seems like a laid back kind of guy. Still, he's in a suit and tie, and his voice is clear and commanding when he speaks. "She's home from the hospital and very weak. Also pray for John who is becoming very forgetful." He backs away and settles into his side chair again.

"Anyone else?" our leader asks. "Let us pray. Father, thank you for this week and the fruits and vegetables are growing. We don't have to do what we did last year in the fields and with our crops...and we do have plenty of vegetables growing..."

Gloria continues, renaming all the people mentioned by others. This close sense of community and concern for each other is really a very wonderful thing. I'm aware however, that if I choose to come to Westover Mennonite Church, I'd have to accept that my life and body might no longer have any privacy as I have known it. I can just hear the announcement: "We went over to Ruth Laker's house. She's back from her trip to the hospital. Turns out it wasn't anything too serious....just a bladder infection that was pretty painful for her...she was urinating blood until they got her on the Bactrim. She was wearing a wet bathing suit for too long and that's generally what happens..."

Well, we're almost a half hour into the service and we've only covered the first few lines of the bulletin: those things listed under "Gathering." Now we're about to start the section "Praising God," which seems to be done only through music.

Eight songs of music, to be exact.

When you think of good church music, you often think: African-American, Bach and the Lutherans, Southern Baptist Gospel, Mormon Tabernacle. You don't tend to think "Pennsylvania Dutch."

There's a reason for that.

We have two women leading us as we plod through seven songs. Not four songs, not five or even six songs. *Seven.* And the emphasis here is on the word "plod."

The pastor's wife, Marjorie, is one of the leaders, and I have to say she seems like one genuinely sweet, sweet lady. As a songstress and conductor she's cut from the Miss Sally mold. I'm wondering if she is "self-taught" in the conducting department, because of the unusual way that she flaps her arms, kind of in a cross between a chicken and someone who is trying to rally the troops. She really is extremely cute.

It seems that Marjorie has attended some type of church conference in Charlotte just prior to this service, and she is very excited to try out some new songs, which she puts up on the overhead projector. The page is curved and distorted so much, that in order to get one section of the words in focus, another section must be sacrificed.

Marjorie has picked some good ones. The problem for me, is that I've heard several of these songs done in another church. Differently. Like...musically.

The congregation doesn't seem to notice. Mennonites don't seem to be a get-carried-away-crazy-with-God-in-their-music kind of folk, so they are happy to sing the songs in a steady, but low-key kind of way.

What I notice most of all in this part of the service, is the way that the pastor is watching his wife as she talks with the congregation. When she smiles, he smiles. When she laughs, he laughs. He is totally in tune with her in an adoring, adorable way. It's so sweet to see. I hope my husband will stare at me with such eyes of love when we are in our sixties.

We're on song seven. Still. But it is the last song, and it will have to end sometime....*won't* it?

"That was five verses!" Marjorie exclaims as we finish flogging the last section of the horse. "I hope it wasn't too long for you...but you did very well! Thank you for hanging in there!"

The only thing missing from that last sentence was "boys and girls!" Marjorie was born to be a nursery or Kindergarten teacher. Still, when she sits down, I miss her already.

The pastor's massive body heaves up into the air and walks down a few steps to the side of the front area. He calls to the children very matter-of-factly, "Okay boys and girls. Come up front." It seems to be a custom with the PA Dutch that they sometimes dispense with little things like "please" or "would you?" Like their German cousins, they have no trouble issuing commands.

As the children weave and scurry to the front, Pastor Walt looks out a window over the cornfield...wistfully. It's like he just wants to climb through that window and walk out into the stalks, never to look back.

But he's still got a job to do.

"Okay boys and girls...what happens when someone does something you don't like? What am I doing here?" Pastor Walt has started to stack cardboard boxes, one on top of the other.

"You're building a wall!" one of children calls out.

"That's right! And when someone does something you don't like, and you start building a wall, eventually you may just build a wall so big you don't even see them anymore. Jesus says we need to communicate with each other."

It's funny how Pastor Walt is saying all this behind the boxes as a disembodied voice.

"What we need to do is this." The pastor starts taking down the highest boxes until he has made them all level. "What have I just made?" he asks.

"Boxes!" one of the littler tots observes.

"Yes, but the boxes are now a *table*. We need to discuss things around a table. If Jason Prizer's sister says something you don't like, say, 'Megan, I didn't like that. Let's talk about that.' Jesus wants us all to come together at the table....men, women, Jews, Gentiles, young and old."

The pastor's body looks freakishly huge amidst these little tykes.

"Let us pray. Father we thank you for these children. For their lives and for what they bring to the table. We ask you to bless them and be with them in the week ahead. Amen."

Walt hauls himself up from the floor, with a significant amount of grace for a man of his size and age. Being married to an equally large man, I'm well aware of the issues of the "gravity-challenged." When my husband walks, at 6'6, he's so tall, and his knees are so stiff from years of athletics, that he kind of has to sway side to side, Frankenstein-like.

Gloria's voice booms out over the pews. "Our scripture reading is Luke 14:1-14." She begins, again with the confidence of a well-seasoned sportscaster, but with what must be known as classic Gloria-isms. Like when she says, "...and he read this Pharisee....oh shoot....I mean parable..." It's kinda neat how Gloria flirts with swearing in the pulpit...she even comes close to taking the Son of God's name in vain every time she mutters "Jeez!" And it's really very admirable how she admonishes herself right then and there after each slip of the tongue. There is absolutely no need for anyone to fill out a suggestion form or to give her feedback about her slip-ups. Gloria is well aware of them.

As her reading closes, she says with a playful lilt in her voice, "Pastor Wa-alt..."

Pastor Walt walks toward the woman, like Frankenstein's monster toward his master, as she places one arm across his chest and stomach, and another on his back, in a full-bodied, authoritative hold. "God we ask for you to bless the Pastor as he prepares to bring your words to us. Let them be a beacon unto each and every person in this room. Amen."

Our shepherd mutters and fumbles with the pages of his sermon. Then he walks to the side wall and starts flipping switches, looking for the light that will help him see better. People start to titter as every possible light in the room is flicked off and then on, until he finally lands on the wanted switch. It seems very probable that this man has been at this same church for thirty years and is still uncertain of which light switch he needs to flip. He mosies back to his spot, the most unassuming pastor one may ever see.

"Two weeks ago, we had guests here who talked about our trip to Charlotte, and I didn't get to preach. I was all depressed about it and cried that day."

(Sounds like someone might be ready for retirement.)

"Anyway...they asked me to say more about it, and I came to the conclusion that two weeks ago was the appetizer...and I like appetizers, don't you...I like shrimp cocktail....(he sighs)...anyway, I should have a beautiful table here, and by the way, I took a picture of the one they made of maple, walnut and cherry....I'll post it in the back for you to see....it was really something....anyway, WE are invited to the table of God. You know...usually you're invited by a host. Jesus says, 'Come and dine and eat with me.'"

Walt gets out a sheet and puts it up on the overhead. He flips the switch and "viola" we have another out-of-focus sheet to peer at as our worship touchstone.

A thin woman slides over from her seat diagonally behind me, and asks me if I have the "study sheet" to fill out. She hands me one before I have a chance to look and see. I take it from her, smile and say "thank you," cause she's one of the eleven women with the white lace caps, and I'm not gonna mess with any of *those* momma's. She'd probably meet me out in the parking lot if I refused her gift, grasp me firmly around the back of my neck as she led me toward my car, muttering something in my ear like: "So you think you're too good to take my study sheet? Huh? HUH?!" Then she'd probably bash my forehead into the roof of my car, just to punctuate her point that I better never refuse the study sheet again.

I check out the sheet. Good grief! It's another one of those sheets with the fill-in-the-blank spaces, like at Mount Zion Baptist, only this one is a lot simpler. What is *with* this?! Has there been an outbreak of teacher-envy among ministers? Do we need little hand-outs and things to take home to keep people engaged in the service? Is this another manifestation of our Attention Deficit Disorder culture?

I don't want to have to take notes in church! I've been through eleven damn years of college thank you very much, so I'll be damned if I'm going to sit in a pew, at forty-one years of age, and TAKE NOTES!

"Jesus didn't refuse vegetables... children may not like them....there is one vegetable I don't like..."

"BROCCOLI!" A man yells from the back.

"No! Corn fritters! Don't ever offer them to me, cause I won't eat them...I just can't stand them....I can't tell you why, I just do."

Clearly I've missed something while I was ranting about taking notes, but all I can think at this point is: corn fritters are a *vegetable?*

Pastor Walt's sermon style is well.... "casual," would probably be the word. Yet very sincere. He winds through some points about how everyone belongs at the table with God, while throwing in a few good folksy tidbits ("Someone said to me, 'Pastor, I can't come to your church...I don't own a suit and tie.' I said, 'Come as you are! No one wears a suit and tie anyway...except me...'") and a reference to Jimmy Carter ("The word 'Christian' means 'Little Christ.' As Jimmy Carter said, 'What if you thought of yourself that way?' That's pretty powerful.")

You've got to love a man who quotes Jimmy Carter.

We've been in the sanctuary for 90 minutes when the good Pastor finally trails off to an ending of sorts. Apparently, gone are the days of the 60 minute church service, except in the Catholic Church, where I learned that one could easily be trampled to death by the parishioners as they stampede to the exit, that is, if you try to go against the masses.

We end up having to skip three of the blanks on the study sheet, but it's not a problem because Mennonites don't appear to be all about closure.

It's great to finally stand up and stretch my legs and as I twist a bit, out of the corner of my eye I see a woman standing behind me, waiting quietly.

I pivot around. She is smiling at me, her hands clasped neatly in front of her. Her presence is very soft and non-threatening.

"Hi, I'm Ruth Laker," I extend my hand.

"Ruth...I'm Lois Armentrout. It's very nice to meet you."

"Thanks. I live just down the road and I've passed your church many times. I wanted to check it out."

Another woman, of the white-capped variety, comes over and waits politely to greet me. I turn to include her in our conversation.

"Hi, Ruth Laker," I shake her hand.

"Hi Ruth, I'm Fern," she says kindly.

Another woman is standing behind Lois, also waiting to be meet me. I extend my hand to her.

"Ruth Laker."

"Ruth, I'm a Ruth, too," she smiles.

"I don't meet too many Ruths!"

"You don't? We have a few here..."

Another woman walks up to stand near our circle. I reach over to her.

"Hi, I'm Ruth Laker..."

"I'm Mary Zimmerman. Very nice to meet you."

"Nice to meet you."

Yet another woman comes to the circle. Mary introduces her as "Eileen."

Within minutes I have been surrounded by kind, gentle women who seem only to want to say "hello." No one is asking any questions, no one is plugging the church, they just want to stand with me, in this space–smiling.

It feels as though I'm somehow being held in a loving womb.

I smile at all of them and thank them for coming over to meet me.

Fern says, "Well, we're glad your curiosity got the best of you."

"You have a very lovely church," I respond. "The people seem to be a very caring family."

She smiles back.

Out in the lobby, I linger for a minute, picking up some information about Mennonites and their church.

Lois approaches me, again in a gentle way. "This is something we do every year....and people seem to like to come." She hands me something. It's a flyer for their "Arts and Crafts Chicken Bar-B-Q and Antique Tractor Show." Highlights include a slow tractor race, music by "Pentecost," the "Parade of Tractors," a lunch stand with chicken corn soup, hot dogs and sauerkraut, and of course, barbeque, a "Milkshake Barn," horse-drawn wagon rides, and "the Bumble Bee Train."

As I look over the flyer, again, three or four women have encircled me in a very peaceful, unobtrusive kind of way. I keep waiting for the hard sell of the church, but they seem to just want me to feel welcome. And I do.

Walking to my car, I reflect on the feeling I am left with after attending this little church out in the middle of a cornfield. This little church with people who have names like "Ike," and "Shirley" and "Hazel."

And the feeling is pretty darn nice.

Mennonite

#	Dimension of Church Experience	Rating
1)	Is parking close and convenient?	9
2)	How beautiful is the worship space?	3
3)	How comfortable is the seating?	4
4)	How welcoming and friendly is the congregation?	10
5)	How enjoyable and uplifting are the musical aspects of the worship?	4
6)	Does the leader have a pleasant speaking voice and does he/she make sense to me?	8
7)	How clean are the bathrooms?	9
8)	Are the people in the pews interesting to stare at?	8
9)	How tolerant to many ways of seeing and doing things does this group appear to be?	10
10)	Would I feel good about how these people would spend my money?	10
11)	How close did I feel to God in this place?	8
12)	Did I smile more than once during the experience?	10
	Total	93

BROTHER GREEN

SISTER RAMONE

BROTHER WASHINGTON

Jehovah's Witness

When I mentioned to my husband that I would be going to a Jehovah's Witness service that particular day, he was quiet. He scraped the side of the omelet pan, flipped his creation and waited a few minutes for it to finish cooking. Then he was moved to speak.

"Yeah...it's good that you are telling me where you go each week," he observed. "Make sure I always know where you are, just in case."

"Just in case what?" I ask.

"Just in case I need to send for your body."

Something about those two words: "Jehovah's" and "Witness," inspires that kind of thinking.

My first attempts to make contact with the Jehovah's Witnesses, ironically, met with silence. I left two phone messages, asking for someone to call and tell me the time of their services. No one called back. So I drove to the place where I remembered their meeting hall was, only to find that it had moved, and in its place was now a Church of the Transfiguration. I would have been out of luck, had I not stopped at a friend's house and mentioned that I was trying to find the Jehovah's Witnesses and that they were evading me. She knew where their new worship hall was to be found, given that it had been built a mere mile from her house.

So I had already cased Jehovah's joint days before going to the "Public Discourse and Watchtower Study." I had no idea what either of those things would be, but whatever they were, they started at 10:00 a.m. on Sunday morning, according to the sign on the outside wall of their establishment.

The "Kingdom Hall" in this case is brand new, being shared by two neighboring congregations of Jehovah's Witnesses. Pulling in to the parking lot, I am confounded by the total lack of any aesthetics to the building. It is a rectangular brick box with a small overhang near the front door, perhaps to keep off the rain as cars deposit passengers for services. There is not one window in this structure.

The cars in the parking lot don't signal any possible reasons for concern. They are of varying national origins, many are on the newer side (except for mine), and they are clean and well kept. No smashed fenders or bullet holes.

Pulling into a space diagonally near the front door, I spot an African American woman, dressed in a smart black outfit and fashionable high heels, walking toward the door with two clean-cut teenage boys.

Inside, the environs are clean and stark. Everything says "brand new building," like the shiny gold plates that advertise "ladies" and "gentlemen" on the bathroom doors. There is what seems to be a small, motel-style information desk in the lobby, and a few people are walking here and there. I am expecting a full frontal assault by the regulars, me being unknown, and they being JW folk, but not one person even makes eye contact. Many are already in the hall, which as I enter, screams FUNERAL PARLOR, only with movie-style rows of seats bolted into the floor. Long burgundy curtains hang on each side of the pulpit area, which I am tempted to walk up and pull back just to see what they cover. It couldn't be windows, there aren't any in this bunker. In front of each section of curtains is a teal-colored wingback chair, looking fresh off the furniture truck. A small sign in between the two curtain sections declares that if one moves closer to Jehovah, Jehovah will move closer to them. Only one decorative touch exists in the place, a strip of wall paper border with a geometric pattern around the top of the wall.

I find a spot on the right side of the room, where I hope to be able to keep my notepad low on the chair to my right. Unfortunately, the movie-style seats have to be flipped down with weight, so it's impossible to put your things on the chair next to you. I must hold my notepad in my lap and write out in the open, which, at one Catholic Church I attended, really seemed to bother an older man who kept giving me disapproving looks.

Gazing around, I'm realizing early on that this may not be a problem here. No one even seems to notice me, despite the fact that this is a very small congregation. There are maybe forty people total in the space, which is built to hold about 100. The crowd is half Black and half Caucasian, with what appear to be a few Latino folks in the mix. All the men, with the exception of the two teenage boys, are dressed in suits. The women are also dressed quite fashionably, with the latest ruffled polyester dresses and high, high shoes. Many have very neat hairdos and impeccable make-up. There are maybe a handful of mothers with young babies, who are also dressed very neatly.

Something about this group strikes me as odd from the beginning. And it's not because of some predisposed notions about them. I've only ever met one Jehovah's Witness person in my life, and it certainly wouldn't be wise to make judgments about a group based on a sample of one. It just feels as though something is "off," for lack of a better word. Not only are these folks not the least bit interested in a newcomer (if you sneeze, no one even says "bless you"), but there isn't much intermingling among them either. They sit in family units, but separate from each other, it seems.

"Brothers....you can find a seat please, we're going to be starting in just about one minute," a very neat and attractive young African-American man announces into the microphone in the front of the hall.

A few more people come in from the back, and I watch a young mother struggle with her unhappy three-year-old. She finally has to haul the child out, which seems very difficult to do in her three-inch heels. Ah, to be young and willing to tolerate pain from all angles.

"We're going to sing our opening song, "Loyal Worshipers Bless Jehovah."

I'm looking around for a hymnal but there is none to be found. I lean over and ask the woman in front of me where I can find one.

"Oh....maybe there's one in the lost and found....I'll go and look." She heads out of the hall, returns with one and tells me to give it back to her at the end and she'll put it away.

I flip for the page and start to sing along with the group, to flat, lifeless, piped-in, pre-taped piano music with not even an occasional variation in rhythm or dynamics.

The collective sound of the congregation is disappointingly weak. I'm finding myself longing for the Assembly of God right about now. Flipping through the songbook, it's clear that it contains none of the standard hymns one finds in many Protestant Churches. All of these songs seem to have been written specifically for this group, and the names reflect it: *See Jehovah's Army; Waiting on Jehovah, Jehovah's Holy Nation; Taking Sides With Jehovah; Jehovah's "Dewdrops" Among Many People.*

There are other titles that don't include the "J" word, such as: *It is Impossible for God to Lie; Praise Jah With Me ; Loyally Submitting to Theocratic Order; and God's Pretty Things.*

Somewhere I remember reading something about Jehovah's Witnesses being insistent on using the term "Jehovah" for God, and that this fact, along with their vigorous door-to-door campaign of evangelism, seems to make them uniquely who they are.

But what is so all-fired important about the word "Jehovah?"

"Thank you. Now we have Brother Martinelli from the Westover congregation with us today. He's going to talk with us about "Is This Life All There Is?"

Brother Martinelli, a middle-aged white man, takes to the pulpit, and the very first thing I notice, and the thing I continue to notice for the entire time he talks, is that his hair is shiny, poofy on top, and perfectly stiff, like some type of helmet. It looks exactly like the hair on my "Rick" doll from Barbie days of the early 1970s. They could open all the windows...oh wait, there aren't any...they could open the double doors, tornado-force winds could whip into the Kingdom Hall, and Brother Martinelli's hair would remain unaffected by any of it.

"Is dis life all dere is?" the gentleman begins. "A lot of people don't know de answer, but we look to Jehovah to tell us. Dere are udder tings...tings in this life...like wealth. Wealth has contribute to anxiety. Let's look at King Solomon...what was his outcome? King Solomon engage in great works...he build...he *built* irrigation to water great forrestesses that he had...as it says here in da Bible, 'and toward da hard work that I had work hard to accomplish.'"

Good Lord. I am pressed back against my chair in a state of partial catatonia. What tongue is this man speaking? I recognize snippets of English, but it is not any English with which I am familiar. Is it the Old English of Beowulf? Chaucer's Middle English? Clearly he has decided to dispense with the "ed" ending of words which would put them securely into the past tense. He also has an unusual way of making things plural, as in "forrestesses." And then there is the oft-used "da" to replace "the."

"King Solomon had in his reach the asses to do whatever he wanted."

I swear to you–that's what the man said.

"So wealth isn't the meaning of life. What about beauty? Beauty fades...don't I know it. And we're all supposed to be thin. You know dose commercials when Sally Field suggestes we feed the Ethiopian kids? I ask you...dey are skin and bones...are dey beautiful? Absolutely not."

I'm not sure which point would be more important to impart to him at this juncture: that it isn't "Sally Field," but rather "Sally Struthers," or that the plural of "suggestes" is really "suggests."

Probably the latter.

"What did King Solomon learn? He's saying... 'I lived it, I loved it, and then I became to hate it.' Everything Brothers...we die...this is not cynical, because we can cling to da hope of life after death. Jehovah has promised it. What does da Bible say about this?"

Brother Martinelli begins a Bible reading. It's painful to listen to him read in his halting, struggling way. I need to turn my focus away. It's hard to reconcile that a 50-something man made it through the public school system, and then through a good chunk of his life, with these reading, writing and speaking skills. Perhaps he's a former alcoholic or crackhead. The senseless murder of millions of neurons could account for what I was hearing, and it would be so much easier to swallow then this man being a product of our educational system.

Each person in the hall seems to be in his or her own little world–examining finger nails, pulling fuzz off of clothes--but I can tell some part of them is connected to the good Brother every time he asks them to turn to another part of the Bible. Hands dutifully flip through pages until they come to the desired place.

After about 30 minutes, I come to a frightening realization: Brother Martinelli's "sermon" is apparently the meat of the service. He shows no signs of slowing down. With no piano, organ, choir, hymnals, programs, pastor or assistant pastor, it would seem that nothing more is going to happen except more of what is happening right now. There is only one child in the service who walks, so there's little reason to hold out hope for a "Child's Moment." There was the advertised "Watchtower Study" on the bulletin board by the front door, but I'm afraid I may not make it to find out what it is.

Brother Martinelli is now telling a disjointed story about growing up in South Philly and eating breakfast with his aunt, who believed in "transmigration" enough that she spared the life of a trapped bird that particular morning, but not enough to save a horsefly minutes later, which she flattened to death without a second thought. Apparently she told Brother Martinelli that the fly had probably been his uncle, who was a "low life," so it didn't matter anyway.

I stand up and head to the doors. Outside in the foyer, it feels good to stretch and I make for the women's room. Splashing cold water on my face, I stare in the mirror. I look weathered. This searching for the best place of worship can be tedious work at times, but I don't want to skip out just yet. This "Watchtower Study" could actually reveal thinking processes within the group.

Back in the foyer, I stand around, my hands on my sides, still stretching. I just can't bring myself to go back in to listen to the good Brother's voice, which has been going strong for 40 minutes. And when I say "good Brother," I mean that. There is something about Brother Martinelli that seems genuine and earnest...I sense no evil or malice...no big ego trip in the pulpit. He wants to impart an important message–he just lacks the basic skills in grammar, speech and reading to make it a coherent undertaking.

Two young mothers come out of the hall and head toward a glassed-in room with their babies. Presumably, this is where they are supposed to go to hear everything without disturbing the group. There are now four young women with babies in the room, collective age: 20. No father's to be found taking a shift. Maybe this little booth is kind of like the "menstrual hut," and is a female-only affair.

But here comes one now. I want very much to make a human connection, to alleviate this nagging sense that these people may have all been mildly lobotamized. I smile and approach him.

"Hi, how are you?" I ask.

He looks a bit mistrustful; he gives only a trace of a smile.

"Isn't this a fairly new hall?" I'm trying to break the ice.

He nods and looks surprised to be asked.

"I used to live near where your old hall was....over near the car dealership?"

He nods. "The one near the Pizza Hut."

"Right!" I'm making great progress with the man. Time to move in with a burning question.

"Hey, this is my first time, so can you tell me, how come you use the term 'Jehovah'....I mean I know it's one of the terms for God, but what's so important about using it?"

"Because it's his *name*..." He says this with a small smile of disbelief on his face.

Things are now more than a little awkward.

"Oh ....you mean like my name is Ruth and your name is......like that's his first *name*."

He nods again, slowly, as though he's never met anyone who doesn't understand a Jehovah's Witness. A young woman comes up to the two of us, holding a little baby. She seems to be his wife, but since neither of them is introducing themselves, I guess I'll never know.

"Well, thanks for clearing that up," I say, feeling oh-so-very-stupid.

He smiles again, only a fragment of a smile, and turns toward the bathroom. The young woman heads back to the hall with the baby.

It hits me in a new way, this information. So God has a *name*...a *first name*....like Elwin, Tiffany, Bob, Manmeet or Justine. How stupid could I be? As I'm standing there, I wonder: does God like this name? Does God have parents who stuck him with this strange three-syllable utterance or did He choose it for himself? Is He finding this group's overuse of it as annoying as I have been for the past half hour?

Maybe that's what this group needs to freshen up their image: a new way to refer to God. Like when "Prince" changed his name to "The

Artist Formerly Known as Prince," but without the "Prince" part still in it. "The Church Formerly Known By God's Name," for example.

I used to know a man who changed his name from "Stan" to "Forrest." It transformed everything for him. Since there's now an unused "Stan" floating around out there, maybe this group could adopt that name in the spirit of better public relations and a "face lift" of sorts. "Stan's Witnesses." At this point in the service, I need to substitute something for "Jehovah," which if I hear too many more times, might just cause me to drop to the floor and have a seizure.

I make a pact with myself: In my mind, I'm going to substitute "Stan" for "Jehovah" from here on, and perhaps I will make it to the other side of this experience.

With heavy feet, I walk back into the Kingdom Hall.

"What about the person who has died...their body has disintegrated and smells? Here it says in John 11:35, 'Jesus gave way to tears,'....so we know whadda sympatetic King we have....Martha started to back up...da sister of da decease backs up....cause she tinks he probably smells! He's been in dere for *four days*! If Steven Spielberg was dere he'd get a great idea for a movie...the *Return of the Zombies!* Do you tink Lazarus walked like a zombie?" Brother Martinelli holds his arms out on either side of the microphone and simulates his best zombie walk.

"He took da wraps off and he didn't smell! And one day we will be reunited with our loved ones and we'll be able to hug dem and hold dem and dey won't smell....isn't dat a beautiful ting? Again, it's all part of (Stan's) promise to us."

There is a slight crack in our speaker's voice. Yes, the very thought of being able to embrace one's long-departed Aunt Philomena, and knowing that she won't smell of disintegration, is enough to make anyone get a little choked up.

"The creator of DNA has da ability to recreate da person..."

Heavens! Is this man advocating cloning? Was Lazarus perhaps, really *cloned?*

"Our creator, (Stan), wants us to have eternal life in perfect conditions. A lot of people tink we will be like Ken and Barbie–but we will be perfect in obedience...maybe our crooked nose will straighten out...I don't know...be we will be perfect in obedience."

HELP ME STAN! I DON'T KNOW HOW MUCH MORE OF THIS I CAN TAKE!!

"Our copy of da 1973 'Watchtower' tells us dat our version of life has no reverence for life. The Theory of Evolution says we come from animals. In other words...our mommy's a monkey? Come on...there is a blas–a blasmaphous lack of reverence for the Creator. But the Bible always gives man dignity. If dere sayin we come from monkeys...my brodders...I can't even bring myself to say dis...what are dey saying our *Creator* looks like?"

(And in another parallel world somewhere, monkeys are getting very offended at the idea that they were created by someone who looks like a guy in a cheap, wrinkled suit with immovable hair and poor grammar.)

"If we don't have da truth...God help us cause no other religion will help us out there. No other religion speaks da truth like this one. We're not saying we, as (Stan's) people are better, we just know better, so we have a responsibility to share dat with others."

It's now been 50 minutes of this. I want a medal.

"This reporter in Czech–o–slo–vakia...he remembers da communistis tried to force them to do terrible work...to put dem in uranium mines, to build bombs...dey made dem stand in front of da mines in cold 30 degrees below and poured water on dem...but dem Brothers were perfect in their faith."

There is no such place as "Czechoslovakia" anymore. I suppose I could raise my hand and tell him. But since Brother Martinelli is quoting articles from 1973 in a non-historical way, there are probably other things he doesn't know yet. Like that Nixon resigned, Sonny is dead, Cher is retiring and Chastity is now grown up and gay.

"Our associations can spoil our good habits. To illustrate....let's say we're in da Garden of Eden with Adam and Eve. Both Cain and Abel ask us to go for a walk in da dark forest...which one would you choose?" He looks at us silently, nodding his head uh-huh. "I think you get my point..."

Well since no one had yet been murdered in the story, I'm not sure I'd make any distinc–OH GOOD GOD IN HEAVEN! THIS WILL ONLY END UP LIKE THE BIBLICAL VERSION OF "WHO'S ON FIRST!" GET A HOLD OF YOURSELF Ruth!!

"So friends....how do we feel now? We know we will have paradise. (Stan) will give us a world with no sickness and no death."

Everyone in the hall claps.

I'm in such a state of mental exhaustion from trying to put some type of frame of logic over this oozing mess that I can hardly pull myself up in the chair.

The handsome young African-American man is back at the microphone. "Thank you Brother Martinelli for teaching us that this isn't all that there is. We're going to have a song and then our Watchtower study."

A half dozen people or so leave, not waving or acknowledging anyone as they head out.

I welcome the opportunity to stand and stretch my legs again, as the next song is being sung to another taped accompaniment. That was the longest "sermon" I had ever heard in my life, although I'm not sure they call it by that name. It would appear that this church is run by the people and that there is no one head or leader. I'm more than grateful for the change of speakers, and hope that the black man will lead the next part. He has a very articulate manner and great speaking voice. And he knows how to form plurals.

The song ends.

"Open your Watchtowers to page nine please. We will be studying the section 'Look! This is Our God!'"

Everyone has a little magazine of some type, and again, I am without the necessary materials. No one seems to notice or care. Two men are holding microphones in the back...some type of deacons, probably. I get up from my chair and kind of poke my head around like a pigeon, trying to let them know that I need a 'Watchtower.' One young woman with a baby gives me a glazed-over smile, but no one offers me any assistance.

Finally, I go directly to one of the men with the microphone and ask where I can get the book. He points me out toward the lobby. I walk out to get one thinking that this is not exactly how I was expecting to be treated as a first-timer. I'm almost offended at the lack of intrusive pushiness about pulling me into the fold. I mean, come on, people. I need Stan as much as the next person.

"The Watchtower"–the object of the entire second half of this service, the sacred writings that are so important that they are listed on the side of the building as in "Public Discourse and Watchtower Study at 10:00 –this "Watchtower" is a 30-page, skinny little magazine that looks like something you'd be handed as a "freebie" as you walked out the door on your last day of Sunday School when you were in fourth grade. The pictures and reading level are right around fourth grade level as well.

I walk back in to the Kingdom Hall, feeling somehow both over-fatigued and under-stimulated at the same time, sit down again in my movie theater seat and flip to page 9.

"Brother Jackson will now read for us the first two paragraphs." Another well-groomed young black man in a suit stands at an adjacent microphone and reads two paragraphs of the article:

"My friend. That is how Jehovah, the Creator of heaven and earth, referred to the patriarch Abraham (Isaiah 41:8) Just imagine–a mere human enjoying a friendship with the Sovereign Lord of the universe! You may wonder, 'Is it possible for me to be that close to God?'

The Bible assures us that a close relationship with God is within reach. Abraham was granted such closeness because he 'put faith in Jehovah.' (James 2:23)"

The young man finishes his reading, folds his hands together and stands quietly. I breathe a sigh of relief that he was indeed, able to read.

Our first moderator now asks questions of the group. "How did Jehovah refer to the patriarch Abraham, and what might this cause us to wonder about?"

At the bottom of the first page of the article one can see that this Brother has just read a study question already provided, exactly as it is printed on the page.

A few people raise their hands.

The moderator calls on someone. "Brother Green?"

A large man with a loud voice takes hold of one of the microphones. "He called him 'my friend.' And it makes us wonder if it is possible to be that close to God."

"Very good," the moderator says. "How does the Bible assure us that a close relationship with God is within reach? Sister Simion?"

"It tells that if we 'put our faith in Jehovah,' we can be that close to God.

"Yes. Very good."

The Watchtower study progresses on in this formulaic manner, through 24 paragraphs. Yes, you read that correctly. It was the same thing over and over and over again: The paragraphs read by the one young man at the microphone, the questions asked by the other young man at the pulpit, the answers provided by those in the congregation, taken word for word from the same text we had just heard read out loud, and then the Brother moderator would say "very good," with almost the exact same inflection to his voice every time. Once or twice he might have said, "that's a good point," but almost always it was "very good."

Read-question-answer-very good.
Read-question-answer-very good.
Read-question-answer-very good.

This process did little to ease my mind about the possible mass lobotamization of this group.

There was one shining moment in the two hours that I spent at the Kingdom Hall of the Jehovah's Witnesses. Twelve paragraphs into our Watchtower study, this question was asked: "What tender word picture shows us Jehovah's willingness to protect and care for his worshipers?" Since there was only one picture on that page--a picture of a smiling shepherd holding a little smiling lamb under his cloak--it wasn't likely to stump anyone. Well, then again...

The microphone was handed to a Latino woman who said, "I really like that leetle picture, and way the shepherd is holding the leetle lamb. I wro my name on the lamb's forehead, cause I want to think that God eese taking care of me like that."

Everyone in the room chuckled. I saw smiles of understanding in the group. She had a good idea, that woman. I decided to copy her, and I wrote my name on the forehead of the little lamb as well. And it did make me feel better.

When the "Public Discourse and Watchtower Study" were finally over, I was drained and without much motivation to stick around. No one stopped to introduce themselves, although I got the sense that the moderator might be making his way over toward me.

A sudden burst of energy took me out the door, and I found myself running toward my car. Not walking, but running. My eyes winced to see the sun, and the wind was in my face, and it all felt fantastic. I stopped and stood by my car. The view from the parking lot was beautiful–fields of wild grass sloping downward and then up again, toward bluish hills.

If Stan is anywhere to be found, for me, He is somewhere out here. In the light.

Jehovah's Witnesses

#	Dimension of Church Experience	Rating
1)	Is parking close and convenient?	8
2)	How beautiful is the worship space?	1
3)	How comfortable is the seating?	4
4)	How welcoming and friendly is the congregation?	1
5)	How enjoyable and uplifting are the musical aspects of the worship?	1
6)	Does the leader have a pleasant speaking voice and does he/she make sense to me?	0
7)	How clean are the bathrooms?	10
8)	Are the people in the pews interesting to stare at?	1
9)	How tolerant to many ways of seeing and doing things does this group appear to be?	1
10)	Would I feel good about how these people would spend my money?	1
11)	How close did I feel to God in this place?	1
12)	Did I smile more than once during the experience?	1
	Total	30

Quaker

"Quaker Meeting has begun, no more singing, laughing, talking, chewing bubble gum!"

Growing up, my neighbor Dwayne Austin and I used to play that game routinely on the strip of field behind our houses that ran alongside the railroad tracks. I don't remember how we ultimately created the outburst from the other, thereby winning the game, but if memory serves, victory was often obtained by speaking in strange accents or, in Dwayne's case, making fervent farting noises.

My two stepsons have been involved with Quakerism since they were very young, and through them, I have gained some appreciation for the values and practices of the Religious Society of Friends. I know that worship is a meditative affair, not led by anyone in particular, and that Quakers are the ultimate "walk what they talk," kind of people. Actually, they are "walk much more than talk" kind of people.

I've seen little old Quaker women standing out on the curb, smiling and waving signs that say "Peace is Patriotic!" It's hard to dislike people who do that.

Still, I wasn't overly excited about going to a meeting–after all you sit for an hour in silence, with none of the things that I have always liked the most in a religious experience: music, stained glass, inspirational messages from various people, flowers and candles. Call me spiritually shallow, but I like all the trappings of worship–the bells and whistles.

Pulling into the little parking lot of the old local meeting house, only one other car is there. The message on the answering machine had said that there was an adult discussion time at 9, followed by the meeting at 10. Entering the building at five minutes to nine, only one person is inside, an older woman with short white hair and glasses.

"Hi," I greet her. "Is there an adult meeting time at nine?"

She looks a bit surprised. "No. We haven't had that in a long time. Everybody works and they like to sleep in on Sundays, you know..." she smiles pleasantly.

"Oh. Your answering machine indicated that you had a meeting at nine."

"We have an answering machine?" she asks me.

"Yes, you sure do," I inform her. Already I'm getting the sense that Quakers might be more about the forest and not so much the trees.

"Oh my. Well, I'll be....I didn't know that. I'll make a note to myself to get that message changed. Thank you so much for informing me!" She laughs.

We share introductions and she invites me to sit and wait for the ten o'clock meeting. I tell her I'll just take some literature and find a nice place to sit and read until the meeting. As I pick up this and that, she shares with me about a speaker from a Quaker retreat who would be coming the following week. A writer and poet, this woman is well-known in the Quaker community.

I thank her for the information and leave. Luckily, there is a spacious park near the meeting house so I drive there, find a spot with a nice vista and park my car. Looking around, one can see many deer feeding in the fields. When joggers come near them, they bound away, their fluffy white tails sticking straight up behind them. I think about what I've read about deer sightings, from a Native American perspective–that if you see one, it means you must be more gentle with yourself.

I start to read about the Charlestown meeting house and its history. Although it is two hundred years old, there aren't as many interesting tidbits as one might expect from its past. I thought more Quaker names would be dropped: you know, "Warner Mifflin came by to worship after giving his antislavery petition to congress in 1790," or "Susan B. Anthony attended meeting here while crusading for women's rights." Maybe they don't want to show-off.

Another pamphlet contains an extremely well-written essay by a Quaker gentleman, describing what it is like for him to be at meeting. His advice is that the most important thing in preparing for Quaker worship is not to come to meeting planning to say anything, and not to come planning *not* to say anything. Just get in touch with the Spirit and see what happens while you're sitting there.

I flip through other literature in a cursory kind of way: A call to volunteer at a hospice; an advertisement of an upcoming conference entitled: Quaker Families: Impacted by Prison. It reads: "If you have been in prison or your loved one has been, is, or may be in prison, come to this conference. You will meet other Quakers with similar experiences."

If we were to play the adjective game where you ask me to say the first three words that come to mind when hearing the word "Quaker," "prison" would unlikely be one of them. Then again, they are known to be deeply socially conscious people, so perhaps they are often being sent to jail for standing up for their beliefs.

Or, they could be a bunch of crack-smoking hoodlums who traffic in arms and prostitution.

It's time to drive back to the meeting house.

Several cars are now in the parking lot. Bumper stickers appear to be popular with Quakers: "Commit Random Acts of Kindness and Senseless Beauty;" "Support the Disabled;" "My Other Car is a Pair of Boots," and "Redefeat George W. Bush in 2004," are a few of the ones I notice as I head to the old screen door again.

This time it's straight into the old meeting room itself. Benches are arranged in a square, facing each other from all sides, with an open space in the middle. About ten adults are sprinkled throughout the room. With them are a fair number of children.

I slide into the back row to a corner spot. Looking around, I see that many of the adults are sitting with their eyes closed. The children are all very alert, but extremely quiet. Most impressive. It's amazing to think that these little ones will sit through an hour of near total quiet.

The screen door shuts rather loudly and the old floorboards creak every time someone enters, but I've decided that I will try to get into a meditative space. I have come committed to the idea of focusing on God and God alone.

I close my eyes and instantly, my body gives out a long, involuntary sigh.

Clear your mind....focus on God.

Prayer has always been a somewhat spotty affair for me. There are times when I've felt that I've gotten a good thing going with God, but it doesn't last for too long. I just seem to forget that I can talk to God.

Okay. I'm going to imagine God with me in the room right at this very moment. Sitting right next to me. I'm having difficulty with the gender thing. Should God be a man or a woman? I kind of want God to be both at the same time–a hermaphroditic God, if you will. Perhaps I could make God into a centaur of sorts; the head and chest of a woman and below the waist, a man. No. I decide I will imagine God first as a woman, and then as a man.

It's taken a while to sort that out in my mind, and as I'm about to get into it more, a man stands up in front of me.

"Once a month, our meeting reads a query," his voice says calmly and quietly. "How does our meeting work to assure justice for those in the world who need help with political oppression...who need help in having their basic needs met for food and shelter? How does our meeting work to help secure justice in education and health care for others in the world? Does our meeting encourage the prayerful openness to the Light?"

He asks a few more questions of a similar vein and then sits back down. I reflect for a minute on the nature of his query. Pretty heavy stuff.

Suddenly, half the people in the room stand up and head for the door–the half who are children, along with one adult man. As the door closes behind them, they erupt in a shower of chit chat and laughter out on the lawn. Well, that explains why they were so able to sit quietly; it was only a ten minute Quaker Meeting for them. Their voices fade away until all is quiet again, and only we adults remain.

Where was I before being so rudely disturbed by that talking Quaker?

Oh yeah....God is sitting beside me. As soon as I imagine God sitting next to me, Her body glowing through soft folds of a flowing white gown, I want to melt into Her. I feel a strong desire to lean into the space next to me, but it is difficult with these unyielding old benches. I rest my head in my hand and pretend it is God's hand, comforting me.

For the next twenty minutes or so, I deviate a bit from this potential communion with God. I review my grocery list; I think about the political situation and marvel that out of 300 million people, this is the best we can do with some of our leaders; I check out the clothes and in particular, the shoes being worn by the other people in the meeting house; I chastise myself repeatedly for having the "monkey mind" that won't seem to settle down. Finally, I think I almost fall asleep.

Suddenly, there is movement of bodies all around me, and I open my eyes to see people up from their seats, hugging and greeting each other. The couple in front of me turns and introduces themselves. They look familiar and we realize that our children go to the same school.

Someone starts to make a few announcements. He asks if there are any new people in the group. One woman from a distant Quaker Meeting says she is visiting relatives. The man in front of me says, "we have Mary here," and points back toward me.

"Actually, my name is Ruth–Ruth Laker," I correct him.

"I'm trying to change your identity," he chuckles.

"Maybe I have a glowing aura about me, like the Divine Mother," I suggest. People laugh. "My stepsons, Justin and Eric were involved with this meeting when they were younger," I tell the group.

"We love them!" one woman says enthusiastically.

The moderator carries on with his task: that of orienting the group toward a business meeting. One woman asks to make a report on her attendance of a regional Quaker conference. She shares with the group in an impassioned way–challenging them as to how much they really want to be involved with a larger body of Quakers. I can see that she takes her job as representative very seriously.

I really don't want to stay for this business. I don't want to do anything but go home and sleep, which I do.

It was helpful to be able to stop the world and get off, which the Quaker meeting definitely promotes. That's something we should all probably do a lot more of. But I'm just not sure if Quakerism is for me.

Maybe I'm somewhat "spiritually materialistic," if that's possible. I need music, stained glass, flowers and padded seats.

Quaker

#	Dimension of Church Experience	Rating
1)	Is parking close and convenient?	6
2)	How beautiful is the worship space?	2
3)	How comfortable is the seating?	1
4)	How welcoming and friendly is the congregation?	10
5)	How enjoyable and uplifting are the musical aspects of the worship?	1
6)	Does the leader have a pleasant speaking voice and does he/she make sense to me?	5
7)	How clean are the bathrooms?	7
8)	Are the people in the pews interesting to stare at?	5
9)	How tolerant to many ways of seeing and doing things does this group appear to be?	10
10)	Would I feel good about how these people would spend my money?	10
11)	How close did I feel to God in this place?	10
12)	Did I smile more than once during the experience?	3
	Total	70

African Methodist Episcopal

I'm not sure how the AME church was founded, but I'd have to imagine that a group of African-Americans who had been converted to Methodism were living in close proximity to a group that had been converted to Episcopalianism and that the two collided somehow–not unlike when peanut butter and chocolate became Reeses.

My experience with African-Americans has been fairly extensive in my adult life. Still, only once have I worshiped with Blacks at a predominantly African-American church, but it was so remarkable and uplifting that I never forgot it. In any search for the right church, African-American churches should be on anyone's list to visit.

That one experience to which I just referred, was at an American Baptist church in a southern city. My neighbors, natives of Oregon, were the only two whites in the membership. They invited my husband and me to go one Sunday, which we happily did. There we sat in a pew, four white onions amidst rows and rows of potatoes. It was a vibrant, wonderful worship time, and my husband, who had been jaded toward church for the most part, said he really felt the Spirit for the first time.

I had no idea if an AME congregation would be anything like a Black Baptist group, but I wanted to check it out, so off I headed on a rather gloomy fall Sunday morning.

The AME church I visit is a cute little shoe box of a building, and I do mean shoe box. The dimensions of the shoe box are like those that might hold a pair of men's work boots, as opposed to a box that might hold slippers or a pair of women's AAA loafers. The most notable features of the church are simple blue glass windows and a spacious and spotless playground as part of its yard. There seems to be something for everyone on this playground: a freshly painted basketball court with bleachers, many swings, an elaborate jungle gym with slides and little car and bulldozer rides for the tots.

Making my way to the front door, several very neatly dressed people are merging toward the same place. Everyone smiles at me as I head up the steps--a young man opens the door for me and says hello.

Inside, several kids are playing around, jumping back and forth through a door, while a woman at the bottom of a staircase motions for them to be quiet and come downstairs.

I head into the sanctuary and see a circle of men and women sitting up behind the pulpit. One woman in particular is talking with a fair amount of passion about her own spiritual journey, and how Grace is growing in her more and more every day. She seems to have a certain amount of authority in her voice, which is noteworthy.

Another very attractive and neatly dressed woman slides in beside me and introduces herself as "Joyce Smith." I shake her hand and tell her my name. "I've been wanting to come and visit an AME church for some time," I tell her. "A friend was at an AME wedding and the bride's father is an AME minister. They suggested he come to a service. From the way he described things, I thought it sounded like a good idea, too."

"And you picked us...isn't that nice?" she smiles.

"Well, you aren't too far from my house."

"Let me get you a bulletin," she says. "They're finishing Sunday School up there, and then we'll get started." She goes out and a minute later returns with a bulletin, a newspaper and a beautiful AME calendar for 2004, featuring the poetry of Langston Hughes and the art of Benny Andrews. The art is original and compelling–a mix of oil painting and use of collage. Each picture is fresh and interesting.

"I see Mayor Street is featured in this paper....he's having his troubles, isn't he?" I observe.

"Well, aren't we all...." she says.

I nod. She's got a good point. I've certainly had my share this past year.

"That reporter came here when the Iraq War started and interviewed me. They had an article and my picture in that paper," she said. She was smiling and proud, but certainly not bragging.

"Good for you!" I smile back. "And if I may ask, where did you come down on the war issue?"

She hesitates for a second, obviously more sensitive to issues of tact than I am. "Well, as a Christian, all I can say is that I think we should pray. It doesn't seem to make sense that anyone would kill anyone. All this killin' isn't getting us anywhere."

I nod agreement. "It's a big mess over there, isn't it?"

"Um-hum. I just heard on the news about more Americans and Iraqis getting blown up yesterday. It's just such a shame."

I like this woman. She is really easy to talk to.

Just then, another woman comes over and introduces herself as "Millie Fredericks."

"Are you a friend of Joyce's?" she asks me.

"I just met her," says Joyce. "She's my friend now."

We laugh.

117

Joyce invites me to come and sit with her in her "regular" spot, and I thank her, but tell he that since I've got all my stuff spread out, I'll just sit here and read some of this literature for a minute. "I'll visit with you again after the service," I tell her.

"Well I'll just be right in front of you if you need anything," she smiles.

"Very nice to meet you," I tell her.

"You, too."

As she starts to walk away, the authoritative woman from the Sunday School circle comes over and looks at me in a half-friendly, half-quizzical kind of way. "I'm Brenda Hicks," she says as she leans over a pew to shake my hand. Her voice is no nonsense and strong.

"That's *Reverend* Brenda Hicks," Joyce adds.

Well, that explains the commanding air of this woman.

Another woman comes over and stands in front of me, waiting to introduce herself. I noticed this particular woman the moment she walked into the church because of her confident and peaceful air, and her magnificent leopard skin hat, fanning out from her head to one side. She is trim and wearing a smart, tailored dress with several substantial gold chains hanging around her neck and something that looks like a military medal pinned to her bodice. Her demeanor seems to say "Dressed Up and Ready!" The other two women leave and she leans over to shake my hand.

"I'm Ethel Sales," she tells me with a very welcoming smile.

"Ruth Laker," I take her hand.

"It's so nice to have you here," she says warmly.

"It's really nice to be here," I tell her.

"You just make yourself at home and do whatever you want," she throws her arm up in the air. "Whatever the spirit moves you to do!" She walks away smiling.

Well, I certainly feel welcomed by this group. I look around and at this point, about twenty-five people have meandered into the room, five or six of them, children. It looks as though I'm the only onion in this group of potatoes.

I take a brief look at the paper Joyce gave me: *The Black Suburban Journal.* I manage to read a few headlines: *Katz and Limbaugh: Birds of a Feather?; A More Humble Washington Negotiates its Place in the World; The Mixed Blessing of Affirmative Action; Karaoke Finals Crown Champion Senior Idol; Sickle Cell Disease Affects All of Us.*

I can't resist flipping to the "Ask Deanna!" section, which features the picture of a strikingly beautiful Black woman, whom I presume is the advice columnist–Deanna, herself.

Her first letter: *"Dear Deanna: My homeboy just told me he's gay. I'm tripping and can't deal with this information. He's handsome and I always thought he was a stud. He seemed comfortable when we were out playing the field and running games on women. How can he snuggle up with a man? Very Straight, Dallas, TX."*

Deanna responds: *"Dear Straight: You're not the only one who doesn't understand why two, big, hairy, ashy men with rough feet want to play footsies together. However, it's no ones business to question anybody's love life regardless of gender and who they fall in love with. If he's content, celebrate his happiness. By the way, you think he's handsome–you sure you don't have a little sugar in your tank, too?"*

Although I've always prided myself on strong communication skills with many kinds of people, I have to admit that this letter and response leaves me feeling out of the loop. What would "running games on women" be? Who are these "ashy men with rough feet?" And, what exactly does it mean to have "a little sugar in your tank?"

Another woman writes that her man is too good and that it bothers her. Deanna tells her to be grateful and to consider that she could be married to O.J. Simpson, Scott Peterson or Robert Blake.

"PRAISE THE LORD!" Reverend Hicks yells from a microphone in the corner.

"Praise the Lord!" several people answer.

"I SAID: 'PRAISE THE LORD!" she booms even louder.

"Praise the Lord!" a few more join in.

"I CAN'T HEAR YOU PEOPLE!! LET'S TRY THAT ONE MORE TIME: PRAISE THE LORD!"

I think I saw her glaring at us at one point, so I jump in on the last one with as much feeling as I can muster, given my fear and all....

"We're gonna sing *'What a Mighty God We Serve'* so raise your voices to the Lord!" Reverend Hicks starts singing directly into the microphone. With her strong, excellent voice, and her rhythmical clapping accompaniment, she creates a veritable One-Woman-Band.

Others start to sing along. I notice that no one seems to need a hymnal, they just know the words. I start flipping through an AME hymnal, hoping to find the song somewhere. I like the titles of the different hymns I see: *My Hope is Built; I'm Gonna Live So God Can Use Me; Dere's a Star in de East; Rejoice, Rejoice Believers; There is Sunshine in My Soul Today; I Have a Friend in Jesus.*

Joyce walks back to orient me to the bulletin. She helps me find the hymn. Then she walks back to her place.

After the song, Reverend Hicks asks if someone has a testimonial. Before anyone can respond, she says, "Well I have several. I want to thank God for this beautiful day, and for the Sunday school group we had, and for all the people I see in this room, especially the children." She goes on a bit longer. "Who else wants to testify?"

"Learning to lean....learning to lean," an older Black man starts to sing.

"UM-HUM!" many of the people respond. There is clapping in the group, and everyone joins him in singing. Again, no one needs music–they just know it.

After the song is over, the man stands up. "That is the lesson we learned about this morning in Sunday school...."

"Tha's right! Um-hum! Amen, Brother!" several people respond.

"I'm finally realizin' at this point in my life, that I have *got* to lean on God. And it hasn't been easy to get to this point, let me tell you!"

Again the group calls out various words of support and encouragement.

Now we move into another hymn, this time led by a middle-aged Black man who has taken a seat at the piano in front of the church, his back to the group. And I might add that he has a very muscular back. As he starts to play, it is clear that this is not your average church pianist. Hell, this isn't your average pianist anywhere. The man is *amazing!* Flying all over the keys he is, making every song a feast for the ears! He sounds like someone who could have played with Duke Ellington or Louis Armstrong. Now the church picks up even more with the energy of the music.

"YES LORD JESUS WE THANK YOU!" the Reverend yells at the end of the song. "I am grateful for Jim, our ever faithful piano player, for being here this morning. And now, Mr. Stokes....our professor....(she laughs), is going to lead us in prayer this morning. Mr. Stokes...."

An older gentleman walks to the front of the church and kneels on a prayer bench. "Lord, there are so many people who laid down last night, and did not get up this morning...."

"Amen! Tha's right!"

"We thank you for giving us another day of life. Lord, we ask you to watch over us today. I ask you this morning to touch my wife and heal her....walk by my house and heal my family....Lord, I just love you so much...."

Through the entire prayer, the piano man is tinkling the keys, kind of the way you'd hear them being played in a saloon from the old west. The instrument is an ancient upright, and sounds like something that probably was in a saloon in the old west.

"Thank you, Lord, for letting us improve every day...there are so many problems in the world....our leadership is going down....thank you for our food and our shelter...Lord, go into the hospitals and mental hospitals...there is nothing you can't do....we ask you to let the Pastor bring us the message today and that we have a good week, Lord. Amen."

It goes without saying at this point, that throughout the prayer everyone has been calling out and offering words of encouragement to Brother Stokes. This, in fact, is one of the most prominent features of the African-American worship services that I have attended: this continual free-association of words and utterances from the congregation.

I realize that this is one part of the service I haven't tried to get involved in. I'm just afraid my responses will draw too much attention to the fact that I am the only White person in the room. Most likely to come out of my mouth would be things like: "Go ahead...I'm listening," or "Yes, I've felt that way too," or, because I'm not always patient, "Could you consolidate this a bit and get to the point?"

"PRAISE THE LORD FOR THAT FERVENT PRAYER, BROTHER STOKES!" the Reverend gives him a winning smile. She's got great teeth, that woman.

It's time now for worship through music, brought to us by the "Choral Ensemble." This consists of four women, one of whom is Reverend Hicks. They start a song in what seems to be an unusual beat– 2/2 time, maybe? Is there such a thing? *"Praise Him –Praise Him – Praise Him –Jesus our blessed Savior is worthy to be praised!"*

It doesn't seem possible that there are only four women singing and one piano as an accompaniment. With the sound those women make, the tambourine shaking and the muscle man pounding on those keys, you'd think it was a full choir up front.

As the group performs, a Black man, who must be close to seventy, enters and walks to the front of the church. He is wearing a gray cape of some kind. This goes nicely with his hair, which is sculpted in the shape of a mushroom cap. Something about the gray of his hair, dotted with so much white, reminds me of a yummy nonpareil candy.

He sits down on what looks like a modest throne behind an altar table, and I can't see his face. Only the top of the nonpareil mushroom cap thingy.

After the song from the "Ensem," Reverend Hicks calls the ushers forward. Two boys in white shirts, black pants and white gloves walk forward. One has been standing along the wall through much of the service thus far, and gave me the friendliest smile when he first saw me. I always notice when boys smile, because as a group, they don't do it nearly enough.

They start to pass the collection plates around. Joyce comes back to show me that this is a special mission collection, and that the regular church collection is done by having us all walk up front and put our offerings in a locked box.

When the one boy gets to me, I put my money in the plate.

"Do you need change?" he asks me.

"....Excuse me?"

"Do you need change?"

"Um...no, thank you."

Now that is something I've never been asked before in a church. I did happen to notice that all the money in the dish consisted of one dollar bills. My five dollar bill must have seemed like a big contribution to him. That sure puts things in perspective. I was feeling like my five was cheap, but that's all I had in my wallet.

Wow.

The "Hospitality Committee" is now giving announcements. A young woman in her 30s is at the microphone in the corner, telling us important things about what's happening, including the "Annual 100 Men in Black" service and the "Annual Men's Day REVIVAL."

"We'd like to ask any visitors to stand up and make your self known to us at this time," the woman says.

A boy of about ten raises his hand and then stands up. "I'm Andre and I'm here with Bobby. Praise...praise God up in the sky!"

People laugh and clap.

That's a tough act to follow.

I stand up and say, "I'm Ruth Laker and I'm here visiting. A friend told me to check out an AME service and you all are just down the road from me, so here I am..."

"Tha's alright! Yeah! Glad to have you!"

Everyone is smiling at me and I feel totally welcome. Even the big Black man sitting behind me, who scared me when he first came in because he looks so much like the actor in *Pulp Fiction* who says "I'm gonna get meDIEval on yo' ass!" He's looking at me with a huge, beaming smile, nodding his head in approval that I've come.

Another gentleman gets up and asks for the group to bake things to bring to a fund raiser in front of Wal Mart. I like the way he nudges the group: "You all know I wouldn't ask you to do anything that I wouldn't do myself...and there isn't anything anybody's ever asked of me that I've said 'no' to."

There's something very refreshing about that. Plain and simple: you *owe* me.

The old Reverend in the gray cape finally stands and moves to the pulpit, a bit slowly, like the senior elephant of the herd, ever responsible....ever faithful.

"We ask that you...ahem....uphold these announcements....ahem..."

(In the bulletin, that was the part called "Pastoral Emphasis.")

He continues: "I was at a church banquet last night and they had a packed house. If they can do, we can do it. And our food will be better cause we're gonna make it. Us is some good cooks, ain't we?"

"Um-hum! Tha's right!"

"I ask that you be at the board meetin'....we're gonna take the rolls and see who is and who isn't gonna be there. When they call out 'Preacher,' I'll say 'Here,' and we'll see who else is there, too."

Another very refreshing approach: Be there or we'll all notice you blew us off.

"I feel kinda good this morning," he smiles. Everyone claps and yells out. "The Lord hooked me up this morning...and you gotta be grateful, 'cause he don't have to hook us up!"

"Tha's right! Um-hum!"

"And I'm grateful for the World Series. The Yankees can't buy everything!"

The piano player has moved to the organ, where he is giving background music. He breaks into a little ballpark theme.

"Now I got a problem here...we got to pay our budget and we only got a little money in the treasury....if you can loan us $500.00 we can pay you back after Men's Day. I'd like to have it by next Sunday. And if you love God, and appreciate me just a little bit, please give it. We ain't gonna rob anyone...but we need it, and God will bless you."

Never in my life did I wish so much that I had a lot of extra bucks. Nothing would give me more pleasure than to leave $500 on the Reverend's desk, then hide outside the door to see his happy face--just like when the elves made the little pair of shoes and watched from behind the curtain.

At least ten more people have filtered into the church since it started. It's interesting how people just come in whenever.

"It's prayer time now," our elephant leader says. "Everyone needs some prayer. God is listening and waiting for us to come to Him. The only communication we have with Him is through prayer. You say: 'I've been prayin' a long time Reverend, and He ain't come...give Him time! He has his own time! Pray for those who are hungry...pray for the folks who have AIDS...the Devil got so many tricks out there...he's got a new one every day...and they're so enticing...they don't even look like a trick, but they are. Like them companies that send you checks to cash...I throw them right into the trash...like they think I'm a fool! And I use a word, and it ain't no *Sunday school* word!"

A few people smile and look at each other.

I, unfortunately, have this problem with laughing out loud. When something strikes me as really funny, I just laugh out loud. Even in church. And what that man just said strikes me as way funny. I hold my hand to my mouth, trying to keep it in. The momentum has to go somewhere and I start shaking with silent laughter.

Suddenly, something catches the corner of my eye. I turn and see the scary man diagonally behind me, quietly laughing and shaking his head. He gets it.

Joyce comes back again and tells me that I can go up to the altar and kneel and say a prayer if I want to. A group of people go up and form a row in front of the Reverend.

Just then the boy usher comes over with a pad for me to sign as a visitor. He sits right down next to me as though we are old buds who go way back.

"I really like your white gloves," I whisper to him.

"You can write that in the 'Comment' section," he tells me with a little grin.

"What's your name?" I ask him.

"Robert," he tells me.

I fill out my name, address, visitor status and on the line where it says "Comments," I write, "I love Robert's white gloves!"

He peers over my hand as I write, checking to see if I am, indeed, taking his suggestion.

When I finish and hand him the pad, he reads it and smiles approvingly.

I go up and join the last group kneeling at the altar. As I'm about to close my eyes and pray, I notice a locked box under the altar table, labeled "Answered Prayers." That's a nice idea. I like being at the altar with this group. I feel like I could kneel here for a long time and offer up my concerns to God. In this room, with these people, it all comes so easily. Unfortunately, my conversation with Robert put me at the tail end of things, and when I open my eyes, I see that everyone has left the altar but me. The lone White person is holding up the works.

We have another offering and then a song: "The New Jerusalem." I notice that almost all of the songs that have been sung by either the congregation or the Choral Ensemble are not the ones that were printed in the bulletin. In some cases, the group just breaks into a song because someone starts to sing it.

As we finish, the Reverend heads toward the altar table, but one of the women from the Choral group says, "Wait right there Reverend...we've got another song...a special song to do. We're gonna do it just for you!"

"Alright then," he says, turning and smiling at the woman who is commanding him from her microphone. "Lay it on me...sock it to me ...."

"Sock it to me!" a boy mimics in the pew in front of me. Joyce turns and puts her finger to her lips. I've noticed how all of the adults in this group have tended to the children, in a gentle and caring way. This is a good thing to see.

The Reverend is sitting back down as one of the women from the Chorale Ensemble comes to the microphone and adjusts it slightly.

"Sock it to me, Sister Yvonne!" he says again.

He would date himself less if he said something like, "Play on, Playette!"

Yvonne starts to sing a song in a slightly off-key voice, but pleasing nevertheless. She feels moved to act out the various words she is singing, for example, when she sings, "I'm gonna prepare my mind," she points to her head, and "I've got strength to pass any test," she makes a fist and shakes it.

The song ends thusly:

>   I'm gonna be ready
>   I'm gonna be ready
>   I'm gonna be ready
>   I'm gonna be ready
>   I'm gonna be ready

I'm gonna be ready
I'm gonna be ready
I'm gonna be ready
I'm gonna be ready
I'm gonna be ready
I'm gonna be ready
I'm gonna be ready.

But will she be willing and able?

After all the clapping and hollering has ended, the Reverend again trudges to the pulpit. "I thank you for that beautiful song–we all thank you. Time has almost gotten away from me, but nothing can take the place of preachin' the word...so I thought I'd preach a little. So grab your bibles."

"Um-hum! Preach on Preacher!"

"Jesus told his disciples, 'I need to go to Samaria.' He had a divine appointment. I sat here this morning with a divine appointment...we all got all kinds of appointments: the foot doctor, the heart doctor, the eye doctor....I better stop there. Jesus had a divine appointment, and you should have one too. 'But Reverend, what kind?' Well every Sunday you should be in church–God will meet you...He does show up. You ought to be in the choir or sittin' in a pew. YOU GOT A DIVINE APPOINTMENT WITH GOD AND ONE DAY GOD HAS GOT A DIVINE APPOINTMENT WITH YOU!"

"Tha's right!"

"Jesus comes to a well....let's see what happens here...a man goes to the doctor for problems with his memory. The doctor says, 'We can fix it but you'll lose your eyesight. Which would you rather have?' The man says, 'Doc, I'd rather see where I'm going than remember where I've been.' Many of us have things to remember, but the life of Jesus was perfect."

I'm not sure how we got from Jesus at the well to the man at the doctor's office, but this preacher man is indeed, preaching on.

"Many of us have things to remember, but the life of Jesus was perfect. His mission was twofold: redemption of man and reconciliation back with Him again. Man thought that God was remote, but Jesus came and explained: 'I and the Father are One. God is me, and I am Him.' Jesus asked a woman at the well for a drink of water...people were amazed that he would ask her, him being a Jew. But he MADE all the water! He didn't NEED the woman to give him a drink, but because of heavenly apPOINTment, he NEEDed to have a converSAtion with this Woman!"

The Reverend carries on with his sermon, offering parallels between the initial attitude of the Samaritan woman, and the prejudices that people in the room may have faced. I can't relate to this experience based on race, but I was picked on for being in band and watching Star Trek.

The volume level of the sermon has been quickly rising, and we are now at a point where the good Reverend is officially shouting: "The Loooooooooord is the Giver of Life! Jesus is the strength in the heart of the believer! He done gives water to our soul! The woman began to get stirred up about Jesus–she gave testimony—she said, 'COME AND SEE A MAN WHO CAN RESTORE SIGHT TO THE BLIND!! COME AND SEE A MAN WHO CAN GIVE LIFE BACK TO THE DEAD! COME AND SEE HIM WHO WE CALL THE 'MESSIAH!'"

The Reverend starts to rock rhythmically.

"LOOK AND LIVE MY BROTHER! DRINK AND LIVE MY BROTHER!! SOMEONE SAY 'COOL WATER! SWEET WATER! COOL WATER....RIGHT HERE WATER....WATER JESUS....WATER HERE....JESUS GOT THE BEST WATER THIS MORNING! HE GOT THE BEST WATER IN THE WORLD!! LET YOUR BUCKET DOWN!! LET YOUR SOUL DOWN! GIVE ME A DRINK! I WANT A DRINK! OOOHHHHHHH, WASH ME IN THE WATER!'"

He stops and it is quiet for about three seconds. Then he closes: "You ought to have a divine appointment. It's yours just for the taking."

Looking spent, the Reverend sits down.

This final part of the sermon, stylistically, was kind of what scat singing is to jazz. Many in the congregation had been giving him the "yeahs" and "um-hums" for some time, but at the very end, only Reverend Hicks seemed to be able to serve as chorus. She alone responded after every other word. Personally, I was unable to give feedback due to both my Whiteness and the pain in my ears.

I wondered as I watched this aged man of God, if he is one of a dying breed. I felt as though I was watching him do what he had done for forty-five years...what was expected of him by the small but loyal following in the pews....but is it what the next generations will be looking for? Maybe young Black preachers are still doing the same thing, I don't know. But of the forty some people in the church, most were older and had probably grown up on such a style of preaching.

Many young Blacks have rejected the Christian faith altogether; after all, it was the faith given to their people by oppressors. You can't blame them. Still, it would be a shame to see the charismatic Black Christian preachers fade away. I don't know why, but I find them more earnest than their White counterparts. Maybe because I assume that more Whites than Blacks are building palatial temples, taking lavish trips in the name of evangelism and hosting TV shows, while this humble man has to ask to borrow $500 dollars by next Sunday.

We stand for the Doxology and then everyone starts to mill about.

I walk over to Joyce and a friend of hers. She turns and gives me a big hug. We talk about this and that. I comment on how amazing the piano player was and she tells me that he is a music professor.

"Thank you for making me feel so welcome," I tell her.

"Oh, we loved having you! Come back again!"

"I'd like to. I'd like to bring my daughter with me–she's twelve. I'd like her to experience all types of worship."

"Yes...it's good for them to see all the different cultures," she smiles.

As I leave, I think about what she just said. It almost makes me a little sad. Does this woman think she and I come from two different worlds? Do we? I'm half Hungarian, but I can honestly say that I have more in common with Joyce than I do the demure, oppressed women of my father's homeland, wobbling around on three-inch high heels and dressing in the seemingly mandatory quasi-prostitute garb of the Euro woman.

Still, she and I live in different neighborhoods, and all my neighbors look like me. Our children go to different schools. We may have our Christianity in common, and maybe she likes to watch *American Idol* and eat Indian food....but I'm afraid she might be right. We might be from two different cultures.

I climb into the front seat of my car and notice the clock.

Good Lord! It's 1 o'clock p.m.! I've been sitting in that church for two and a half hours! Suddenly, I feel exhausted and hungry.

It's hard to say if the African Methodist Episcopal Church would meet my spiritual needs. I certainly would feel comfortable going back to visit again. Now I think I know how Darryl Williams might have felt in my Middle School. He was the only Black kid in the building.

For me, in the end, it might be important to see at least some other onions in the potato patch.

African Methodist Episcopal

#	Dimension of Church Experience	Rating
1)	Is parking close and convenient?	8
2)	How beautiful is the worship space?	2
3)	How comfortable is the seating?	4
4)	How welcoming and friendly is the congregation?	10
5)	How enjoyable and uplifting are the musical aspects of the worship?	10
6)	Does the leader have a pleasant speaking voice and does he/she make sense to me?	4
7)	How clean are the bathrooms?	7
8)	Are the people in the pews interesting to stare at?	8
9)	How tolerant to many ways of seeing and doing things does this group appear to be?	9
10)	Would I feel good about how these people would spend my money?	8
11)	How close did I feel to God in this place?	5
12)	Did I smile more than once during the experience?	7
	Total	82

Another Presbyterian Carried Away By Religious Ecstasy

Presbyterian

As the daughter of a retired Presbyterian minister, obviously, I'm going to know a fair amount about how things go in a Presbut service. I just made up that word, "Presbut." It's not a nickname used by the group, or by anyone outside of the group that I know of. The only nickname I've ever heard for Presbyterians is "The Frozen Chosen."

Because of schooling, I moved around as a young adult, so whenever I'd come to a new community, I'd check out the Presbut Church first, in an obligatory kind of way. Often I didn't feel the group would meet my needs–they were too conservative, or didn't have enough younger members, or the minister's sermons were lacking–so I didn't always worship within the faith group of my childhood.

Now, as part of my quest for the right church, I will again visit a Presbyterian congregation. Living in suburban Philadelphia, there are many choices. I opt to go to the church where my father was "processed" when he first came to America as an escapee from a Communist country. A wealthy church on the Main Line, "Middleton Presbyterian," as I'll call it, is imposing from the outside.

It is a gorgeous fall day when I head toward the Main Line. Going down one of the primary boulevards, I realize that the scenery never gets tiresome in this area: beautiful mansions grace the thoroughfare, and magnificent, gated lawns stretch out for acres and acres. The sunlight playing off the fall leaves is giving everything a magical luster. Nearing the destination, I am immediately struck with the number of people walking toward the church from all directions.

Alright. The first thing we need to talk here is clothes. Whoa. Ninety percent of the men are dressed in suits and the women are all smartly dressed in serious, tailored clothes. There are very few prints anywhere: we're talking solid colors, people. And the colors aren't hot pink, lime green and purple. It's all about grey, black and cranberry.

Not red. *Cranberry.*

I find a parking space along a residential street several blocks away. As I make my way toward the church, using the massive stone steeples as a guide, I come up behind several families with young children. Again, we're talking serious clothes–serious kid clothes. And those aren't easy to come by unless one has do-re-mi. Do not attempt to dress your child with dignity and quality at most stores in America: our children are being used as walking billboards for companies from GAP to Osh Kosh, and above all else–THE DISNEY *MACHINE*. Fabrics are cheap, colors loud and boys and girls clothing perpetuates powerful stereotypes: like in the sweatshirts parents put on three-year-old boys that say "Philadelphia Eagles," and on girls, "Princess." It's no wonder we have a culture of men who sit around watching sports while the women whine that they're not getting enough attention.

At Middleton Presbyterian, there are no "Barbie" or "Spiderman" sneakers on the children. Only black leather and patent leather shoes. Perfectly shiny black patent leather shoes. Without-so-much-as-one-little-scuff-mark black patent leather shoes.

Approaching the church area, it becomes clear to me that this is not just a sanctuary, but a complex of buildings, all of them connected by arched stone pillars and walkways. Everything is old and big. And did I mention stone? One has to hike up many stairways to get to each building, and when you finally reach the plateau which holds the magnificent cathedral-like church, you feel as though you have just ascended to sit at the right hand of the Gods and Fathers of Business and Industry Almighty.

Entering the sanctuary is a breath-taking moment. The church is like a miniature combination of some of the most impressive cathedrals in the world: Cologne Cathedral, Westminster Abbey, St. Peter's Basilica. And it's really not all that miniature.

A crisp young man with an effeminate voice asks me where I'd like to sit. "As close to the front as possible," I say.

"Alright. We have several seats near the front still available."

I sit down on the end of a pew, beside an older couple dressed to the nines. "Good morning," the woman says to me, sideways out of the corner of her mouth, as though we are sharing a little joke between us.

No sooner has my posterior met the pew when a hand bell choir breaks into song. It is directly in front of me and the beauty of the sound they are making is overwhelming. Never before have I heard such a hand bell choir! Thirteen men and women in white shirts and white gloves waving their arms back and forth creating sounds that could call angels to earth! Their precision and polish are mesmerizing, as is the melody of the piece they are playing. The bulletin indicates that it is something called "Lux Aeterna (Light Eternal), composed by Cathy Moklebust and performed by "The Ringers of Middleton."

And what a piece of work it is!

The highest four bells are in a constant state of motion, moving from highest to lowest in a one-two-three-four pattern which creates the backdrop for the melody. It is so unbelievably gorgeous and ethereal that I am moved to tears just listening. It's a complex piece that lasts for at least ten minutes. When it's over, the cavernous space is quiet.

"Wow," I can't help but say, loud enough that others close to me hear. No one moves though, or affirms that that was, indeed, amazing. I'm sensing that one isn't expected to make any ad hominum comments in this church. I'm also sensing that one isn't expected to do anything but sit stiff and straight in one's pew.

Maybe they are the "frozen chosen," to some extent. Or the "not easily thawed."

An attractive young woman in a black robe comes to one of the pulpits and gives the "Call to Worship." Her name is listed as "Ms. Peterson," and I note that she is one of two women ministers at the church. There are seven ministers in total. I also note that all the women in the bulletin are referred to as "Ms."

This is interesting because didn't "Ms." totally bomb as an alternative to "Miss" and "Mrs.?" No one seemed to get what it was intended for, which was to be one title for all women, the way men are all "Mr." Instead, it became the calling card for feminists and women who had an attitude. So many women are hell-bent on keeping their "Mrs." title, that it was doomed from the start.

Personally, I guess I can live with the "Miss" and "Mrs." distinctions. Maybe what we should do is develop two titles for men that signal who is married and who isn't. We could use "Mr." for married men, and "Free" for unmarried. At a party, introductions would go something like this: "This is my friend Free Larry Fittapaldi, and over here is Mr. Bob Tryjankowski." The single women could then encircle Larry, while Bob would be able to spend the evening without any temptations or unwanted flirtations. What piece of mind married men could finally have! It's a wonder they haven't done something like this already.

The congregation rises to sing the first hymn, "For All the Saints," by Vaughn Williams. Vaughn Williams, as I learned singing in the Western New York Chorale, is to religious music what Elvis was to rock. Again, the sound that breaks forth as everyone begins singing is amazing. HUGE, would be the word. A mighty organ booms and I can hear a powerful choir of voices coming from somewhere. I turn and see a balcony in the far back of the church, which is massive in size and filled to the edges with robed choir members and musicians sporting cellos, flutes, violins. There are two huge tympani drums–the anti-aircraft missile of drums. They go straight to the heart and break it into pieces.

I can't help but look around as everyone sings. There is so much impressive stone and beautifully carved wood in this place–and the stained glass windows! There must be hundreds of them–little ones, big ones, round ones, rectangular–all of them with intricate pictures that I can't even begin to decipher from this distance.

Again my eyes wash over the crowd. How many people are in this place? Some quick math is needed: roughly 60 pews on the lower floor, about ten people in a pew, two side balconies packed with people, about 40 more pews between them. We're talking about 1000 people in the church right now, and there is still another service after this.

Being a color-minded person, I can't help but perseverate more on this issue of what people are wearing. Looking back over my shoulder, I can see all the colors of the clothing en mass and again, it's all about gray, black and cranberry. It's like there was a phone chain, 1000 names in length that passed along the message to everyone that those were the three colors to wear this Sunday.

What I really want to see is the bright red Republican power suit on at least one woman. I mean, come on....there have to be some Elizabeth Dole wannabees in this crowd. Surely this is a breeding ground for Republicans. But no....I see no red suits. Or royal blue. Or even navy blue. This group seems to be saying, we are too distinguished and serious to be seen in anything but the colors of death and blood.

One of the phrases from the Vaughn Williams hymn strikes me as non-applicable at this particular moment: "We feebly struggle, they in glory shine...." He's referring to the Saints as those who shine in glory, but he is *not* referring to Presbyterians when he speaks of people who "feebly struggle." This is a comfortable, powerful, self-assured group. The kind of comfort that comes with a loooooong heritage of wealth. This is where the old, old money is. Money so old, some of it probably predates Christ himself.

Here comes an anthem by the choir: Requiem Aeternam. Oh my...it is so lovely. It has a haunting melody which I never tire of hearing. It isn't recommended though, for anyone who is feeling suicidal.

Our young Ms. Peterson is at the podium again. "If we say we have no sin, we deceive ourselves and we are not living in Truth. But if we confess, God will forgive us and wipe away our sin. So let us confess our sins together..."

Ah yes. *This* is what I remember and loved about being a Presbyterian: all you have to do is say, "So sorry" and you're done. It's all *wiped* away! You don't even have to put that much feeling into it because the Presbyterian God is just waiting up there in the heavens to pardon you for anything.

The Prayer of Confession is a short matter–it includes this line: *"....that joined with those from ages past...we may inherit the kingdom you promised in Jesus Christ."* All churches try to shape their messages to meet the parishioners where they are. Catholics speak of obedience, African-Methodist-Episcopalians of joy in the face of oppression, Presbyterians of expected inheritances.

This Prayer of Confession is supposed to end with a moment of silence for personal reflection and confession, but after a mere five seconds a lone cello begins to play a solo which builds as one instrument after another is added and then the choir sings, *"Out of the deep, have I called unto you, O Lord: Lord, hear my voice. O let thine ears consider well the voice of my complaint."*

Here comes the Assurance of Pardon, given to us by a Ms. Lehman-Joseph: "Hear the good news! Who is in a position to condemn? Only Christ and we who live in Christ are pardoned. We *know* we are forgiven and we are at peace!"

Yes–we who amass gobs of wealth, we who live in houses big enough to comfortably provide three or four homeless families each with a suite of private rooms and a bath, we who drive cars that cost more than most people's homes, we who send our children to private prep schools in order to be sure they get into ivy league colleges in order that they might continue on in the family way of making more and more money–no one can condemn us but Christ and we know He is too good of a guy to do that, don't we?

Moving right along, it's another offering from our top-rate, professional-level choir and instrumentalists. This one is called "Pie Jesu" and features the lovely solo voice of a young soprano. What I really like about her voice is that she is able to sustain all her notes without vibrato, giving them a hollow and haunting sound in this magnificent space.

So far, the service has been about 90% fabulous music, 10% telling us our sins have been wiped away.

Now it's time for the "Welcome, Concerns of the Church and Offering of the Tithes." The welcome comes from Ms. Peterson again. "I'd like to take this opportunity to welcome you and we hope that you find this a place where you are welcomed warmly. At this time, please fill out the welcome pad and pass it along to those in the pew with you. Please note that there is an exhibit in the Conference Room on Nepalese Thangka Buddhist and Hindu Art. This is open between services or after the second service, when there will also be a performance by Nepalese dancers. Also, there will be a "Global Mission Celebration" today at 11:00. Please join us in the Congregational Hall for this interesting event."

What, no Nepalese clothing boutique?

"Freely and graciously we have received....let us now generously and joyously give."

Well, I'd say she has probably just described how most of the people in this congregation have come by their wealth–they've freely received it from their parents and grandparents. In reading a few things about the church, I notice that their annual budget is four million dollars. That says nothing about their endowments, of course. Unless I missed something, I didn't hear any "Concerns" of the church. With their annual budget and resources, the only concern is probably that they don't know how they can possible spend all that money in just twelve months.

Guess what happens while they are taking the offering?

Did you guess that people in the congregation start standing up and giving reports on those in the hospital? *Noooo.....*

A slide show presentation is made of a shelter for domestic violence and the volunteers who work there? *Noooo.....*

We reach out and hug our neighbors and offer them love and greetings? *Noooo.....*

The choir and small orchestra offer another piece of incredible music to help soothe and elevate us in style as we open our wallets?

That would be correct.

This piece is titled, "The Lord is my Shepherd," and starts: "The Lord is my shepherd: therefore I can lack nothing. He shall feed me in green pastures and lead me forth beside the waters of comfort...."

I'm sensing a theme and a book here. It could be titled: *"Comfort and Luxury: It's God's Will For Me."*

Every minister knows that there are limits to ideas he or she can introduce to their congregation, based on each group's values. Some can't talk openly about homosexuality without half the people walking out, others about a woman's right to choose or divorce as a social institution that offers people freedom from oppression.

In this church, here are some of the sermons the ministers have had to reject over the years: "The New Spirit of Minimalism: Leave it All and Walk Naked into the Woods Forever," and "Sinning: Beyond Spending Principle." This one was put in a locked vault, never to be even breathed of again: "It Is Not God's Will That Some of Us Should Be

Filthy Rich While Others Need to Dig For Couch Change to Pay For Their Children's School Lunch."

We've been well massaged and lubricated by the grand music. It's time for the sermon.

Now what I've noticed about Presbyterian ministers in my time, is that eight out of ten are distinguished-looking older men with gray or white hair, but not decrepit by any means. At the bigger churches, they have doctorates. Here at Middleton Presbut it's no different: a "Dr. Marshall Adams" is our head minister, and he's got the obligatory white hair and crisp, robed demeanor.

"The scripture reading comes from the Revelation to John. Here is the call to the endurance of the Saints...(blah, blah, blah)...and I heard a voice from heaven say, 'Blessed are the dead who die in the Lord.'"

I'm sensing a "Saints" theme.

"In the calendar of the church, November 1st has always been 'All Saints Day.' Protestants have altered it to be the first Sunday in November, and in our congregation it creates a head-on collision with our Pledge Day."

There is an ever-so-slight rumble of polite laughter. It's moments like this when I wonder what would happen if someone just started laughing hysterically until tears came out of their eyes. This must be some type of Turrets of the imagination.

Dr. Adams tells us in a very clear manner, with flawless Main Line diction, that he had asked the choir to perform the Requiem in honor of those who have died as saints, as well as those who have died in Iraq. He speaks of those who died in their faith, but then stretches beyond this theme: "This morning, I have in mind, not just the exceptional, but the ordinary....the likes of you and me."

Does this man seriously believe that anything about this church and these people is "ordinary?" "Ordinary" is Wal Mart, blue jeans, Miller beer, McDonald's, old people singing "Rock of Ages" in a half-empty small town church.

"Ordinary" is *not* adult education classes entitled, "Wisdom from the Past: Great Sermons Preached in Turbulent Times," an evening of "Walking the Labyrinth," a Macular Degeneration Support Group meeting in the Congregational Hall, a Presbyterian Women Event: Silver Polishing, and Nepalese art for sale, such as the picture entitled "Buddha with Gold and Black Background" for $1400.00.

"There is something more to this day than a grateful remembering: a call for the endurance of the Saints. The scripture says it is now *our* endurance and faithfulness which are at stake. The writer wants us to ponder not just what we have received, but what our legacy will be. The author of Revelations knows that endurance is essential for anyone who will uphold the legacy of the Saints and of Jesus Christ. As our African-American Christian friends are apt to say: 'Just keep on keeping on...'"

Well, I was hanging out with some of those African-American Christian friends recently, and I bet you that it would be a whole lot easier for them to "keep on keeping on" if someone would make a donation to their church of $1400.00, rather than purchasing "Buddha with Gold and Black Background."

"You and I have been passed the baton...we are the Saints of the next time...we are to serve those who come after us. The endurance of the Saints is ours to undertake. May we be so inspired, that one day it will be said of us, 'Blessed are those who died in the Lord.'"

He sweeps around in his robiness, and reassumes his seat on the throne-like chair behind him.

Well, I'd give it an A-. He made his points well...fine delivery and nice sentence structures. The minus is because when he said, "Just keep on keeping on," he didn't do it with a soulful, gettin' down kind of voice, but in a very stiff Presbut manner which was kind of like hearing a James Brown song done operatically.

We sing one more hymn together as a congregation, and our distinguished Man of the Robe comes to a microphone to give us the benediction, which he delivers with perfection. If he were an Indian, his name might be "Stands With One Arm in the Air."

Believe it or not, we have another anthem with multi-instrumental accompaniment. "Lux Aeterna"-- the talkie version this time. Three soloists are featured, their voices weaving around those of the primary choir. This is the seventh musical offering from the choir. How on earth do they do it? Each and every one was flawless and of a caliber that one might enjoy at Carnegie Hall or the Academy of Music.

I honestly can't say I'm tired of the music–it has just been so amazing. I can't say I'm tired of hearing the leaders talk–they didn't say very much and what they did was concise and exactly what I would like to hear when I come to church: no one can condemn me and all my sins have been wiped away. I am a tabula rosa. A blank slate. I'm like a virgin, touched for the very first time.

Well, it's been a great free concert.

When the choir stops, I position myself to start running down the center aisle the moment the Postlude begins. It's a looooong aisle. True to memories of Presbyterianism, not a single person stands up until we hear the first note of the organ. I book down the middle, not wanting to get wedged in between six hundred Presbyterians all clogged at the end of the aisle because Presbuts always like to shake the hand of the minister. How else will he know that you were in church?

I make it about three quarters of the way and then the jam begins. Oh well, this will be a good opportunity to hear what obscenely rich people chit chat about. I make a concerted effort to eavesdrop on various conversations.

"Wasn't that Rutter incredible?....well, *everything* that Rutter composes is incredible...it was absolutely haunting!"

"OH my GOODness! MISS MINdy! WHERE have you BEEN?...it's SO great to SEE you!"

"Well, we just bought the shoes last night so there was no way she wasn't going to wear them to Sunday School today..."

"You know those special Delta Force guys aren't even wearing uniforms...they're just wrapped up like Arabs....it makes sense, I mean, wearing a uniform is like having a bulls-eye on your chest."

"We had it catered at Angelino's....they do a nice job. I don't cook anymore–who am I kidding...I never really cooked!"

I finally get through the doorway out into the foyer and break from the stream of bodies. I end up in front of the visitor's table, where an intelligent-looking young woman with hip glasses smiles and asks me if it's my first time. We chit chat for a moment.

"That was some music this morning," I observe.

"Well, that isn't typical of every Sunday," she tells me.

"Oh. You don't normally have that many people in the choir?"

"Yes, we do."

"You don't have special instrumentalists and soloists?"

"Well, yes we do," she laughs. "They were featuring more music than usual because of All Saints Day."

"Oh." I guess nothing says "we miss you" like seven pieces of classical music.

A robed choir member comes up to my hostess and gives her a big hug. She turns right away and introduces me to him. That's some pretty impressive manners. I could imagine if I had her gig, I'd get tired of all the faces and names and let things slide.

I thank her again and move on outside. Boy, it's a beautiful day. It seems more glorious than usual, which I'm attributing to all the grandeur around me. Fabulous architecture, landscaping and perfectly dressed, wealthy and well-educated people can, I'm guessing, enhance any kind of weather.

I start to feel alone in a crowd, so I decide to meander over to the Nepalese exhibit. I ask a few people where it is, and they are very attentive and helpful in showing me where.

The building which houses the church offices is another impressive, bustling space. I walk down a small flight of stairs to a glassed-in conference room, the walls of which are lined with colorful art for sale. I start to stroll around the perimeter when I see something much more compelling and important: a punch and food table.

I walk over and look at three baskets on the table, each of which holds some type of comestible, totally unfamiliar to me.

A stately older woman is scooping out punch.

"Is this Nepalese food?" I ask her.

"Well, they're Indian....*snacks*," she says with a smile, as though she's not sure that is really the right word for them.

One of the baskets has some little ball thingys, which are covered with some little sprinkle thingys. I decide to go for one of those. I bite down and my teeth meet what feels like a chalky brick. I don't want to be rude, but I can't tell which is more vile–the texture or the flavor.

Another woman is standing beside me, and she bites down as well. "Eeeehhhh," she says without any restraint. "I expected something soft and chewy, but this isn't. I don't like these at all." She tosses the ball into a small trash can near the table. Must be a big contributor–they don't have to care what others think.

I put my ball into my napkin–as though I'm going to stroll around and munch on it while I look. I reach for a glass of punch.

"Were you at the first service?" the serving woman asks me.

"Yes, I was."

"How did you like it?"

"Oh, well...the music was amazing."

"That's what I heard," she smiles.

We share introductions and she asks me what I do for a living.

"Well, I'm a retired psychologist and now I'm starting a business designing clothing for children and I'm doing some writing."

"Clothing for children?"

"Yes. I'm designing and making clothing for dress-up and fantasy play....period pieces and what not. All out of really sumptuous fabrics."

"No kidding!" she says. "What a great idea for a business. Where are you selling them?"

"Well, I'm trying to get some exposure at fine craft shows. Eventually I'd like to sell them in stores and maybe on line."

"Really! Well, I'm on the selection committee for the Middleton Hospital Show....I'd love to see if we could get you in–that sounds like just the kind of thing we're looking for. Something unusual and high quality for children."

What luck! I've been trying to find the folks with money and resources to help launch my business and here is a woman with a seat at the grown-ups table.

She asks for a business card, but I don't have one. It's probably best because networking and passing around business cards at church seems a bit like hitting on someone at a funeral. She suggests I speak to a woman who works over in the nursery area, and tells me her name. This other woman also knows of fine craft shows in the area.

I thank her, tell her I'll be in touch, and make a quick round of the art. It's pleasant and colorful, but not particularly challenging to my eyes for some reason.

Over at the nursery area, several young mothers are watching their children in a well designed playground space. I ask if any of them knows a "Caroline Chase."

"Here she comes now." one of them tells me.

A leggy blond woman in her early 30s comes toward us, wearing a grey, lightweight wool skirt and a pale pink cashmere sweater. "I'm being summoned?" she jokes.

I introduce myself and tell her that another woman suggested I talk with her. I explain what my business is.

"You know, I am on the committee for the Philadelphia Orchestra Craft Show. I'd be happy to put in a good word for you. Do you have your business card?"

"No, I'm afraid I don't."

"Well, bring it next time."

She tells me of other shows I can check out, and I thank her. I leave with at least five solid leads on top-of-the-line shows where people with money stroll around just looking for places to put their disposable income.

I have to admit, these obscenely rich, conservatively-clad, subdued Presbuts are actually not such bad people once you stop criticizing them and telling yourself that you're really superior to them because you watch a 20-year-old TV with only one bent antennae.

And I think I just learned something very important at this church: on earth, as it is in heaven, it's not *what* you know, but *who* you know.

Presbyterian

#	Dimension of Church Experience	Rating
1)	Is parking close and convenient?	2
2)	How beautiful is the worship space?	10
3)	How comfortable is the seating?	6
4)	How welcoming and friendly is the congregation?	6
5)	How enjoyable and uplifting are the musical aspects of the worship?	10
6)	Does the leader have a pleasant speaking voice and does he/she make sense to me?	8
7)	How clean are the bathrooms?	9
8)	Are the people in the pews interesting to stare at?	9
9)	How tolerant to many ways of seeing and doing things does this group appear to be?	8
10)	Would I feel good about how these people would spend my money?	5
11)	How close did I feel to God in this place?	5
12)	Did I smile more than once during the experience?	2
	Total	80

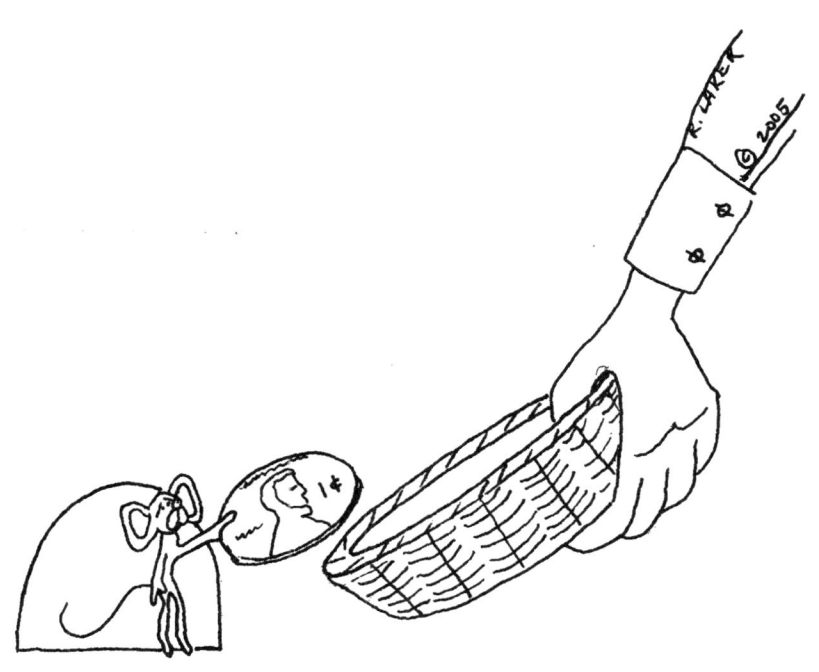

CHURCH OF THE NAZARENE MOUSE

Church of the Nazarene

Heading home from a visit to my parents in Buffalo, my husband and I decide to take in a church service together–another stop in this journey of exploring and researching as many faiths as possible. My husband suggests we go to a Church of the Nazarene–something small and humble in a little town in the middle of the country, where the people are likely to be unpretentious and deeply committed to their faith.

Did you buy that?

Suckers!

Here's the truth: my husband has to be dragged into the church and only after I bribe him with promises of three chicken sandwiches and a mega cup of coffee immediately after the service. He fears the worst: snake handlers or people rolling down aisles. I tell him to think of it as an anthropological experience.

"Anthropologists study people who shrink heads. I rest my case."

"Please try not to look as though you have diarrhea," I ask him as we walk toward the simple glass door. "An important part of my making the right decision is to be as open and unbiased about a place as I can be. If I like this church, I'll check out another Nazarene near us."

We walk into a dingy looking lobby. You can see the sanctuary ahead, up a small flight of steps. A woman comes up some stairs from a lower floor and looks at us with a touch of surprise and then a smile. She introduces herself as Susie. We tell her our names.

My husband cuts to the chase. "Is there a bathroom here?" he asks.

Susie points the way.

I start to follow him because it has been a long trip so far.

A very bouncy man comes around the corner and nearly jumps out of his skin at the sight of us. "Hel-LOO!" he exclaims with way too much enthusiasm, especially when one has a full bladder. "I'm Craig Ludwig–the Pastor!" His face is in total shock, moving toward delirious joy, as though he's just seen an apparition. My husband has continued to walk on, leaving me in his dust.

"Hi, I'm Ruth Laker, and you'll have to excuse my rudeness, but I need to head in that direction." I smile.

"OH! YES!" he makes way for me to pass.

I've got a bad feeling already.

Walking down the hallway toward the bathrooms, I feel as though I'm in Baghdad or some similar place where nothing can be kept nice. The furniture is early seventies and in bad shape: rusty metal legs, nothing upholstered or comfy-looking. Rugs are filthy and buckling up all over the place–all of them a caramel hue. Obviously purchased during the color year 1971. I see several buckets in unexpected places, catching a variety of drips. Whole ceiling tiles are missing and insulation is hanging down from the crawl spaces. It doesn't seem as though these are projects in the works, but rather emergency triage measures.

The bathroom is at least usable. The wall "art"–two small cardboard plaques which show scenes of smiling lady bugs crawling on flowers- frightens me, but if I keep my eyes focused downward I don't have to look at them again. The plastic flowers in a skinny white vase on the sink are a blue color not found in nature.

Strolling back down the hallway, the bulletin boards need to be surveyed. Not much is on them. Many are empty. This looks like the last day at a going-out-of-business church.

Ah, here is one that's filled in. Polaroids of teens grace the board, and a "Students Bill of Rights" is proclaimed in the middle. Items on the list include: *Students have a right to pray in school. Students have a right to wear T-shirts which proclaim their faith in Jesus Christ and God. Students have a right to point out that our country was founded on religious principles.*

I'm looking for: *Students have a right to disagree with the Church and form their own opinions about Christ and God.*

It's not up there.

Walking into the sanctuary I feel a mixture of pity and dread. There are no more than ten people in the pews and one overly talkative, self-conscious minister with a forced comedic style who is trying to work the crowd, such as it is. Oh dear. I may owe my husband a lot more than chicken sandwiches and coffee. We could be talking that thing that women hate to do but men love so very much: stopping to buy plastic twine for the weed whacker.

I find a spot near the back and my husband joins me. We've both taken the two meager flyers that were lying on a ledge as we came up the stairs. One says "Welcome to the Horseheads Church of the Nazarene: Your Family Can Be Part of Our Family." The other offers one page of information about the history of the Church of Nazarene movement. This I'm curious about. My husband and I both hypothesized that they were formed as some type of splinter group that didn't want to be dictated to by some guy like Luther or Calvin–these folks probably wanted everyone to know that the man *they* answer to is the man from Nazareth.

I'm about to find out if we're right, when one of the older women in the congregation comes over to shake my hand. Immediately after introductions the woman says, "We hope you'll come back-we need you to come back!" She moves on. Another woman, Ellen, walks over and shakes our hands as well. "We hope you'll come back again–our poor church is in trouble...."

"Oh, what's the trouble?" I ask her.

"LET'S GET STARTED FOLKS!" the Pastor calls out.

Ellen leans over a bit to confide in us: "Everyone is going to other churches...."

The look on her face is so desperate I feel obligated to tell her that we're just passing through.

"Oh, that's a shame..." she says, her face crestfallen. She stands and lingers, as though she isn't sure what to do. She keeps looking at me as though she can't accept what I've just said, and I half expect her to ask if she can come with us.

The Pastor begins. "WELL....a few of us met Wednesday night for prayer group and guess what we prayed for? No winter! That's one prayer that probably won't be answered! Amen? Hey, if you're new here you'll see that we aren't a quiet bunch, amen? How many of you came to see each other?"

Pastor Craig puts his arm up in the air to demonstrate how one raises their hand.

"How many of you came to see Pastor Craig? Our worship team? That's right...you didn't come for any of those things. You came to be with Jesus Christ our Lord and Savior, amen?"

A few people echo his "amen."

When the Pastor mentioned the worship "team," he pointed to one skinny teenage boy at a microphone with a guitar on his lap. He's the only other person up front except for a teen girl sitting on the floor, putting up the transparencies on an overhead projector. As we later came to find out, those two teenagers are the children of Pastor Craig and his wife Susie, whom we had met before. They also have one other child in the pews. That means that of the fifteen people in the sanctuary, one third are the Pastor's family.

"If you see any new people, say 'hello,'" he looks back toward my husband and me. "They just *look* scary...just kidding! They don't look scary!"

My husband, who has been reading his pamphlet, glances over the tops of his glasses, giving the Pastor a look I can't see, but I'm concerned could be in the scary vein. I try to compensate by offering a big, beaming smile at the handful of people looking back at us.

"We need to thank Jesus for letting us be here, Amen? Lord Jesus, we feel the cold and we know that this is when things lay dormant. We come here, not to hear the Pastor, or the music, but to be with you....we've been in a dirty world all week, Lord....give us a *hug*."

I can't help but get the feeling that Pastor Craig's approach to this service so far has been one big disclaimer: The Pastor assumes no responsibility for whatever experience people may have at this church.

"Folks, get up and greet your neighbors in Christian love!"

The other five people come over and shake our hands before the Pastor himself comes to us.

"So...are you folks from the area?" he says, moving his hands around in a circular motion like beaters in a mixer.

"No, we're from outside Philadelphia," I tell him.

"Outside...." again he's beating his hands, blending the cookie dough.

"Near Valley Forge," my husband says.

"OH! Yes! I used to go to Cape May a lot," he proclaims in his bursting-out-of-his-skin way. "Well, we're so glad you're with us today and we wish you safe travel," he says. Pastor Craig's nonverbals are very disconcerting: he seems on edge and slightly agitated, as though he may be on a mild amphetamine. His speech is very fast and pressured and his attempts at humor painfully forced. I have to feel sorry for the man.

What really seems sad is how much everyone hungered for us to be new parishioners in their tiny group. Now that they know we are travelers just passing through, you can sense the disappointment.

Do they really think that two middle-aged people who just walk in off the street are going to save this church, even if we are wearing fairly nice sweaters? What do we look like–the Gates? The word "congregation" implies numbers–bodies–more than a handful if one wants to maintain a church building and repair the leaking roof.

A song is projected onto the little screen up front, right near the neon cross on the wall. The neon cross. Yup. It's neon.

"Explain to us why you picked this song today Justin..." the Pastor addresses the teen boy, who speaks smoothly and eloquently. "Well, it just says to me that all that we have, what we think of as gain, is really nothing compared to a relationship with the Lord."

I like this boy's style. I'm tempted to stand up and say, "How many of us would rather hear Justin give the sermon than Pastor Craig? Amen?"

We sing the song and the Pastor breaks right into another prayer at the end: "Lord Jesus...you're our joy...you're the *best*...(he whispers 'best')...if we took everything and compared it to you, there'd be no comparison...everything isn't worth a hill of beans...we think of those fighting on distant shores...they might be in a foxhole, or police station....Lord, would you take the ones who don't believe that you exist and give them a strange feeling so they know you exist? We think of the Supreme Court...we ask you to help them reconsider the Ten Commandments. Let 'em know that the founding of our country was under God....Lord, let 'em know that the word 'God' is meant to be there on the tombstones of those people who wrote the Declaration of Independence..."

My husband nudges me while the Pastor continues with this prayer. He points to some information typed in the church flyer. Specifically, the Stewardship Report. It reads:

Weekly amount needed	*$900.00*
Last week	*$ 79.00*

Please remember that when we do not have enough tithes and offerings come in. Pastor Craig, the Electric Company or the insurance, etc. do not get paid. This amount is a minimum amount not a suggested amount.

Underneath these cheery words are some more: *Please keep liquids other than water out of the Sanctuary. This will help keep our carpet from being stained. The Pastor and Church Board are asking you and the ushers to help us this way. Thank you*

This is so sad. This is so very, very sad. And not just because there *are* no ushers.

The "Church News" part of the bulletin says only the following: *1.) Need people to count money.*

Perhaps someone jumbled the word order. Shouldn't it read: "Need money for people to count?"

Pastor Craig starts to lead us through a study of Isaiah. He attempts to explain the difference between suffering and punishment. I'm thinking that whatever form of ADD or hyperactivity he *suffers* from is starting to be experienced by me as very *punishing* indeed. I can tell by the way my husband has the preacher in a locked gaze, he's trying to stare him down until the man falls to his knees and admits his incompetence. When it comes to religious leaders, my husband has never suffered fools gladly.

Personally, I feel too sorry for the guy to want to intimidate him in any way.

"We all know about punishment, amen? When the kids go bad, we think we're being punished? Jesus knows every little wrong thing we've ever done and he's ready to lay down his life for us. Now granted, he didn't have children...I know many try to say he had a child with Mary Magdalene or one of the other ladies from his band-but let me tell you that is a LIE from the Devil!"

"The ladies from his band?" Does he mean that Christ was like Mick Fleetwood and we will not believe that he had sex with Stevie Nicks or Christine McVee?

There are three things I really want to say to this man at this juncture: 1) Stop saying "amen" in the form of a question. It's really annoying. 2) Please write your sermons ahead of time. You are not good at improvisation, segways or developing points to their logical conclusions. 3) What on earth is so awful about the idea of Jesus having been married and fathering a child?

This last point really does stay in my mind as the preacher keeps bouncing around. I mean, think about it: images of Jesus carrying his child around in a snugli, pressed up close to his chest, could do a whole heck of a lot for the institution of fatherhood. Maybe people just don't like the idea of having to share Christ–I mean he came for *us,* right?

As the preacher continues, a woman comes by and hands us a pew pad on which to sign our names and where we're from. My husband opens the cover, then leans over and whispers in my ear: "I expected to see a note on the inside of this pad that said, 'Please help, I am seeking asylum!'"

"How many of you are happy to be adopted?" Every time he asks us a question he does the arm raising demonstration. "I've been-not by my parents, but by my God." Pastor Craig keeps saying things like Guber from the old *Andy Griffith Show.* He assumes a Guber smile too. "How many of you know family does stuff for you?" Again with the hand raise. "Now I'm from a German family. We don't talk a lot, we might not see each other or talk more than once a year, but if someone dies, we're there. We'll drive from anywhere to get to the funeral."

So what this man is saying is that his family only wants to be around their kin when they are lying flat and stiff.

"Jesus wants us all not to....what?"

"Perish," a few of the elderly woman say.

"Perish! Obviously, not in a physical sense....if we had walked around from the dawn of creation–WRINKLES! How many aches and pains do you think you'd have after 2000 years? Ellen says, 'I've got enough now!'"

Pastor Craig is laughing forcibly at his comment about Ellen, but he's the only one.

I glance back at my pamphlet–desperate for any diversion that will pull me away from this awkwardness. I notice something called the "Silver Sword Award." It reads: *The names on this list have told Pastor Craig all the books of the Bible in 2005.* There are six names on the list: two of them are members of the Pastor's family, and here's the really curious one: Pastor Craig. Yes, Pastor Craig has told himself all the names of the Bible. I think after services I'm going to suggest that he give back his Silver Sword Award. Clearly, this award contest has been tainted with nepotism or worse, downright corruption.

Back at the ranch, Craig is now discussing the crucifixion and demonstrating with his body how Jesus hung on the cross. I've noticed over the years that a certain percentage of male ministers seem to like to step right into Christ's shoes and have little hesitation to do it. Once I saw a minister act out Jesus calling Lazarus from the tomb. His interpretation was not quite how I have always envisioned Jesus, but hey, none of us really knows for sure just how Jesus was day in and day out, right? This man portrayed Jesus as a macho, swaggering, demanding, cocky loudmouth who yelled, **"LAZARUS....COME OUT!"** while thrusting one arm dramatically toward the tomb and holding the other hand casually on his hip.

Our leader is now waxing philosophic. "I think for Jesus the real hurt came when he was feeling alone, without God, and asked 'Why have you forsaken me?' But by light and life He had knowledge in the end. And hey, I thank God President Bush banned partial birth abortions–I'm gonna go on the record saying it right now."

Yes, I remember seeing a photo of the event. I don't recall one person with a womb in the picture.

A woman near the front is coughing steadily. Pastor Craig stops and stares at her. Strange, but he just stares for a moment, almost as though he is looking at her but doesn't see her. Finally, he says, "Would you like a tic-tac Ellen?"

Ellen can't answer because she is coughing. She keeps her head down and attempts to deal with it privately, despite the fact that the

Pastor has just stopped the entire worship experience and focused a spotlight on her discomfort.

When she doesn't look up or respond, Pastor Craig says, "Okay," in a slightly offended way.

I start thinking about the ride home to try to take my mind off the pain of the Pastor's need for validation. Neither my husband nor I got much sleep the night before so we'll be struggling to get the driving done in the final stretch. Maybe we can pull off the road and take a half-hour catnap together. I'm having trouble imagining this. My husband is taller than most people and he can barely drive comfortably, let alone stretch out and sleep in the car. I smile thinking about a time that we tried to have "relations" in the car. It was quite a fiasco.

My husband looks over at me and raises his eyebrows at my smiling face.

"I'm thinking about that time we tried to have sex in the car and you kept banging my head against the roof," I lean over and whisper.

"I'm glad to see you're using this worship time constructively," he responds.

"People think they've got to be tolerant-that's what God loves in people. No he doesn't! He likes people who are *right*! And if you're not right, God will discipline you just like you sometimes need to discipline your kids."

So let's see....God is intolerant of tolerance....I always thought maybe it was the other way around. Well, he's the guy who went to seminary....

"Some of you don't know that I work 40 hours a week with juvenile sex offenders. They say 'MY way! I don't care what God says'....that's the SIN. Adam did it with the apple too. 'MY way!'" The Pastor takes a bite out of an imaginary apple, making a loud biting sound. He does it two more times. "'MY way!' 'MY way!' We've got to be willing to say, 'I've done it wrong,' and He'll forgive us. Isn't that cool?"

I did sleep very successfully in he back of my Volvo one time when we went camping. My husband and daughter and I were in this little pup tent kind of thing, and I was pressed up so close to the wall that I had an attack of claustrophobia. I squirmed out of the tent and went to the back of my Volvo. It was great inside for sleeping. Soundproof and everything. Those Swedes...

"If everything I've said is Greek, Latin, Jibberish–remember this: Jesus *LOVES* you!"

Oh Craig. Craig, Craig, Craig. If this was the point of your sermon, you could have said it a half hour ago and my husband and I could be in Binghamton by now looking at the puppies in the mall.

"We're going to end a little differently with our offering...." Craig is holding an offering dish and circling around the front of the church as though he's trying to figure something out. Finally, he walks to the back and sets the dish down near the door. "The finances of the church are poor but....God will take care of it all....Come on up here Justin, we're gonna do one of the easiest, babiest songs we know. Anyone know what I'm talking about?"

"Jesus Loves Me!" one of the elderly women calls.

"That's right!"

After the song is over, we slide out of the pew. I throw an arm up at Pastor Craig and tell him "thanks." My husband tosses some money in the offering dish, over which the Pastor's wife, Susie, is hovering. Yes, she's actually watching what people put in the dish.

I'm getting the feeling that Pastor Craig is somewhat angry about the money situation. What he may not be realizing is that it's probably not a good idea to browbeat the last seven parishioners who haven't yet jumped ship.

When the Pastor said that the church finances were poor but that "God will take care of it all," I'm wondering if he has considered all the ways that God might do that. Specifically, I'm wondering if he has considered the fact that when a church shrivels up and there are no more people (despite the fact that the planetary population has doubled from 3 to 6 billion in the past thirty years) and no money and the building is falling apart, that it might be God's way of saying "This isn't your calling Craig. It's time to do something else."

Amen?

Church of the Nazarene

#	Dimension of Church Experience	Rating
1)	Is parking close and convenient?	10
2)	How beautiful is the worship space?	1
3)	How comfortable is the seating?	3
4)	How welcoming and friendly is the congregation?	10
5)	How enjoyable and uplifting are the musical aspects of the worship?	2
6)	Does the leader have a pleasant speaking voice and does he/she make sense to me?	0
7)	How clean are the bathrooms?	4
8)	Are the people in the pews interesting to stare at?	2
9)	How tolerant to many ways of seeing and doing things does this group appear to be?	1
10)	Would I feel good about how these people would spend my money?	1
11)	How close did I feel to God in this place?	1
12)	Did I smile more than once during the experience?	1
	Total	36

Methodists

It's good to go to a Methodist Church after experiencing many religious groups, some of which have left you scratching your head, or worse, your body. Of all the denominations, Methodists are probably one of the least scary to me. They are the whole wheat bread of churches–substantive enough but not too complicated. "Accessible," that would be the word that comes to mind for me when I think of Methodists.

I've been to several Methodist services in my life thus far and they were always pleasant. The only negative thing I ever heard about a Methodist was from my grandmother. She was very put out by the Methodist minister who had lived on the same street as we did, Kent Morris. Apparently, he ran off with "some Black woman," leaving his wife and three children, and began selling cars out on the edge of town at Stiles Ford.

I never did ride my bike out there to see if it was true. He was a pariah. We were never to speak of him, except when my grandmother wanted to. Now as an adult in middle age, there is something compelling to me about Kent. I mean, who is more confined than a minister? Who lives in more of a fishbowl? Who has a greater expectation to be perfect and beyond reproach? For him, as a minister, a father and husband, to just chuck it all...and as a White man in a southern town, to run off with a Black woman, well, I can't help but marvel at the part of Kent that couldn't be contained anymore.

Anyway, it's another lovely fall day as I pull my car into the Westover Methodist Church parking lot. It's between services and I'm hoping to jump in on a Sunday school class. Methodists are known to be fairly socially progressive, so there might be some neat offerings like: "Cleaning Out Our Closets: Gay Clergy in the Faith,"or "Raising Your Drug Addict Daughter's Children in Christian Love."

The facilities at this church are comfortable but not overdone. Walking down the hallway of the education building, I can hear the murmur of classes going on. Oh good, the classes are labeled with signs on the doors. "Social Justice".....nah. Here's one that's interesting in a slightly mysterious way: *"ConverSAtions..."* Oh-la-la.

There's no window so I can't see what's going on, but I'm feeling game for anything this morning so I open the door and walk right in.

Oh dearie me.

I've walked into what looks like a great-grandparents support group. There are about sixteen people in a circle, average age seventy-five, most of whom are sitting on comfortable couches. Not one person is under seventy. There is only one empty seat and it's right up front next to the leader. I sit down somewhat awkwardly, aware that many eyes are upon me: eyes that have seen the Depression, the rise of Adolph Hitler, WWII, Elvis movies, Vietnam and the hippies, Jimmy Carter's gas lines, Reaganomics and the closing of the twentieth century. Their century.

I look around slowly, trying not to draw attention to myself as the leader reads something. There are equal numbers of men and women–all of them dressed carefully in their Sunday best. Some of the women are looking at me, most with smiles on their faces. One man looks at me furtively. Two of the men have their eyes closed, one's head is nodding forward.

"And that, to me, really captures Galatians like nothing else," the leader concludes. "Comments?"

It's quiet for a few seconds.

"Sounds about right," one of the women on the far side of the room chuckles.

"That says it all," another woman offers.

Our leader waits for another minute and no one has anything more to offer. I hear the slightest snoring of a man on one of the couches but no one else seems to notice.

"Well," let's move on....Hell-o ..." he says to me as he is flipping a fresh sheet over on his giant writing pad. "I didn't see you come in!"

"I guess I just snuck in..." I smile. I hate being the center of attention when I'm the "new kid."

"I'm Larry Tyler, the facilitator...."

"Ruth Laker."

"Well, we're so glad to have you!"

The woman sitting next to me pats my arm and smiles. There is something very comforting about that one little motion coming from an older woman. Nice older women have that wonderful something about them, what you might call the "Every Grandmother" quality.

Larry has his marker poised and is ready to write on his big pad. "How would you define love?" he asks us.

"Fifty years of marriage," a man says.

"That's dedication," another woman laughs.

"How about fifty-two?" someone else says.

"We can beat that: fifty-four," yet another voice calls out.

I'm reeling at the very thought of so many years of marriage. I'm on my second marriage so it's unlikely I'll ever have those kind of statistics, but good heavens, fifty-four years! I guess I shouldn't be surprised; my grandparents and my husband's grandparents all had numbers like that. My mother's parents made it to sixty-four years. But....they all kind of, well....*hated* each other. None of them believed in romantic love, self-fulfillment or growth. Marriage was something you just did and stuck with no matter what. It was like doing time, it seemed. Were all these couples in this room happy to have been with each other for so very long?

"Well there's so many different kinds of love," a woman observes. "There's family love, mother love..."

"Agape," a man offers.

"I think it's an emotion," another woman says.

Larry is writing all of this down on the paper.

"There's unconditional love," someone says.

"Can't you people come up with any easy words," Larry chuckles as he tries to write the word.

A woman with a strong German accent complains that there should be more words for love in English. It's too general for her.

The group goes on and generates a list that includes: love of money, self-love, God's love, love of God, friendship love. Strangely, no one mentions romantic or physical love. I'm tempted to say it, but I'm afraid I'll just seem like another one of those "young people" with sex always on the brain. I *do* feel very young in this crowd. Hey, maybe that's the secret to "staying young." Just always hang out with people who are older.

Larry flips over the paper. "There's three types of love for the Greeks: Eros, Phileo, and Agape. Anyone know what these different types mean?"

"Eros is physical love," someone says.

"What we might think of as sexual," Larry says as he writes.

Well good. I wasn't the only one thinking sex.

How many books in the New Testament speak of Eros?" Larry asks.

No one answers. I'm thinking Song of Solomon, but I know that's not New Testament.

"Zero. That's how often Christ talked about it."

Well, that's how often the men who wrote the books about Christ's life talked about it.

"What about this next one?" our leader asks.

"Phileo–isn't that a kind of dough?" a man says, deadpan.

"The class clown," the woman beside me says.

"It's companion love–love between two people like friends," someone calls from the other side of the circle.

"Okay, what about agape?" our leader asks the group.

"Unconditional."

Larry nods. "I love you without expecting anything in return...that's the kind of love Christ talks about." He flips the pad to the next page. A question is printed out which Larry reads: "What kind of love has affected you in your life?"

"Family..."

"God's love..."

"Well I'm going to have to go for Eros," a man in the back says.

Larry writes it all down. I know this is church, but the last man's comment begs elaboration. What erotic love is he speaking of? Is his wife in the room and do they have this amazing chemistry which has sustained a lifetime of great sex? Did he have a whirlwind romance in Korea with an army nurse, or better yet, a prostitute who broke his heart?

"Friends..."

"Christian friends..."

"Well I probably shouldn't say it, but some people love their animals an awful lot," a woman interjects.

Now why is that a problem? Animals are awesome! In our family, we're proud to say it: we love our poodle–all five fuzzy pounds of her. Unconditionally. It doesn't matter that she yaps constantly and poops her little pellets in the corners of rooms–we're crazy in love with her! And *God* loves our poodle, too. Just as much as us...cause we said so.

Our leader asks us, "Who has given you agape love in your lifetime? Ministers do, don't they?"

"That's not always true," the woman beside me mutters.

"Some ministers, right?" he clarifies. "What about teachers? Did any of you have a teacher who gave you agape love?"

"Mrs. O'Neal," a man says without hesitation. It's so cool that here this man is, probably eighty years of age, and he remembers this woman as though she was teaching him just yesterday. Another man questions whether a teacher's love is really love, or just liking a lot. Several former teachers share that they did, indeed, love many of their students.

"I wasn't a teacher in a school," one woman says, "but I taught Brownies and Girl Scouts and I have to say, I loved those little girls. I mean I *loved* them! I'd come home from those meetings just feeling so good–they just made me so happy!

Geez. I wish I had had her as my Brownie leader. I went to one Brownie meeting and the woman was so mean I never went back. My father wasn't too happy about it because she was a parishioner in our church, but hey, he got over it.

"Doc? Did you want to get in on this?" Larry asks a man two seats over to my left. Doc, a very senior citizen, senior even in this crowd, is mouthing something but no sound is coming out. Then, he pulls it all together.

"I'm trying to think of something intelligent to say," he says, giving the leader a provocative look.

People laugh.

He speaks slowly. "When I was at Normandy, we were worried about how the Jewish guys would do in battle. But there was this one guy who would go out and collect the frozen bodies, even under gun fire. He'd be out there again and again...he was very brave. And I loved that guy. He just died....what was it?" he turns to the woman beside me.

"Two years ago," she reminds him.

"Two years ago...and I really miss him. Yep, I really loved that guy."

A woman across the room in a bright red blazer says, "You said because he was Jewish you were worried about how he would do...why?"

"Oh, they just had a different way of seeing things than we did. But he was very brave...he did a great job."

Like that woman, I had the same question in my mind. But I wasn't thinking that they wouldn't be brave. I remember reading about several Jews who killed themselves to protest the lack of support for the plight of Jews in Germany. That seems like an act of tremendous courage.

The same woman who prodded him about the Jews is now asking him, "Do you think it's love when the terrorists gave their lives to kill all the Americans on 9/11? They thought the best of each other..."

She's got some mocksy, this woman.

The man from Normandy doesn't say anything. Judging by the look on his face, he didn't hear her question.

The leader steps in. "Me personally, no...killing others isn't love...unless one has to do it in self-defense. Killing others to promote your way of thinking is not love."

The German-American woman chimes in. "Well, Christian churches have done it a lot through history–they kill in the name of their beliefs."

"Sure, but that's not what Christ taught, is it?"

"The Crusades were pretty brutal," a man observes.

Our prodding woman in red continues. "Well, if we're going to go this far out, if we have soldiers fighting for our country and killing other people, is that love?"

Now there's a silence. A very awkward silence. An uh-oh-now-we're-not-talking-history-anymore-silence. It's wartime and we're an occupying army in another country and yes, we're killing people.

One of the men who had been nodding off starts to speak with a slow, far-off quality to his voice. "It's a different kind of love in the military. In Korea I had all Blacks under me. I never feared that they'd shoot me because we were in the same conditions. But I wouldn't call that love."

Hmm. Where'd that come from?

I want to get back to the lady in red. What the heck, I'm going to finally open my mouth. "Do you think Christ wanted us to go into Iraq?"

Again, silence.

"Well, when three thousand people have been killed on our soil..." the leader says to me.

"There were no links found between Iraq and any terrorist groups," I interject. "Since we invaded, terrorists have been driving into Iraq to kill Americans, and Iraqi terrorist groups have been forming..."

"Yes, I see your point. Maybe Afghanistan would be a better example..."

"I just wish the politicians would start telling the truth," a rather crusty-sounding man says from his couch.

A woman swats his leg. "This isn't a political discussion..."

"Well actually Betty, I think you can't separate religion and politics...they are almost always connected," Larry says thoughtfully.

A woman addresses a comment to me. "But you could see how awful life was under Sadam. I mean, those poor people needed to be liberated..."

"I don't know the answer," I tell her. "I just asked a question..."

"I think we have to help people when they are oppressed," she follows up.

I can see that a man across the room–the one who has had great Eros love experiences–is nearly jumping out of his skin to say something to the woman who is defending the war. The woman beside him is holding his one leg down. I wish she'd just let him speak. Maybe he'd say something like, "So why aren't we invading half the countries in Africa to free the poor, oppressed people? They've still got *slavery* in parts of Africa."

Well, at any rate, I'm impressed by the diversity of opinions in the group. I have the bad habit of clumping all older people together, as though they are of one mind and way of living. Obviously, they're not.

The leader speaks. "Our time is nearly over, but I wanted to ask: what differences do you see between agape love and that practiced by most people today?"

No one says anything.

He continues: "Mother Theresa would probably be the most perfect example of agape love. She's not getting anything out of doing what she does in terms of herself personally. There are people in this church who are saints, if you ask me. They are more concerned about others than themselves."

The German-American woman speaks. "Jesus said love your neighbor as yourself. So you have to love yourself in order to love others."

"Well, I was going to read Corinthians to you, to remind us all what true love is. I suggest you all go home and reread it. Bob, what are we doing next week?"

"Mr. Albrecht is going to talk about Christmas."

"That's timely. Okay. Let's end in a word of prayer. God, we thank you for the love you give to us every day. Help us to practice agape love–the kind of love that expects nothing in return. We are all worthy of love as you have shown us through your son our Lord, Jesus Christ. Amen."

Two of the women from the class come up and welcome me. We exchange greetings.

Larry might not be happy that I brought up the Iraq thing so I start to tip-toe out.

"BYE Ruth! Thanks for COMing!" he calls to me with a big smile.

Well, that was sure nice of him.

I decide to stroll down the hall to the women's room and freshen up a bit. Passing the Pastor's office, I notice several cartoons taped onto the door. The best is a Gary Larson: a person is entering heaven and an angel says "Welcome to heaven, here's your harp." Another person is entering hell and the Devil says, "Welcome to hell, here's your accordion."

The hallway is a bustling place. There's a great deal of diversity in ages at this church, although not races, unfortunately. Maybe that's why the man from the Korean War felt comfortable sharing that no Blacks shot him in the back because they were all in the same boat.

Various Christmas crafts are laid out on a table with sign up sheets next to each. Apparently one can come to these events and make a polymer clay snowman ornament or decorate a plastic table tree with babies breath and ribbons. I don't mean to be a craft snob, but doesn't anyone like to take their time anymore and make beautiful things that take more than 20 minutes and a glue gun?

After freshening up, I head back to the sanctuary. A grandmother and her little grandson shake everyone's hands as they enter. He is absolutely adorable with his perfectly combed blond hair and little black shoes. His grip leaves something to be desired; I've felt more life handling my dish sponge. The sanctuary at this Methodist church is very large and modernish...probably built in the 1960s. The stained glass is definitely of a modern style, while the wood is all light in stain.

Hey, here's something interesting in the bulletin: the Senior Pastor is a woman. That's cool...I've been wanting to hear a woman give a sermon and so far, much of the Pastor scene still seems to be a men's club.

"Good morning! Welcome to First United Methodist Church! I'm Cassandra Wilson, the Senior Pastor. We're happy to have you, and if you are here for one of the Baptisms, a special welcome. Please note that during advent we will be doing fewer announcements so please take your bulletins home and study them....there's a lot going on here!"

Well, speak of the devil...or angel, I guess would be more appropriate. Cassandra is a pleasant-looking woman in a long cream-colored robe. Her cheeks are very red at the moment, and her voice is nicely soft and feminine. While she is speaking, the pews are alive with chatter. Kids, adults, everyone is talking, and they're not making any great attempts to tone it down on her behalf. I guess that's a sign of a congregation where people like each other. Or they were all raised in a barn.

The Pastor introduces a strapping middle-aged man, Jeff, who gives the stewardship report. That's interesting–the money news right up front. Usually parishioners want to be lubricated before they have to think about that stuff.

"Pastor Cass is very brave to give me a free microphone without any idea of what I'm going to say," Jeff says in a blustery style. "We started out this year $40,000 dollar shy of the $330,000 it takes to run this place. Then we made some calls and people really came through and we ended up the year even a bit on the positive side. For our next fiscal year, we've already got $193,000 pledged and only 42% of the pledge cards have been turned in. That is great news. You people didn't just step up–you leaped up to the plate. We also have 33 new members, 18 Baptisms, so this is a growing church in every way."

What a relief. I can't remember the last time I was in a church of moderate size in a middle-class neighborhood where the financial news was good. Churches always seem to be strapped for cash these days.

There is a call to worship and we sing the opening Hymn, "To God Be The Glory," while the choir processes down the aisle and sits in their special pews up front. I always like it when the choir walks in during the first hymn. When I was a child, I would listen for the individual voices of the singers as they passed, and decide who I thought was the best soprano, alto, tenor and bass. Often Mr. Sprague was the best bass. Often Mr. Sprague was the only bass.

Our opening prayer is particularly well-written, in my opinion: "Wondrous and unwearied God, breathe deeply into us, so that we may be eased into this holy time." The theme of the prayer is about how harried people tend to be around the holidays. I can't say that I'm feeling very stressed because I have been part of a simplicity movement and I have cut back on what I do enormously. Here's how I did it: I told my husband that he was in charge of everything. He has to do the food shopping, make the Thanksgiving meal, buy gifts, wrap gifts, organize cookie baking, get the tree, decorate it, make the Christmas Eve meal, the Christmas Day meal and organize all aspects of the trip to Indiana to visit his family the day after Christmas.

So far, it's working great. I feel no stress at all. But I do plan to cover all of Valentine's and St. Patrick Days, provided they don't get too out of hand, as they are wont to do.

It's time for a multiple Baptism event. Apparently two babies are being baptized and two small children are reaffirming their faiths. As I watch Pastor Cass pour the water from the silver pitcher, and lay her hands on the babies heads, for the first time, I have mixed feelings about it.

It all started when I saw these two young Amish guys building a roof at a small organic foods place. I needed to hire some people who could sew and I thought, what the heck. I walked over and introduced myself. They had just sat down to eat their lunches and nodded their heads.

"I'm looking for some people to sew for a small business and I wonder if you know of any women in your community who might want to do some work at home. I'll pay them well."

The one man scratched his head. "I dun't know, but I live near a Mrs. Stolzfus who might be interested," he said in an incredibly thick Dutchy accent. This was like conversing with someone from another country.

"Does she have a sewing machine?" I asked.

"Every Amish woman knows how to sew," he says, with an slight smile of amusement on his face.

"Yes, I know, but I mean, does she use electricity? How does she run a machine?"

"Some are powered by air..."

"Oh. Great...well, let me give you my card."

"She doesn't have a phune so I'll get her address, call you and you can send her a letter."

"Okay, well here's the card."

The other young man was now standing near me, having walked over so quietly that I didn't realize he was there.

"I'll take one of those tue, my wife might be interested, but I dun't know."

And that's how it all started. The one young man called me back the next night and gave me the woman's address. It was so much fun talking to an Amish man on the phone...he took his time and was in no hurry to hang up. When I finally said "good-bye," he signed off by saying, "all right, then."

A few weeks later the wife of the other young man called me, Judith Lapp. She sounded as sweet and enthusiastic as could be. "Is it really very hard?" she asked in her sing-songy accent. I told her she could try it out and see what she thought.

My first trip to an Amish house was quite thrilling. These were genuine Old Order Amish and I was getting a chance to experience something not that many people do. The house of this young carpenter and his wife was modern with a small barn and fenced in grassy area for their horse and some chickens and turkeys. The buggy sat in the barn, looking like something out of history. Just beside the barn, next to a plastic Graco stroller, was a tree with a dead deer hanging from it, upside down.

A sweet-faced young woman with brown hair and a cap opened the door, holding a beautiful little blond boy in a blue shirt and black suspender pants. Yes, this one-year-old was wearing a little miniature Amish man's outfit. He was so cute I could hardly stand it.

Judith started sewing for me and we developed a good working relationship. Over time, I've gotten braver about asking questions about their lifestyle, and she asks me questions about mine. One of the things that is really cool about their religious practices is how they do baptisms. No one is baptized until they are nearly out of their teen years, in other words, on the threshold of adulthood. The decision to be baptized is entirely theirs and they take the vow to God and community very seriously.

A small percentage don't feel they can do it; they usually end up at a Mennonite Church and they are shunned from their community. The Amish seem to be lovely people, but there is a certain harshness to it all, too. I'm not into the concept of shunning, but I do like this idea of deciding for one self whether or not to be baptized.

And so, now that I've talked with Judith and Benuel about their faith practices, and as I watch the minister rub the water on the head of the child, I'm not sure I like this idea of deciding for a baby.

At any rate, the baptism goes off without a hitch. All four of the little ones are cooperative. No one cries, spits up, falls asleep. The Pastor is terrified of holding one little boy because he is wearing a two-hundred year old baptismal gown, passed down through the generations. She does just fine.

After the baptism applause has died down, a young woman comes to the front of the church and announces in a clear, confident voice: "This morning you are going to see sacred dancing. This might be new to you. This group is called 'Faith Factor,' and the song they will be dancing to is 'Tomorrow,' which tells us that there is always another chance and another way. I hope you enjoy it."

Six thirteen-year-old girls are standing on the altar area, with their backs to us, wearing black jeans, different colored stretch tops and no shoes or socks. I try to remain open to what I am about to see but a dark sense of foreboding comes over me.

Tomorrow, tomorrow, gonna be a way...Tomorrow, tomorrow, it's a brand new day.

The girls start to move.

Yikes. I don't know how the rest of the congregation feels, but for some reason, I'm embarrassed watching. The "sacred" movements look like those used at cheerleader try-outs.

I decide to venture a glance over my shoulder at the rest of the congregation.

Many faces are frozen. No one is smiling. Some people seem to be deliberately looking away. Other faces assume the expression of those who have just sniffed something unpleasant. I turn back and close my eyes. That helps for a minute or so, but there is still the piped-in bubble gum music with its trite lyrics being played in *church*.

I chastise myself for not being more open to this experience. I know when I was a thirteen-year-old girl, my friends and I were always working out dance routines and we loved the chance to try out things with our bodies. It is a form of expression popular with girls.

And then there's the whole thing of the feminine energy reclaiming the sacred places within the church. Six young maidens, writhing around in their bare feet on the altar of a church harkens back to the time of the tribes, when God was a woman and the female power to give birth was rev—oh please! Please make them stop! You just don't DO things like that on an altar for goodness sake! (And if you're going to, at least pick some bitchin' music like Prince or Cold Play.)

Well, if they form a human pyramid, I'm walking out.

When it's over, there is applause, but I can't tell if it's "thanks-for-being-innovative-applause" or "praise-the-Lord-it's-over-applause!"

Another young woman comes to the altar and says, "That was GRE-eat! Could the children please come forward?"

The children's message is given by a young woman who has great skill in managing the little ones. For her, it's all about the kids and it's nice to see her work.

She defines the word "provoke" as used in the Bible reading, and suggests that God calls us to "stir up good!' After they have a short word of prayer, the kids stampede out to their Sunday school classes.

We're on to the "Sharing of Joys and Concerns." Pastor Cass tells us that two couples had babies. There are a lot of concerns about different people in the military. She also says something intriguing: "We'd like to ask you to pray for the staff of the Eastern PA Methodist Conference. We've made some extreme changes which will be difficult for some people to take."

What? What extreme changes? What will be difficult to take?

Talk about a cliff hanger! I want to know what changes, for goodness sake! Is it the classic "Should gays be ministers?" issue, or have they done something even more radical like making teen dance mandatory at all Methodist services?

Now we move into some of the more traditional musical offerings. A healthy-sized choir performs during the offering, singing the song, "I Want to Be Ready." The lyrics are basically *"I want to be ready, I want to be ready when Jesus calls my name,"* repeated over and over. The melody is simple and peppy, not unlike the tune you'd hear for a car dealership.

The conductor is a middle-aged woman with a pretty face and huge eyes who seems to have a passion for her work. Her arms move with deliberation and great strength. I like watching her. She's believable. When the choir is finished, the members disband, half of them moving into the pews to sit with loved ones, which really seems like a great idea to me. I settle in, ready to hear a sermon from a feminine perspective for a change.

The Assistant Pastor stands at the altar and reads the New Testament Lesson from Hebrews. Now he's starting to tell a personal story, the way minister's often like to open their....sermons, hey....wait a minute... I look at my bulletin and see the sermon title: "Our Able Response," given by Assistant Pastor *Tim Austin.*

Oh great. She's not preaching today. And what's worse, this Tim seems to be doing his entire sermon in a quasi-shout. Oh, Good Lord.

I sit in my pew, stewing. Yup, I'm having a full blown pew stew.

Well, I can see that I'm going to have to return when I calm down a bit. I enjoyed hanging out with the seniors, and I'm glad to see a woman minister as shepherd of a thriving, vital church. It's worth another look.

I didn't get around to returning to the Westover Methodist Church until many months later, what with visiting other churches and missing the pastor on other occasions, but eventually it happened. Pastor Cass was giving a sermon called "From First Breath to Last." I settled into the pew, confident that it was really going to happen this time.

The Pastor started with a story about her uncle who had a serious heart condition as a child. The doctor told her grandmother that she could hold a mirror up to his mouth to see if he was breathing. Life and death were measured that simply in those times. She shared that when he finally died, times had changed.

"Instead of being cared for at home, he spent his last weeks in a hospital bed, hooked up to monitors and tubes that measured every bodily function. If his breathing stopped, they would put him on a respirator; if his heart stopped, the crash cart was standing by ready to shock his heart back to beating again. Wire leads ran from his head to machines beside the bed to measure his brain activity. Only when those machines shoed no activity in his brain was he finally pronounced dead.

In the five and a half decades of my uncle's life, medicine had come a long way. But as it moved that great distance, as it offered hope for extending life, it also raised new questions, questions that had not been necessary in 1924. By the time of his death we had begun to face questions like: When does death occur? What does death mean when we can extend bodily functions indefinitely with machines and drugs? And those kinds of questions lead us to an even bigger question: What is human life?"

Well, Pastor Cass knows how to get to the meat of the matter.

"We heard those kinds of questions being asked recently in the Terry Schiavo case..."

Here's a minefield. I wonder how she's going to step through this one. Terry Schiavo has been so controversial, I know two friends who stopped speaking because of their different views on it.

"I'm not planning to give you the answers this morning. I'm not sure there is one right answer for all people and situations. But I do want to help us identify some of the considerations that Christians will want to take into account when making their own end of life decisions or decisions on behalf of loved ones."

Sounds reasonable to me.

"The creation stories in Genesis remind us that life is not something we earn or deserve. Life is a gift from God - the breath of God that enlivens and animates us is something we cannot control as individuals or as a society. We can clone life, we can facilitate life through in vitro fertilization, but we cannot create life from nothing."

I was afraid this would happen. I was dreading the moment when the word "clone" would be used in a sentence as something commonplace. I would have preferred it if she had shuddered as she said it.

"The church has wrestled publicly with the question of when life begins. But what about life at the other end? What about those whose life potential doesn't lie ahead of them as Jeremiah's did when God commissioned him in the womb? What about those who are too weak, too old, too disabled to contribute to the life of the community? What then?"

Nobody is answering her.

Pastor Cass goes on to talk about how we are charged by the bible with taking care of those who need our help–the widows and orphans, beggars and lepers. She shows us how life is portrayed as something very special in the bible. Not something to terminate carelessly. She's articulate and she's definitely got the flow factor goin' on.

"But, and there is a very large but to be spoken here, the bible is careful not to raise our appreciation of life up into an idol or worship. Life is not God, and life does not need to be continued at all costs. The 23rd Psalm reminds us that each and every one of us will walk through the Valley of the Shadow of death....and we who call ourselves Christian hold ourselves to a belief in eternal life, a life that continues beyond the life we know now in this world.

Proclaiming our belief in eternal life means that death itself is no longer something to be feared. Because Jesus has been raised from the dead, we who believe in him can have confidence that our lives will not end in death but that we will be raised to new life. In First Corinthians Paul says, 'Listen, I will tell you a mystery! We will not all die, but we will all be changed, in a moment, in the twinkling of an eye, at the last trumpet. ...for the perishable body must put on imperishability, and this mortal body must put on immortality...then the saying that is written will be fulfilled: death has been swallowed up in victory!'"

I realize at that moment that there are lots of little Methodists chattering and squirming around and until now, I hadn't even noticed. Pastor Cass's sermon is really drawing me in.

"When we engage in maintaining life or its semblance at any cost, we make an idol of life, and suggest that death is so greatly to be feared that anything is preferable. The Christian faith at its base is built on the story of a man who said he would lay down his life for his friends - he would voluntarily let go of this life. We dare not say that death must be avoided at all costs, or we end up discounting the sacrificial death of Jesus on the cross. And without the cross, without Christ's death, there can be no life in our future."

Wow. She makes a great point. I guess I never thought about it quite that way. Many of those Christians who were outside Terry Schiavo's hospital protesting the removal of the feeding tube had the word LIFE taped across their mouths. If we look at it through the lens that Pastor Cass just suggested, that word should apply to whether Terry Schiavo stays on the feeding tube or leaves her mortal body. In fact, given their ardent belief in heaven after death, wouldn't they have to argue that Terry would ultimately have a better life if they let her go?

After the service, I manage to shake Pastor Cass's hand and ask her if we can meet sometime. She encourages me to call and make an appointment, which I do that week.

A few days later, Pastor Cass was driving out to my home. I was glad she suggested getting together at my house, as it would be a bit more relaxed than the average Pastor's office. We chatted pleasantly for awhile and then sat out on the deck in the bright sunshine. She declined my offer for a pair of sunglasses.

"So, I'm looking for a church," I eventually get to the point, "and I want to be some place where there are rituals and beliefs, but not ones that are too conservative or too liberal, either. Can you tell me what the mix is at the Methodist church?"

"Well, 'mix' is the word, really. We have CEO's of Fortune 500 companies and people struggling on public assistance. We have people who are involved in socially progressive groups and are pro-choice, for example, and we have people who take the opposite view. But overall, the congregation is tolerant and I think a very welcoming place."

"Yeah, I got the feeling of that, especially when I sat in on the Sunday school class with the seniors. That was a really neat experience."

"Oh, what class was this?"

"It was called 'Conversations...'"

"Oh yes...Larry Tyler was running that...he's a very nice man..."

Pastor Cass and I continue to chat about people and events in the church and in our distinctions between those who are spiritually conservative or liberal we invariably end up talking about politics.

"Well, I keep hearing that Hillary Clinton will run in 2008 for President...I guess she's as good as any of the Democrats they might recruit," I observe.

Pastor Cass grimaces a bit. "I'm not sure about having Hillary...I was a freshman at Wellesley when she was a senior, and I have to say that she seemed to be pretty inflexible and wanting to push things her way...kind of like when she came up with the Healthcare program. I don't know that she would be good at compromising."

That's interesting. Someone who actually spent time around Hillary. Of course, that was quite some time ago. Maybe Hillary's mellowed and is less controlling. She'd have to be, living with Bill's foot loose and fancy free antics.

"I'd just like to see a woman be president sometime in the near future...I feel like there's some unspoken prejudice that is still keeping women out of the most choice places of power..."

"Yes, that's probably true. Look at how few CEO's there are of major corporations. And recently, a woman CEO was brought to trial and it felt like it was everywhere just because she *is* a woman."

"Yeah, I know which case you're talking about, but in all fairness to the press, I don't think she's been skewered harder than any of the recent men. I just think we notice it more because she's a woman and it's unusual to us."

"You might be right..."

This is fun. I'm having a real conversation with another woman about life, the universe and everything.

After about a half an hour, Pastor Cass hands me some information about the church and their most recent newsletter. Dennis drives into the driveway, gets out and introduces himself. They chat for a few minutes. We are both encouraged to come back and worship at First Methodist.

Pastor Cass leaves and we agree that we like her a lot. Friendly, intelligent, unpretentious and compassionate: of all the ministers we have yet to meet or converse with, she seems the most true blue.

Methodists

#	Dimension of Church Experience	Rating
1)	Is parking close and convenient?	10
2)	How beautiful is the worship space?	4
3)	How comfortable is the seating?	4
4)	How welcoming and friendly is the congregation?	9
5)	How enjoyable and uplifting are the musical aspects of the worship?	6
6)	Does the leader have a pleasant speaking voice and does he/she make sense to me?	10
7)	How clean are the bathrooms?	10
8)	Are the people in the pews interesting to stare at?	6
9)	How tolerant to many ways of seeing and doing things does this group appear to be?	10
10)	Would I feel good about how these people would spend my money?	9
11)	How close did I feel to God in this place?	9
12)	Did I smile more than once during the experience?	10
	Total	97

Reformed Jewish

I considered it a bit of serendipity that when I called about times for the Reformed Synagogue services, the very friendly office worker told me that there would be a Bat Mitzvah that Saturday and that I was welcome to come. Now I would have the "bookend" Jewish experiences: a Bar Mitzvah and a Bat Mitzvah. You can't have Raggedy Andy without Raggedy Anne.

Given that my daughter is twelve years of age, and was invited to the future Bar Mitzvah of a boy in her class, I suggest she come along and see what the experience is like for a Jewish girl close to her age. She accepts my invitation and uses the occasion to share some insights about herself driving over to the Synagogue.

"You know, this girl is thirteen and now she is considered a woman. That means that I'll be a woman next year."

"Uh, no it does not."

"Why?"

"Because she's not really a woman, they just say that."

"Why? Why would they use the word 'woman,' if she's not a woman? That doesn't make sense."

"Well...it just means that she is...beginning her journey of adulthood...it's just an expression...." I have absolutely no idea what I'm saying and unfortunately, my daughter has radar for these kinds of moments.

"You're just making that up, Mom. If they say she's a woman, then she's a woman, and that means I will be too." She smiles with satisfaction and looks out the car window.

"No, I'm not just 'making it up'...I happen to have studied the Jewish faith extensively...I minored in the Jewish religion as an undergraduate...and I'm telling you that they don't really mean 'a woman.'"

My daughter laughs. There is a long-standing joke between us that I always make up fake credentials and areas of expertise to try to win my point. I'm still speaking fake Chinese because I once told my daughter that the owners of a Chinese restaurant were having a fight. When she doubted my assessment, I told her I knew Chinese nearly fluently. She tried to trap me:

"Say 'cup,' in Chinese Mom..."

"Douh."

"Okay, now say 'spoon.'"

"Chi-ang."

"Now say 'fork.'"

"Weee-at."

"Napkin."

"Chu-oow."

"Now say 'cup,' again."

"Duong."

"NO! THAT'S NOT WHAT YOU SAID! YOU SAID 'DUOH!' HAH! I GOT YOU MOM! YOU DON'T KNOW HOW TO SPEAK CHINESE!"

"Well, cups are very important in China and they have many different words for them. There are cups for tea, cups for...water...."

"MOM! JUST ADMIT THAT YOU DON'T KNOW CHINESE!" By now she's laughing gleefully that she has successfully foiled her mother, who is trying to pretend that she didn't.

I decide to leave this discussion of her near-womanhood alone for now. If she tries to make the point again after her thirteenth birthday, I'll make her do the laundry, cook the meals, wash the dishes, vacuum, dust, mop, clean the toilets, scrub the tubs, pay the bills, do the grocery shopping, the school shopping, the clothes shopping, brush the plague off the dogs teeth, drive four people and two dogs to their doctor and dentist appointments, to sports practices, music practices, sports events, music events, twenty hours round trip back to college, and run a business. Then we'll see if she is ready for all the privileges of womanhood.

I'm getting a bit lost looking for the Synagogue because I forgot to write the street number down. I'm on the right road, but I'm concerned that we haven't seen it yet.

"Follow those people," my daughter says of a middle-aged couple passing us in their Mercedes.

"Why?" I ask.

"Because they're dressed up and they look Jewish. They're probably going to the Bat Mitzvah."

"Honey, we're in a very populated area with lots of people going lots of places. And how do they look 'Jewish?'"

"They just do."

"I can't believe I didn't write the number down ...now we're lost and oh good, here it is. I knew we'd find it. And you were worried, kiddo...."

As we park the car I notice that directly beside me is the Mercedes. My daughter turns and smiles. Another victory over Mom.

Oh, how quickly they topple us, once they're on the threshold of being a "woman."

We walk up the ramp arm in arm. Inside the synagogue, the lobby area is buzzing with happy talk. People are jam packed in the space and I notice my daughter holding back at the door. I walk right in, as though we go to Bat Mitzvah's every day. We meander through the crowd and find the door to the sanctuary. Inside, five or six people have taken their seats, but most remain outside as long as they can.

We sit on the far right near the back. I study the architecture while my daughter studies the other girls as they come in and find seats. The shape of the room is octagonal and windows are near the top, as with the Conservative Synagogue. It is a modern and warm space.

The teen girls present my daughter with quite a study in fashion. Most have very shiny and well-styled hair, much of it in 60s retro style. Lots of little curls are piled high on heads, while some sport wide cloth headbands. All of them look much older than thirteen with their make-up, high heels and glittery clothes.

I study my daughter while she studies them. Already she is falling prey to some of the beauty obsession our culture injects into females. In particular, she is unhappy with her hair. Yes, I can see why she would be. It's incredibly lush, thick, long, wavy and a gorgeous shade of chestnut brown. She wants it to be straight.

"I hate to say it, but some of those girls look really tacky in those sparkly dresses," she whispers.

A victory for mom. I've been pointing out how overpriced and ridiculous much of the clothing is that women slavishly buy and wear. I'm trying to inoculate her as best I can as she gets older and more concerned about such things. We talk about how unnatural high heels are and how many women have to have surgery from wearing them. I share that the tinsel and glitter and boa-like collars, the hip-huggers and mini-skirts and spaghetti straps and the low-cut T-shirts all have one aim: to expose female flesh.

"Look at the row of boys over there..." I point out. "Look at how they are dressed."

She looks over at a row of boys wearing yarmulkes and navy blue blazers.

"When you look at those boys, you notice the boys. When you look at the girls, you notice the clothes and make-up. The boys will be taken more seriously because of it."

"Yeah, but boy's clothing is pretty boring. I like girl's clothes better. They're more interesting," she says honestly.

"I agree. But you have to think about what message you are sending with what you wear."

She nods.

Everyone has filtered into the room by now.

"Good morning and welcome to Temple Bethel. I'm Rabbi Anne Golden. We're thrilled to have you here for the Bat Mitzvah of Rachel Elise Levine. Today signifies Rachel's passage into Jewish adulthood. That means that she is considered an adult within the synagogue and is given all the privileges other adults have in our religious practices."

I nudge my daughter, who looks up at me. I lean over and whisper to her: "She's considered an adult here in the *temple*. She's passing into '*Jewish* adulthood.' That means that when *you* turn thirteen, you will be considered a woman if you convert to Judaism and can get someone to give you a ride over here."

My daughter rolls her eyes ever so slightly. Thank goodness we got that matter of womanhood at thirteen settled. It figures that the Rabbi has a way to explain it so that the parameters are well understood. Chances are my daughter is not the first young person to try to assert adult-style rights because of that phrase, "today I am a woman." Jewish kids strike me as a pretty savvy bunch.

"If you've never been to a Jewish service, let me explain how the prayer book is structured," Rabbi Golden says.

What a cool last name: "Golden." You could have so much fun with that. Especially if she had opted to use it with another name in a hyphenated way. "I'd like to introduce Rabbi Anne Golden-Pond." "This is Rabbi Golden-Graham." "Rabbi Golden-Oldie will now say a prayer." "Our Rabbi, Anne Golden-Them-Thar-Hills, might know the answer to that."

"I'd like to invite Rachel's parents to come forward and present the Tallit to Rachel. We will start on page 98 of the prayer book."

I point out to my daughter where it explains the Tallit in the program. I thought only men wore the prayer shawls. In the Conservative Synagogue it was only the men. Maybe these shawls put the "reform" in "Reformed" Jewish.

Rachel says a few words in Hebrew and puts on the shawl. She is a beautiful girl with thick dark hair and big dark eyes. Her face has a quality of self-consciousness to it, but her smile is broad and you can tell she is ready for this day.

The Rabbi starts singing "Sabbath Shalom," and many of the people in the Temple join in. I find it in the book and sing along. It's a pretty melody...I just wish I understood the words.

"The Reader's Kaddish is on page 108," the Rabbi announces.

This Rabbi is a very matronly looking woman who must be somewhere in her 50s. Another very hefty woman sits in a chair up front, facing the congregation. I'm wondering if she is a cantor of some type, but she never gets up and leads in anything. She almost looks like some type of security personnel. Her eyes continually scan the room over the top of her glasses, and with her football player build and wide, bull-doggie face, she seems like one woman I wouldn't want to mess with.

"Please stand for the Revelation," the Rabbi continues.

Rachel takes over and reads in a clear and strong Hebrew. Then she says, "we will continue on page 112."

This young girl-woman leads us in a responsive reading. Several of the lines are very poignant given the struggle of their people in Israel: *"Let them beat their swords into ploughshares, let them beat their spears into pruning hooks. Let nation not lift up sword against nation, let them study war no more. You shall not hate another in your heart, you shall love your neighbor as yourself."*

A long, involuntary sigh comes out of my chest for both the Jews and the Palestinians. It's difficult not to get totally dejected about that part of the world. It's so hard to fathom that much daily violence and hatred. How can they live that way?

"Please rise for the T'filah on page 114."

Words like "tallit" and "t'filah" as spoken by this strong, respected woman bring to mind the episode of *Star Trek* where Spock has to return to Vulcan to mate. One of the highest ranking Vulcans is a woman, "T'Pow," who presides over the "califi." It would be kind of neat if Rachel would go into a "blood fever" like Spock did, rolling her eyes backward into her head and then coming out of it only to try to kill anyone who got in the way of her getting her Bat Mitzvah certificate.

The congregation recites a Prayer of Thanksgiving, which includes a thank you to God, "whose presence gives life to the our people in Israel."

Well, that's seeing the glass as half full.

"We will have a few minutes for silent meditation and prayer of the heart," Rabbi Golden says gently into the microphone. The prayer lasts for a good long time. I'm aware of my daughter sitting next to me, and as I have done so many times before, I say a prayer of thanks for such an amazing person having been brought into my life and entrusted to my care. She and Rachel and all the girls sitting in a row with their fancy clothes–these are the next generation of women and I want them all to have strength and confidence.

The Rabbi starts singing in Hebrew and everyone who is Jewish joins in.

"Now I'd like to invite Rachel's parents, grandparents, sister and aunt to come to the front and help us in taking the Torah from the ark."

Those family members rise from the front rows and step up to the area that I've always thought of as an altar, but I'm not certain if this is how Jews refer to it.

Rachel's family appears to be very stylish, particularly her mother. Most notable is the above-the-knee semi-see-through black skirt she is wearing, which looks like something one would don for cocktails at a fancy hotel in Paris or Berlin. Her hair is perfectly styled and she carries herself like a middle-aged model.

Once the family members have all smushed together near the doors of the ark, the Rabbi says, "let us give honor to God and thanks for the Torah."

It seems like there should be a drum roll here.

All bodies turn toward the two wooden doors, then the Rabbi pulls back on them.

Talk about an anti-climax.

The doors slide back with a hollow, cheap sound, like when one opens a closet in a shoddy development townhouse. I was expecting the Rabbi to press a button and for several electronically powered doors to open, one after the other, like in the old TV show, *Get Smart*.

The Torah is passed from grandmother to mother to daughter. Rabbi Golden explains that this symbolizes the passing of knowledge from one generation to another. She says, "and the Torah finally rests in the capable hands of Rachel."

Now we start to sing another little ditty in Hebrew, and the family members begin to parade around the sanctuary with the Rabbi, who is carrying the Torah, leading the way.

People reach out their prayer books to touch the Torah as it passes. Again, I'm struck with Mrs. Levine, Rachel's mother. It seems to take a lot of focusing not to fall off the heels.

As they come to their seats near the front, the family sits down. Rachel and the Rabbi go back to the podium. Two little cousins of Rachel's are asked to come forward and help prepare the Torah. This involves screwing off the tops of what look like two big thermoses, and taking it out of its' case.

A succession of relatives and friends are called forward to do six readings of the Torah. All are sung in a strange melody and rhythm which definitely brings to mind the exotic Middle East. Rachel's parents are the last to read before her, and her father, in particular, has a huge smile on his face.

Finally, it is Rachel's turn. With the help of the Rabbi, she finds the place in the Torah where she is to begin reading. As with the others it is all sung, and with a great deal of confidence in the case of this girl. As she continues on with the singing, her voice grows and grows in passion. She uses vibrato, her words are clear and strong–there is absolutely nothing tentative about this Torah reading. The sheer force of her delivery makes me want to know what she is saying.

My daughter looks over at me and raises her eyebrows.

When she finishes, the Rabbi comes to her and says, "Rachel, I have a special blessing for you on this occasion of your Bat Mitzvah. May you grow in graciousness, humility, service to others, and continue to bring joy to your family and friends."

The cousins return to put the Torah back in it's casing. There's a fair amount of clanging as the silver tops are screwed back on. Who makes these things, I wonder? What are they called? Torah Thermoses? Torah Firmas? The Acme Wonder Torah Holder?

Rachel now tells about the Torah reading. Apparently part of it was about Sarah and Abraham and that whole baby at 98 thing, and another part was about Lot and life in Sadam. Rachel poses the question as to whether or not it was a good idea to destroy Sadam. It must be a rhetorical question because no one, including Rachel, answers. Instead she tells us that this part of the Torah teaches us about the importance of kindness to others. She offers Bob Dylan, Elton John and the outpouring after 9/11 as examples of kindness in people.

"How do I help the needy? My family gives to many charities, including Amnesty International, the United Way and AIDS research. I also help my friend who is in a wheelchair, by taking her places and helping her with assignments when she needs it. In closing, I'd like to thank the Rabbi for her support and my family, even though my sister always tried to boss me around!" She smiles and looks directly at her sister. It seems almost as though she had been waiting through the entire Bat Mitzvah to make that one statement, which she did with great relish.

Well, from my perspective, the talk wasn't as inspiring as Alan's at the Conservative Synagogue, although her Hebrew reading was head and shoulders above his. If you could combine her style of Hebrew delivery with his talk, you'd have one kick ass Mitzvah.

"I want to say that it has been a pleasure to work with Rachel," the Rabbi says with a smile. "Those of you who know her aren't surprised at the confidence and seriousness with which she approached her Torah reading. She is a very special young woman. Now Rachel, I'm going to call on your parents to say a few words."

Rachel's mom takes to the podium first. "I need to put on my glasses," she says aloud. "Rachel you did a beautiful job. I'm not surprised because we worked-you worked so hard. We want you to be strong but not tough, gentle but not weak, conscious but not self-conscious and when you speak, may all your words be ones of friendship and love. I love you."

Her mother steps to the side and the dad comes forward. "Now it's my turn....I need visual aids," he says as he pulls out his paper. "Are you okay?" he turns and asks Rachel. "You can take a deep breath now—just relax. The only concern you have now is that your cheeks will survive the pinching from your grandparents. So just relax."

Rachel is standing beside her father, looking perfectly calm, as he repeatedly tells her to relax.

"Last night I went in to your room when you weren't there...I tripped over a pair of boots, a book bag and landed in a pile of clothes. I wanted to think about the past thirteen years and how much we've seen you change and grow. You're mom and I always considered you a special child...you weren't like the other kids. What should we expect from someone whose first word was 'Clinton.'"

(Clinton. That man really has a way with the females, doesn't he? Even the one-year-olds can't resist him.)

"You stepped out of the mold and got a black belt in karate. Your restless spirit has always challenged the status quo. Then you moved on to sky diving. I watched you surrounded by 40-year-olds with tattoos and piercings...your new friends. By the way, let me see your tongue..."

A black belt in karate? Sky diving? I have to push my daughter to try to do a cartwheel.

"Seeing you jump is such a wonderful thing for us. Nothing you have ever tried has been easy. This hasn't been easy, but it wasn't supposed to be. We have some gifts for you. Since you always want to fly, we're giving you something to help you have wings."

Her parents hand her a six-pack of an energy drink and a fancy water bottle. A curious way to give "wings," it seems. Then again, when my husband has more than one cup of coffee, he'd be the first to admit that his tongue seems to take flight.

The Rabbi asks her older sister to come up and offers a blessing on the whole family. The bouncer woman with the huge shoulders makes a presentation on behalf of the congregation: a Bat Mitzvah certificate and a gift certificate toward a trip to Israel. She says, "Hopefully peace will come and some day you'll be able to go there."

Everyone stand for a last song. My daughter and I decide to slip out. We look around at the information in the lobby for a minute: a flyer about a bowling event for Jewish Youth; the women's reading group; the clean-up of a local road.

I decide not to ask Kate for her impressions right away. Let it sink in for a few minutes. We drive to the nearby mall, where I promised to buy her lunch before a music rehearsal she has at her school. It's a rare occasion for us to be at a mall together, and as we walk toward the food area, I'm aware that this really is feeling like a special day.

"Oh, look Mom! *My Big Fat Greek Wedding* on DVD! I have to buy that!"

"Why?"

"Because I have to have it."

"Why?"

"Because I have to."

"You'll watch it maybe three times and then be tired of it. We can rent it for that many times, save money and not have the DVD laying around cluttering up the house." As soon as I say this, I feel kind of bad. I know that spiritually, it's important for me to let go of things, but is it really fair to ask someone who is still incarnating into the material world, who still gets excited about "stuff," to stifle her desire to possess?

I decide to try an experiment. "Okay, let's say you had one hundred dollars in your pocket right now. Let's walk around for a few minutes and see what you think would be really smart purchases with that money."

"O.K," she says gamely.

We pass by a shoe store. "I guess I could buy shoes for next year...but I don't know what my shoe size will be so that probably isn't such a smart idea. Camping stuff...nah, I hate camping and I'd never use it. I never really spend money anyway, Mom. That DVD is like the first thing I've ever said I wanted in the mall, so it's not like--"

"Oh my gosh! They've got a 'Hello Kitty' store here! A whole store devoted just to 'Hello Kitty!'" I exclaim.

"Mom, you don't need any of that stuff..." she tries to steer me away from the store but I pull her in.

"Look! It's a 'Hello Kitty' lunchbox! A 'Hello Kitty' radio! OH MY GOSH! A 'HELLO KITTY' ALARM CLOCK!! Kate, you have to tell someone to get me this alarm clock for Christmas!"

"Moooom....do you really *need* that alarm clock? Don't you have an alarm clock already?"

"Yeah...but I bet this one *meows* when it wakes you up..."

Although my daughter concedes that she doesn't need the DVD, I am not willing to concede that I don't need the meowing Hello Kitty alarm clock, which I am still expecting to see under the Christmas tree.

We find a nice sandwich place, order some soup and rolls and sit down in the midst of a small crowd of people taking a break from their shopping.

"Well, what did you think of the Bat Mitzvah?" I ask her.

She shrugs. "It was alright."

"I thought that girl was really good, especially reading in Hebrew."

"Yeah...she was. Her sister probably went through the same thing. She was really pretty."

"Yep. She looked a few years older."

"It was funny when she told her sister that she tried to tell her what to do."

"Yeah."

We eat our soup quietly for a few minutes.

"Well, could you ever see yourself being Jewish?" I ask her.

"No."

"Why not?"

"I don't want to give up Christmas."

The classic reason.

I think about my own feelings. I could probably give up Christmas, at least the way we hold it in this culture. At this point, I'm jaded by all the commercialism. Some years it's a downright drag. If we celebrated it every two or three years, I could keep up more enthusiasm.

But in the end, Christmas or no Christmas, I realize that like my daughter, I can't see being Jewish, as much as I would love the regular company of Jews.

I fully respect that Jews worship God without any middle man, but I guess I've gotten kind of attached to the New Testament and Jesus over the years.

Reformed Jewish

#	Dimension of Church Experience	Rating
1)	Is parking close and convenient?	7
2)	How beautiful is the worship space?	7
3)	How comfortable is the seating?	7
4)	How welcoming and friendly is the congregation?	4
5)	How enjoyable and uplifting are the musical aspects of the worship?	6
6)	Does the leader have a pleasant speaking voice and does he/she make sense to me?	7
7)	How clean are the bathrooms?	9
8)	Are the people in the pews interesting to stare at?	8
9)	How tolerant to many ways of seeing and doing things does this group appear to be?	8
10)	Would I feel good about how these people would spend my money?	7
11)	How close did I feel to God in this place?	3
12)	Did I smile more than once during the experience?	4
	Total	76

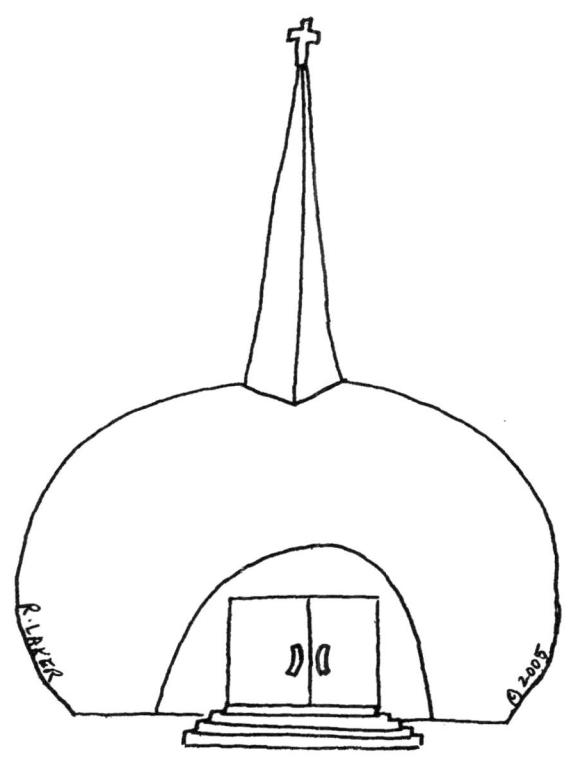

WILLIE WONKA AND THE LUTHERAN BON BON.

Evangelical Lutheran

Strangely enough, I know a fair amount about Martin Luther, and almost nothing about the church which is his namesake. Luther was one intense monk. He took his religion so seriously that he was willing to sacrifice everything and put himself through all sorts of martyrdom. Unfortunately, or fortunately, depending on your perspective, that set him up for a big fall. He was utterly shattered when he finally got to visit Rome and saw how corrupt and jaded most of the men in the upper ranks of the church were.

When he posted his 95 points on those mighty wooden doors, Luther rocked not just a nation, but the world. Nothing would ever be the same.....well, except for the Catholic Church.

I know that a lot of Lutherans hail from German and Scandinavian stock, and Garrison Keilor often pokes fun at them on *A Prairie Home Companion,* but that's about all I have as a foundation from which to build.

So on a bitterly cold winter day–we're talkin, 6 degrees outside– it's time to head to Flint Evangelical Lutheran Church on the other side of the town. There are many Lutheran churches to choose from in the Yellow Pages. If one thought in terms of store chains, the Lutherans might be considered the Sears of churches. I'm not sure why-to me, they just do.

Flint Lutheran sits in the middle of a spacious suburban community which looks to be circa 1960s. The building is a modern structure, which, from the outside, looks somewhat like a big brown bon-bon. Emphasis on the brown. Inside, more brown.

I don't care for a brown church. I love brown in my coffee beans, my soil, brown in people, and of course, in chocolate, but if I had my druthers, a church would never be brown. Particularly not outside and in.

The inside of the bon-bon is, not surprisingly, round in shape. To break up the vastness of the brown there is some cold-looking gray stone here and there, and simple stained glass windows which are composed of rectangles in–and maybe it's just the weather–icy shades of pink, gray and teal. The aesthetics are totally disappointing and I'm having to try to psych myself up to find things to like about this chilly Wonka-esque environment. It doesn't help that I'm sitting in my pew shivering, even with a heavy coat, scarf, earmuffs and gloves on.

A bell choir starts to play and that helps to take the edge off the cold. They're not as keenly polished as the group at Middleton Presbyterian, but not bad for a congregation that probably doesn't have a budget of 4 million dollars. Notable, is a man of considerable age in the row of bell ringers. He's got to be at least 75 and stands like a perfect statue. The bells they have given him to ring are two of the largest in the group, and as I continue to gaze at him he becomes more and more intriguing. He never actually rings the two bells he's holding. I watch him for minutes on end, and still, not one ringy-dingy. Maybe he's a "token" in the group. Kind of like the woman construction worker who holds the "SLOW" sign.

"Good morning," a woman's voice greets everyone. I look around and see a middle-aged woman standing at a pulpit diagonally across the room. She's got a very strong and enthusiastic voice, with just a hint of a lisp.

"Welcome if you are new to Flint–we're so happy to have you. The temperature in here, believe it or not, is 10 degrees warmer than it was at 8 o'clock." She laughs a hearty laugh. "Next week, worship is when?"

"Nine thirty." the congregation answers her.

"Nine thirty! We will be doing 'Visioning Sunday,' when you will share our dreams as a congregation and come up with a plan for our future as a church! Even if you can't be here fill out the blue Vision Statement in your bulletin. We need to hear from everyone!"

Sounds like a fairly democratically-oriented church...coming up with a "vision statement." Adams and Jefferson would approve.

"This Sunday is your last chance to buy wine-tasting party tickets and we have only five left, so if you want to go, you'd better run to the back when church is over and sign up!"

I've been studying the people in the pews as the minister suggests that they run to the back, and I'm having difficulty imagining many of these people running. Not that they don't seem physically fit, it's just that they seem, well, contained. I don't know how many really are from German or Scandinavian stock, but sitting with this group reminds me of the time I ate at a German fish market and watched the people in the restaurant. Most ate their meal in silence and with heavy expressions on their faces. I was tempted to jump up on my table and shake a tambourine or do a little jig, just to see if I could make anyone smile.

"Wednesday the Women's Bible Study group will resume in my office and the Grief Support Group will meet on Thursday. If you didn't see the worship booklet for this week, take a look at the fabulous art on the cover! Sarah Weaver drew it and it is just fantastic! I love the way you included the dove coming down from the sky....girl, you are just too much!"

I pull a booklet out from the rack in front of me. The picture is sweet–three men in a boat and above them is a big heart in which Jesus is depicted being baptized by John the Baptist. Above the heart is a lopsided star. I'd say the artist is three or four. Very nice for such a little tyke.

"Sarah–stand up so people can see you," the pastor exhorts.

Sarah has stood up and appears to be about twelve. Whoops. I guess I've been spoiled sending my kids to a school where every child is taught to draw and draw well from a very early age. Art isn't seen as something that only a fringe group of freaks dabble in, but rather is viewed as a skill that can be developed in every person, just like reading and writing. Suddenly Sarah's drawing stands as an indictment against our public school art programs. But it is a cute concept, and Jesus has a particularly sublime look on his face as he tilts toward John to receive the water, his eyes closed.

"Let's begin with confession and forgiveness," the Pastor says.

I'm having trouble figuring out my bulletin. There's just too much stuff all packed into it. And you have to jump to other pages to follow along for certain parts–it's not nice and linear, the way a woman needs things to be in the morning–especially a woman who is so slow-starting that she walks into the groomer's in her pajamas to drop off the dog.

On one part of the bulletin it indicates something called the "Psalmody" and tells you to see your insert sheet and read responsively. What the heck is a "Psalmody?" As this staid group of Lutherans keeps marching forward through their service, I'm flipping back and forth and forth and back, looking for something that might be Psalmodish.

I never do find it, and now a young woman is giving the first reading from Isaiah. She's dressed in one of those long white monkish robes, in fact, all of the worship leading-type folks are in these robes. The young woman makes a mistake reading, a big enough one that she laughs and people in the pews laugh with her.

Good....they are a people not unfamiliar with laughter.

Another woman comes forward and leads us in responsively read Psalm 29, which indicates that the voice of the Lord is so powerful that it breaks cedar trees, splits the flames of fire, shakes the wilderness, makes oak trees writhe and strips the forests bare.

Sounds like an argument for preemptive clear-cutting.

We move on to the second reading, and then the children are invited to join Mrs. Holoman at the baptismal font. A small crowd of children, bundled in warm clothes, circle around a young woman at the front.

"Well, I should have a clicker to count the people as they come up," Mrs. Holoman offers. A curious statement. Maybe she works for the Census.

"Today is a special day–does anyone know why? Yes, we are celebrating the baptism of Jesus by John....that we have new members....the Eagles are playing the Packers, yes, I'm going to come back to that because it's about teams.....Do you remember your Baptism? You do? You have a tape of it? What did they do? Dumped water on you? Yes, you became a member of Jesus' team and here at Flint you are a member of our team–maybe we should come up with a Flint Lutheran team cheer....well here's some stickers to remind you that you're part of God's team and the Eagles..."

Mrs. Holoman makes some more team analogies. It forces me to once again meditate on why I'm so opposed to pro-sports. I just don't get it. It's about a ball and a bunch of bodies smashing into each other, and men who make sinful amounts of money and never smile when they're being interviewed. Must we all be forced to think in terms of their brand of "team," even in church?

I did like professional sports once upon a time. I remember as a youth watching the Baltimore Orioles and really enjoying it. The team at that time had Jim Palmer, Boog Powell, Brooke Robinson at third base...they were nice guys and they didn't do any grandstanding. They just played baseball–quietly, and without a lot of hoopla. Now it's all so in-your-face.

Well, the stickers must have all been passed out because all the little cherubs are trotting back to their seats and some are leaving for Sunday school.

The Pastor is now saying a few words from the pulpit and ending with "In the name of the father, son and Holy Spirit, Amen." She crosses herself as she says this. I'm definitely seeing some residual aspects of Catholicism which Martin Luther must have brought with him to the new church.

"I know this isn't the Jerry Springer Show, but I have a confession to make," the good Pastor begins. "I'm nervous about next Sunday, when we meet, when?"

"Nine-thirty," the congregation answers.

"I'm nervous that people won't come–that they'll decide to worship at St. Mattress by the spring....but let me assure you–God is always here!"

That's a cute one. I heard something similar, but it went, "did you hear about the two bed bugs who got married in the spring?"

"I'm also nervous because someone who is 70 told me that he was too old to participate. Now, studies show that those who worship live longer and Lutherans seem to live the longest. In fact, I went to visit Minnie Dawes who is 104-years-old. She told me that she didn't want to complain, but that she was starting to feel her age. But we need the voices of EVERYone–the Holy Spirit doesn't just give visions to the young!"

The minister goes on to share how she feels about the "Visioning Sunday" they'll be having the following week. I'm not as into this as others probably are–not being a regular member of the church. I glance around and study the group. This congregation is so unexpressive that Pastor Susan seems even more bubbly and "out there" in juxtaposition to them.

"As the leader it is important for me to have a vision-- this woman did have it right to ask me how my visioning process was going. Three things have influenced my visioning: Jesus, the Gospel of Luke and the music of U2."

The loquacious lady shares examples of Jesus' ministry that should impact the church's future, from her view. Then she shares that the Gospel of Luke also figures in prominently. "I like Luke—it has so many neat things about women and the poor," she shares.

Hey, this is cool. Luke is really one of my favorites, too.

Susan shares a story about a Rabbi who tells the priests of a monastery that the Messiah is among them, which causes them to treat each other much better, she talks about a woman who told her that Flint Lutheran saved her–she shares about a girlfriend's kitchen sign–she talks more about how big their vision could be and how much everyone could do to help make Flint a vital place of worship for the good of God.

When she wraps up her sermon, I've been impressed by three things: she laughs a lot in the pulpit, and does it with abandon; she speaks with confidence; and she mentioned women. The entire gestalt of Pastor Susan is interesting–she really does seem like a lively waterfall toppling into a calm lake below.

More prayers and Lutheran-type stuff. I'm expecting the benediction but it never seems to come.

I opt to steal out the back and meander around the halls a bit. There is a table with all sorts of handouts about upcoming events and service opportunities. I'm really not in the mood for any of it. I think it's all the brownness.

Strolling down a curved hallway, I glance at several bulletin boards. Here's an interesting one: newspaper articles about accomplishments by members of the church. There's an impressive array of articles, all of them current. Lots of cheerleader and sports items, even a member who as a lawyer wrote a book about how parents can communicate better with their children. He claims that his years practicing law have taught him critical aspects of communication that can be carried over to our dealings with our children.

I can just hear him with his kids: "Johnny, if you continue to pursue that aggressive behavior with your brother, I'm going to make you sit down and read Section 4, Subsection 3 of the family penal code and then present your arguments as to why your mother and I should not commence with a punishment."

I find a room along the curved hallway, some type of parlor. Oh, it's so refreshing to be in this space! There are white sheer curtains along a huge window and the sun is pouring in. It's like an oasis in the midst of a dark underworld.

Well, I've perused the hallways and there's nothing too controversial or eye-popping about this place. I'm waiting outside the brown doors in the brown foyer but no one is coming out. I thought I'd wait until everyone started flowing out and ask a few people what it means to be Lutheran. I tap my foot. I look at the table of pamphlets. I stare at the "Visioning Sunday" announcements lying on a podium. I walk out the door. I get in my car. I drive home.

Well, the environs and the people might not have stimulated any of the emotion centers in my brain, but the minister did. She is intriguing. I call the church and ask if I can meet with the Senior Pastor. The secretary asks me to hold on for a minute.

"Hi Ruth!" a friendly woman's voice greets me.
"Hi....is this the pastor?"
"Yes! Susan Beck."
"Hi. I worshiped with you on Sunday and I was interested in learning more about the congregation and I was wondering if I could come and chat with you for a half hour or so."
"Absolutely–I'd love it. Now, are you the one who has the long brown hair?"

"Well, it's not that long, but it's brown."

"The red coat?"

"No, I was wearing a black coat." This woman remembers people's hair and coat colors. I should have said, "I had the pink hair and orange coat," just to mess with her a bit.

Susan asks me where I live, we talk about my children and where they go to school. Her best friend's son goes to my childrens' school and she raves about the kind of education he is getting. She tells me how impressed she is that I'm about to color wash all the walls in my house. Obviously, this is a smart and insightful woman.

We arrange to meet in the upcoming week and on Thursday I pull around the icy circle in front of the church. The big brown bon-bon doesn't look that much better in the afternoon light, but I'm happy to be on the trail of a woman who projects her voice and isn't afraid to laugh out loud.

I meet the secretary, who has a very pleasant, non-threatening demeanor.

The pastor comes through the front door of the office within minutes of my arriving. "Hi, Ruth?"

"Yes. Ruth Laker, it's very nice to meet you."

She introduces me to the secretary, whom she says is second in line after God. We walk down the hallway to her office, and she is chatting nonstop as we go. I sit down in the obligatory wingback chair of the Protestant minister's office.

She sits across from me and looks at me expectantly.

"Well, I've never been to a Lutheran church. I've been worshiping here and there for some time, I grew up as a Presbyterian...I was baptized by one of the first ordained women ministers in the faith, and delivered by a woman doctor...this was in 1963....my mother is a self-made woman and a very strong role model...sooo, I'm very happy to have the chance to sit down with a woman minister. I was really happy to hear you make reference to how much you liked Luke because it has all these neat things about women..."

"...and the poor..." she quickly interjects.

"Right...anyway, I guess I'm wanting to go to a church where there is some progressiveness in the thinking and your church seemed intriguing to me. The last church I went to with any regularity was an American Baptist church—on and off with some friends, and although the minister seemed somewhat progressive in his thinking, a good percentage of the congregation seemed fairly conservative and Bible-bound. And there were all these other ordained American Baptist ministers and missionary men who were often preaching and running the show...no women to speak of. I don't know, it wasn't me. I've been looking around at a lot of churches this past year."

"Yes, well you'll find that our congregation is more left of center than right. We are a fairly liberal congregation." Reverend Beck jumps right in to talking about the Lutheran traditions, how this particular church reflects the people in the surrounding community, how the church has elements of the Catholic liturgy because Martin Luther wasn't upset about everything, how they are behind the Presbyterians on some issues but still a progressive church in many ways. She shares that they are friendly to gays, have several gay members and are a place where gay couples can have their babies baptized. She talks and then talks some more. In fact, I'm realizing that Reverend Beck is, well, talkative. And all I had to do was make one opening statement and off she went. At one point, I try to jump back in.

"Well that all sounds great," I quickly interject. "You know, I'm so tired of going places where they are afraid to talk about some of what I think are the most pressing issues of our time. Have you been able to give any sermons on homosexuality?"

"Yes, I have."

"That's great! What I'm wondering is: everyone is talking about the book *The DaVinci Code*, and I have yet to hear or see or read one thing about a minister incorporating the debate about the exclusion of women in the Bible, the possibility of a Gospel according to Mary, how Mary Magdalene was railroaded and turned into a whore when it's almost certain she wasn't....I mean, this is a great chance to empower women more and more in the churches and ministers aren't doing it....why not? And then I heard you make that statement about Luke including women and I thought: 'Now here's a woman minister who doesn't shy away from the fact that she's a woman.'"

Susan sits still for a second or two. "Yes, I mentioned women and the *poor*," she stresses poor again, "because I thought that that was a good opportunity to educate people about the Gospel according to Luke...the truth is, I don't talk a great deal about women's issues in the pulpit because I have to be pastor to *all* the people, and if I became a pastor about women, then I wouldn't last very long."

"Well, I'm not looking for a pastor who is *about* women, I just want a pastor who incorporates women and their struggles into their sermons as much as they do homosexuality, racism, the poor, the unemployed, the abused– just to identify that many of these issues affect women in a big way. I think we should be talking about women as much as we do any other oppressed group. I mean, we are talking about over half the people on the planet."

"There are associate pastors who are more on the cutting edge on these issues. They can be out there on that edge. As a head pastor, I can't be. I try to create the space for there to be dialogue about those things. We have a women's Bible study group and we just read *The DaVinci Code,* and they all asked me, 'why can't we incorporate the Gospel according to Mary, and I'm thinking, most of you don't even know what the Gospel according to Luke or Mark has to say.'"

Boy howdy, this woman is taking the wind right out of my sails! It sounds like she has no problem being on the cutting edge about gays, but she's not about to use the "w" word.

"I had a friend who was so excited when I became head pastor here," she goes on, "and the first thing she asked me was, 'Susan, are you going to change the gender of God?' and I said, 'Not if I want to remain head pastor.' I mean the reality is that if I tried to bring women's issues into things, I don't think the Spirit would support it."

"The Spirit wouldn't support it, or the congregation wouldn't support it?"

"Both. I just don't think that's where the focus should be. The focus needs to be on God. When the focus goes off of God, then any minister is in trouble. That's what we need to be about."

This woman has me totally befuddled. Aren't intelligent ministers the ones who support social movements, activism and acts of civil disobedience and all that kind of stuff as part of God working to change us and make us better and better? Isn't she the one who bravely went to her church council and told them that she wanted to baptize the babies of gay couples? Why couldn't this woman give two sermons a year on issues specifically plaguing women, like violence to their bodies or the almost total lack of support for motherhood in our culture? I decide to challenge her a bit more.

"I went to the Conservative Synagogue and I have to say that Rabbi Feldman gave the only sermon I've ever heard that was fully devoted to the plight of women, and he did it with passion and conviction. I don't think anyone was put out by it..."

"Yes, I know Rabbi Feldman–he and I are friends. He's a very *raadical* man. Very *raadical.* He's definitely out there on the edge on many issues."

How can talking honestly about obvious oppression be considered so *"raadical?"* My heart has been slowly sinking during our time together, like a car tire going further and further into the mud. What a bummer. I had such hopes for this woman.

"Well, surely you don't think it's radical for women to want to be priests in the Catholic church....being a Lutheran and all....I mean Martin saw some big problems with the Catholic church and if he were here today, I bet he'd identify that as one of them....maybe..." I smile.

"Of course, we know that's where the church should go but it's going to take some time. Sometimes we all get tired of it and we want to say, 'come on, guys,'—even in the Lutheran faith...but everything will unfold in its time."

Well, that's something on her part. I decide to try one more attempt at bonding. "I was thinking that if they didn't want to ordain women priests, and with the shortage of priests and all, they could have priests made out of wax that come up out of the floor, like Lincoln at the Gettysburg Wax Museum, and they could project the mass onto the lips of the wax priest." I smile again.

Susan turns away and looks as though she is actually going to get sick and vomit. "Oh dear," she says quietly. "Ruth," she turns back to me abruptly, "come to us–maybe we will be the church for you, maybe we won't....you'll know before long. There are lots of people in the church who are feminists and progressive on issues and you won't be alone. Maybe you'll find the support you're looking for."

"Well, thanks so much for your time," I reach for my coat. (I don't think the wax priest thing went over well.)

"Let's pray together," she says with a sudden chipper smile, moving to the edge of her seat.

"All right," I say gamely. I'm glad for the reminder that I can talk to God, even in the middle of a Thursday afternoon when it's icy and cold.

"Lord," she starts earnestly, "help Ruth in her search and help her to be patient with us...we always do fall so short. Guide her to where she needs to be and encourage her in using her talents and insights in the best way possible. We ask this in Jesus precious name, amen."

"Amen," I say...but I'm not sure what I've just endorsed. Did she ask God to help a poor lost lamb? Did I just get spanked in prayer?

"Let me get you a welcome package because I'm sure you didn't get one on Sunday," she says. I follow her down the hallway, liking her less and less as we walk.

"Here we go," she says in a busy-body way, as she reaches for a packet of materials on a rack. "And...yes....my sermon on homosexuality is in there ....you can read it and see how I address it," she says.

Can't wait.

We walk back down the hallway together, and she continues to talk non-stop. "My goodness, Mark actually has his office cleaned up," "We have a visiting pastor here," "Oh look, the children are leaving the nursery."

I'm experiencing a low-grade but now constant state of irritation, not unlike when the label on the inside of your collar is rubbing against your neck. I don't know why. I shouldn't be. She's not any worse than the Catholic priest who patted me on the arm and told me to "be good." He didn't irritate me–or rather, I didn't let him. But I expected so much more from her and she turned out to be just another cog in the status quo machine.

I shake her hand and thank her for her time.

As I start the car, I think, well, maybe she is right. Maybe we don't have to push the river, it will flow on its' own. And I can't really fault her for trying to protect her job. Most leaders have to take centrist positions to survive. But most major social changes that have taken place in the world have come at a price. They've required *raadicals*...people to push the envelope...to say "come on, what's with all this?" They've required acts of courage from our leaders and sometimes confrontation.

When a young gay man is killed in a hate crime, or a black person is beaten up by police, many, many people jump on board. There is outrage. Just this past week, the local newscaster told of a fourteen-year-old girl who was pulled around a corner in Philadelphia and gang raped in broad daylight. Her next phrase was, "And now Don Baker will fill us in on those Eagles!" There was no collective outrage. It was just another rape of a female.

Would the Spirit support our religious leaders asking aloud the questions, "Why on earth is this happening to girls and women?" "For God's sake, how can we make this *stop*?" Or, "why have things come to a near standstill when it comes to women's issues?"

The Spirit that I need to believe in definitely would.

I had no intention of going back to Flint Lutheran. I was almost totally deflated by the experience of meeting Susan Beck. The next Sunday, I planned to check out a new church, but I slept in, had a nice chat with my husband over a leisurely breakfast of bacon and eggs, and then somehow I found my car taking me back to Flint. I would be missing the first half of the service, but something was propelling me to go. I told myself that I should at least try to make contact with a few parishioners after the service—to get a better picture of these quiet pew-sitters.

The church was fairly full when I walked through the back doors, so I sat near the front on the side. Just as I started to unwind my scarf, Pastor Susan stepped up to the pulpit and started to give her sermon.

"But Ananias answered, 'Lord, I have heard from many about this man, how much evil he has done to your saints in Jerusalem.'" Act 9:13."

Oh great. This is going to be about Paul. I remember this story from Acts. Paul is not who I want to be hearing about from a woman who has no balls...so to speak. Paul was not particularly female-friendly, and hearing a woman give a sermon about him and singing his merits will be kind of like hearing Hugh Hefner's 50 year-old daughter singing the praises of her Dad's latest relationship with a 23-year-old centerfold.

"I empathize with Ananias not only because he's been asked to do something that seems crazy, but also because I, too, have had my own love/hate relationship with Saul, also known as St. Paul. When I was in college and trying to figure out if God was really calling me to ordained ministry, Paul's warning to the Corinthian women to keep their heads covered and their mouths shut in worship were thrown into my face as proof that God couldn't possibly want women to be pastors. Then I found Paul's letter to the Galatians where he wrote, "There is no longer Jew or Greek, slave or free, male or female, for all of you are one in Christ Jesus...and I found affirmation. And as most of you know, since I have a natural proclivity to always have my mouth open, this is the verse I decided to pay attention to."

I've perked up in my pew.

"The problem is we, along with Ananias and Paul are still stuck in the old. We're body-bound and culture-bound or as U2's Bono puts it, 'we're stuck in a moment and we can't get out of it.'"

That's her second Bono quote in three weeks. I think someone's got a *cru-ush*...

"It was thirty years ago when I first faced the cultural sexism supported by Paul's writings. Since then I have been blessed to be part of a church that has struggled mightily with that and in many ways has moved beyond it. So this past month when three different women from other church traditions confessed to me the hurt and pain surrounding the sexism they experience in their churches, it caught me by surprise."

I can't believe my ears.

"One, a former Unitarian minister who converted to Catholicism after discovering the power of the Holy Eucharist, and even serves on a Church staff as a Minister of Education, shared how her job description which initially included preaching once a month was radically re-defined when the priest discovered she was a better preacher than he was."

The congregation laughs.

"She said, 'no matter how much I love the church and the people, I just can't support this system anymore.' A woman dabbling in the Baptist faith, wondered if she could continue to participate, looking around and seeing how men seemed to dominate, particularly in the pulpit. A member of a non-denominational church asked me about our scriptural justification for the ordination of women. In our conversation I learned that her church uses Paul's admonitions to the Corinthian women as their foundation for discrimination, and increasingly, she questions whether that is the Gospel. Because as she put it, 'Women have the gift of leadership, too.'" All are in churches where they are stuck in a moment that they can't get out of. Now, I don't want to say that because we ordained women in 1970, we're not stuck. I have to tell you, I love being your pastor, but I am the only Senior Pastor in a Lutheran church in much of the state. The *only* one. Like Ananias, Paul and the churches of my sisters in Christ, we are still stuck in the old, ever in need of conversion."

I feel tears welling up in my eyes.

Pastor Susan goes on to talk about her feelings–she openly points directly at herself when she uses the word "feminist." She makes a distinction between Paul the theologian, Paul the missionary, Paul the sexist and Paul the Pastor. She finds value in what Paul the Pastor has to say, and brilliantly ends up using Paul's chiding style as a way of chiding us, in 2005, to change our sexist ways. She ends, "Looking at us, at you and me, and our community of faith, what would someone naturally assume? That we're stuck in a moment we can't get out of? That somehow we've decided to play God and based upon sex, race or orientation have determined who's worthy of grace and who's not? Sisters and brothers, what would *Pastor* Paul take us to task on? Amen."

Through the rest of the service: more hymns, the offering, communion, I find myself feeling as though I'm floating on a cloud. When it's all over, I don't stop to chat with a single person. I head for the doors, bypass the assistant minister and walk straight up to Susan. She sees me coming and gives me a knowing grin.

I hug her. "You know, the Spirit works in mysterious ways," I say. "I wasn't going to come back here today. When you said that the

Spirit wouldn't support you talking about women's issues in the pulpit, I didn't agree with you, and I didn't think you were a pastor for all the people, because you weren't going to be a pastor for women, too."

"You *were* the Spirit," she smiles at me.

Tears well up in my eyes. I pull her head toward me to give her another hug. She bows her head into my shoulder and I rub the back of her head, like a proud mother would her child. Then I let her go.

"You carry on, Ruth," she tells me, a quiet smile on her face.

Fighting back tears, I walk out the door.

When I pull into my driveway, I realize that I have been smiling the entire way home.

Evangelical Lutheran

#	Dimension of Church Experience	Rating
1)	Is parking close and convenient?	9
2)	How beautiful is the worship space?	2
3)	How comfortable is the seating?	4
4)	How welcoming and friendly is the congregation?	6
5)	How enjoyable and uplifting are the musical aspects of the worship?	4
6)	Does the leader have a pleasant speaking voice and does he/she make sense to me?	10
7)	How clean are the bathrooms?	10
8)	Are the people in the pews interesting to stare at?	4
9)	How tolerant to many ways of seeing and doing things does this group appear to be?	8
10)	Would I feel good about how these people would spend my money?	7
11)	How close did I feel to God in this place?	6
12)	Did I smile more than once during the experience?	4
	Total	74

SOMETIMES JESUS LOOKS MAD.

Mormon

What I know about Mormons is this:

1) They settled around the Great Salt Lake cause they figured it was so inhospitable, others would leave them alone.
2) Brigham Young was not allowed to take a seat in the House for practicing polygamy.
3) Donnie and Marie Osmond are Mormons.
4) Donnie hosts the only game show I've ever watched all the way through: *$100,000 Pyramid*.
5) I think I'm going to buy the home version of the *$100,000 Pyramid* game and put it under the Christmas tree, labeled to me from my husband, 'cause he despises board games and won't ever play them.
6) Marie said she was sexually abused as a girl but didn't say by whom.
7) Incest rates are very high in the state of Utah.
8) On *The Big Valley,* my favorite show as a kid, Nick falls in love with a young woman and he gets mad at her father for not letting him see her. Then he finds out that they are Mormons trying to hide their lifestyle practices, and that her father is really her husband. You can tell that she does love Nick and wishes she could leave the old man for him, but he ends up losing her. That was to be expected because none of the four adult children on the show ever stayed in a relationship longer than 60 minutes.
9) I was in love with Heath on *The Big Valley,* and wrote a letter to Hollywood asking them to send me information about Lee Majors. They sent a pamphlet about a wax museum.
10) The Mormons have a great choir.

    I was planning to go to the Mormon Church before Christmas, but as it turned out, I called the number in the phonebook for "Church of the Later Day Saints" for over two months and never received any answer. There was no answering machine. No message telling when the services were. Just seven numbers to punch into my telephone–leading nowhere...signifying nothing. *Finally*, in late January, I tried again on a Saturday morning and a girl answered the phone.
    "Hello?"
    "...Oh....Hi ...Is this the Mormon Church?" I had been peeling potatoes, the phone balanced under my chin, fully expecting to get no answer. I nearly dropped it in surprise.

"Um....yes."

"I'm wondering when your services are."

"Oh, let me get my Mom."

"Hello," a pleasant woman's voice says.

"Hi, I'd like to know when your services are."

"Do you know which Ward you're in?"

"Ward?"

"Yes. If you live east of the Susquehanna River you are in the first Ward, if you live west of it, you're in the second Ward. The second Ward meets at 9 and the first at 11."

"Oh...well I'm not a Mormon or a member. I'm interesting in finding out more about the faith, though. I'd be a first-timer."

"Oh, great! Well, we'd love to have you! We have regular church and then Sunday school classes, where the men and women have their own groups."

Separating the men and women...hmm...maybe that developed as a way to keep the men from checking out each other's wives back in the days of polygamy...no reason to tempt anyone unnecessarily.

She gives me the directions to the church, in a most clear and helpful manner. We're about to hang up.

"Um...I'm not sure if you have an answering machine and perhaps it's not working, but I've been trying to get through to your church for over two months and no one has ever answered."

"Oh, I'm so *sorry*," she says, sounding truly very sorry.

"Well, that's alright. I'm just thinking that you might want to make the information available to people if they call."

"Yes, of course. I'm very sorry you weren't able to get through," she says again.

"No problem....I just thought I'd pass on the information to you, in case your message wasn't working."

That was a *very* gratifying apology–kind of like an emotional facial.

Sunday I head to the 9 o'clock service. It's too much work to try to figure out which side of the river I'm on in juxtaposition to the church, so I opt to go to the 9 o'clock service so that I can get my grocery shopping done on the earlier side of the day. Besides, the whole concept of "wards" is too confining for me, as well as having multiple negative associations: Psycho ward. The warden. Warding off evil. Montgomery Ward (which went belly up).

The church is a modern, large structure sitting back in a pleasant middle-class residential neighborhood. There is a fair amount of land around the building which is always nice. I find easy parking and walk in through a side door.

Everyone is sitting and singing as I walk in to the sanctuary. A young woman with kinky long hair is conducting the congregation in a rather stiff one, two, three, four pattern–just like my old band director, Mrs. Beard.

I find my usual area on the right side, so I can take notes as unobtrusively as possible. I've got one of those seats beside a door, so there is a huge space between my pew and the one in front of me, not unlike when one has the seat by the emergency exit of the airplane. That also means that there are no hymnals to reach for. I take off my winter bundles–it's another absolutely freezing day in a record cold January– and head back out to look for a bulletin and hymnal. Both are sitting on a table just outside the door.

The bulletin has "Susquehanna Second Ward" written across the front with a picture of who I'm presuming is Jesus Christ on front. This is a rather curious rendering of J.C.; he looks stern and very clean-cut, even with the beard and long hair. There's nothing at all Middle-Eastern or Jewish or exotic to this image. He looks like a WASPy model with Jesus-like hair tamed and superimposed on the head. And he looks so serious...no....he looks angry. I don't think I'm going too far out on a limb to say that this Jesus looks truly ticked off.

As the congregation continues to sing *The Spirit of God*, I glance around, taking in this Mormon crowd. I'm feeling like I did when I was at the Jehovah's Witnesses–as though I've infiltrated a cult group and that I have to be careful not to be found out. I was worried about being found out by the Jews as well, but not because I think of them as a cultish; I was primarily embarrassed because everyone in the Synagogue was dressed nicer and had better haircuts.

This group is pretty tidy-looking and attractive. Certainly a very clean-cut bunch. Most of the men are wearing suits or shirts with ties, and there are lots of boys, teens and young men, also decked out in their finest. It's always notable when a church is packed with teenage boys and young men–they don't seem to be among the ranks of big church attenders. They sure are in this Mormon group.

Also notable are the number of babies and children in the pews. Moms and Dads are quietly tending their little ones, and everyone is all smiles. Truly, the vibes I am getting from these family interactions are ones of great tenderness and love. I look at the family in the pew directly in front of me. There is a teenage daughter, a mother, a girl of about twelve and a father, all sitting in a row. What catches my eye is that the mother is playing a game with her twelve-year-old, whereby she spells out words on the girls back. I remember my mother playing that with me when I was a little girl. She'd soap up my back while I was in the tub, and then write out letters. This woman pats the girl's back in between each individual letter. My mom used to run her hand over my back like an eraser on a blackboard.

What's she spelling out? Inquiring minds want to know...

J. Pat. E. Pat. S. Pat. U. Pat. S. Pat. The girl turns and whispers the answer to her mother, who nods.

There's more. L. Pat. O. Pat. V. Pat. E. Pat. S.

Loves? The girl guesses. Her mother nods again.

Y. Pat. O. Pat. U. Pat. The girl smiles at her mom.

Then her mom spells out the word "Spirit."

Clearly, this mother is making use of the game time to reinforce church doctrine. I'm not sure what I was expecting her to spell out, but I thought she might try to make it a bit more challenging–maybe try some words like "spatula," "treacherous," or "species-specific."

The song is over and a young man, we're talking maybe all of seventeen, stands at the podium to lead us in prayer.

"Lord, we just thank you so much for ...ss...po....ty....an....yo... We are so grateful to have ano....me....gether....th.....lo.... Help us to know your truth and to be ev.....ful.....fo....nee.....bro.....ters.....Amen."

"Amen," the congregation agrees to whatever he mumbled.

A middle-aged gentleman now takes to the podium and gives what appears to be the "Ward Business" in the bulletin. He indicates that they have received the membership record of one Allison Bruckner and asks that those who can support her becoming a member of their ward to please manifest it. Everyone raises their right hands.

That's a curious word–to "manifest" their support. It's not one you're used to hearing in such situations; one might expect them to say, "please show your support," or "please indicate your support." But "manifest" is different...so Mormony.

We're about to start a second hymn, *In Humility, Our Savior,* which is actually the "Sacrament Hymn" according to my program. I see a small crowd of boys, ages 10-15ish, heading up front, apparently to get the sacraments. The young woman with the frizzy hair is standing in front of us, her arms held out like an owl or a bat, as she waits to give us the downbeat.

The boys start walking through the church, holding little trays with handles. I'm happy to be receiving real bread, not rice paper like in the Catholic Church, and it's nice and moist! Tastes almost like a good Jewish rye, although I'm guessing it's just a very grainy whole wheat. I think about taking four or five pieces because I haven't had a great deal for breakfast. Probably not good church etiquette.

When the "blood" comes around, amazingly, it's water. Pure, clean water. We drink from our cup and then place the empty in a little compartment under the places where the cups were sitting when they were full. Very clever design.

Man...they weren't kidding when they said that Mormons were squeaky clean and not into tainting their bodies in any way. They won't even pull out a little pretend-grape-juice-wine for the sacrament.

"We're grateful for the reverent attitude displayed during communion," the middle-aged guy says in the microphone. I'm now going to offer you my testimony and then turn the podium over to you. I'd like to testify that there are many blessings that have come from reading the Book of Mormon. At the state conference, we'll have a wonderful opportunity to share more about it with our Brothers and Sisters. Most answers to my prayers come to me when I'm reading the scriptures–maybe I don't pay enough attention when I'm praying, or perhaps I'm a visual learner...they make me think about my children and how I want to be a good father. I was reading in chapter 17...and I'm sure there is no father in this room who wouldn't like their child to be like the sons of Alma..."

I'm assuming Alma is a man, although the only Alma I've ever known of was a woman.

"Anyway....I testify to you that the Book of Mormon is the word of God and I am thankful for the Book of Mormon. We now turn the time over to you for bearing of testimonies. We really enjoyed hearing from so many children last time and we encourage the children to come forward and offer their testimonies as well."

He keeps saying "we," but who is this "we?"

The woman who has conducted us through two hymns takes to the podium. "I've never been in front of you to offer testimony...my heart is pounding...I've never felt this nervous leading you in song...a work friend recently said to me, 'you don't believe in Christ'...and I was dumbfounded. I've been trying hard at work to act in accordance with my beliefs. I just want you to know I *do* believe in Christ...I'm so happy to be a member of this ward...to know that Joseph Smith was a prophet...I told the people at work that I was having dinner with some friends from church, and they said, 'oh, there's more of your kind around?'....when I think of all the mean things that have been said to me...I just want to say again, that I do love Christ and I am so thankful to be a member of this church."

The congregation collectively says, "Amen."

A boy, appearing to be about six, comes to the microphone. In a fast, rote, sing-songie manner, he says, "I'd like to give my testimony that I know this church is true...and...and I'm happy I'm a Mormon." He pops away from the microphone and sits down with his family.

A middle-aged woman is now at the mic. "It buoys me up each week to be here...the scripture lesson we read about the sons of Alma reminds me of people I've wondered about through the years...my heart is so filled to find out when someone is still worshiping and active.." Her voice is trembling with emotion. "My son, who many of you know is now a missionary, tells me that he's been studying really hard so I should look for the blessings..."

Everyone chuckles.

"I encourage all of us to be part of the missionary work...it's the true fuel that keeps us going. I love the church...I love the gospels as we bring in the glorious second coming of Christ..." Again, she is choked up with emotion and has to stop talking for a few seconds. "Amen," she manages to get out.

"Amen," the congregation responds.

A young man, maybe in his thirties, talks of how he travels a great deal for his work and travels "heavy," never able to reduce his loads. But when he looks at his spiritual life, he realizes that the Lord helps him to travel light. He shares his love of the gospels, Jesus Christ and his family. He seems amazingly calm and joyful at the same time.

Another child gives a one-line testimony similar to the one from the other child. He is smiling a very endearing smile the entire time.

An attractive young woman in her twenties shares how grateful she has been for the scripture challenge. Reading them has given her a peace and the knowledge that even if she can't change something, she can change how she reacts to it. Again, she is smiling a big, radiant smile the entire time she talks.

Now a girl of about twelve comes to the microphone. "As some of you know, I have a puppy. She became very ill. I said a prayer that she'd get better and get whatever it was out of her system, and she did. I even said a prayer that God would help me get my sister's shoes on the other day...they just wouldn't come on..." she giggles, "and then they came on!" Suddenly, she starts to cry. "It's so wonderful...no matter what He's there for me....I have a friend who doesn't even know what religion she is, even though she goes to a church...." (she's still crying), "I just can't imagine not knowing about your faith and God...I'm so happy to have this church and to be a part of this...Amen." She walks away from the microphone, her head bowed.

Wow! Talk about intense. I'm finding this all amazing. That girl, that young girl, was incredibly articulate and composed...while crying! She appeared to be speaking entirely from the heart. I can't dismiss it as part of some group hysteria....she really *meant* everything she said. I just can't imagine any of my children getting up in front of a group and sharing from the heart like that. I can't imagine that any of them has such a relationship with God, and this beautiful young girl has me wondering if I've somehow failed them...

A girl of about sixteen shares how she prayed for a scripture verse to help calm her during some intense studying and it came to her. She gets choked up with emotion as she finishes. Another girl, who looks to be about eleven, shares that she knows the church is true and that this is such a great ward and provides such a great example for her.

Here comes a girl I've had my eye on since the beginning of the service. She seems to be about seven-years-old and is wearing a blue Colonial-style dress. I'm getting the distinct feeling that she wears this around because she likes it, not because she is a historical reenactor on her way to Valley Forge. She walks to the microphone with incredible calm and starts to speak: "When I was younger, I used to go on small field trips with my family. We were going to a piano factory in the city and I wanted to take notes, so I put a notebook and pen in my backpack and then I misplaced them. I prayed to be able to find them and then I felt this urge to check in this one location and there it was. I am so grateful to God that He gives me help and guidance everyday and I say this in the name of Jesus Christ. Amen."

"When I was *younger*?" She's seven! "Field trips to a *piano factory?*" "Wanted to *take notes*?" "Prayed and then felt an *urge*?" Who is this child? The combined reincarnation of Nelly Bly, Victor Borge and a Roman Catholic saint?! Never in my life have I heard such diction, such mental clarity and sureness of purpose in one who looks in age as though she should be at Chuckie Cheese sticking straws up her nose with a bunch of other little kids.

Truly, this is all most amazing.

Now a man of perhaps mid-fifty is talking about his encounters with people who just seemed "compelling" and "different" to him....people he then found out were "L.D.S. " I figure that's the lingo for Latter Day Saints.

This man also shares that our spiritual life is vertical, not horizontal, and that we have a direct conduit to heaven. I'm not sure how he knows that vertical thing...is that what Einstein ultimately proved with his E=MC2 dealie?

Here comes another middle-aged man. He apologizes for taking up some time and wants to comfort Sister Lynn who shared about the prejudices experienced against her as a Mormon. "I had a man at my work who thought that our church worshiped the devil and didn't understand how I could be so good."

Again, everyone chuckles. No one seems the least bit flustered- I guess they're used to being misunderstood. In reading David McCullough's *Harry Truman*, I was surprised to find how horribly the Mormons were persecuted until they finally made it out to Utah.

He continues. "A few weeks ago I traveled to Salt Lake City and saw my parents. I was able to work in the home part of the time, and on my way out, I wrote down what I wanted to accomplish with them and my trip. I never had heard their testimonies and so I asked them if we could bear our testimonies to each other, which we did. It was an unbelievable experience for all of us...and it was the first time I ever heard my father talk about his struggles..." His voice gets choked up and he starts to cry a little. "My father had a hard time with church...he just had a naturally questioning mind...it explained so much about him." He drops his head and sighs. "I just wanted to thank the Lord for giving me good parents who did raise me in faith, and if you ever have that opportunity with your parents, I recommend it. Amen."

"Amen," the room answers.

A French-American woman thanks the congregation for being so nice to her parents while they were visiting. She shared that they had such a hard time with her conversion to Mormonism, the "weird religion." She said they were very impressed with the way they celebrated Christmas, particularly all the beautiful singing on the parts of the children.

Three or four more people share their testimony. The final gentleman shares that God performed a miracle for him in trying to help a young woman and her family get into the car, which she had left running with her keys locked inside. Apparently, the windows were all rolled up, and then after he prayed, they noticed that one back window was down nearly two inches. He swore it hadn't been down before.

Testimonial time is over. I'm really quite impressed with the depth of feeling shared by the people. Never before have I seen anything quite like that. There was a reverence for God that was palpable when nearly everyone spoke. And they were all so solid and articulate.

As we sing the closing hymn, several people pass by, heading to their various Sunday school classes to prepare for the others. According to the bulletin, we are to remain seated to let them get there in time. Everyone who passes me smiles a big, bright smile. They all have perfectly white, straight teeth and are neatly groomed. If Hitler really had wanted to put all his efforts into cultivating a "master race," he might have found what he was looking for with the Mormons.

No sooner has the final organ note been played, when the young woman who was sitting next to me turns and introduces herself. I shake her hand.

"Are you a member of another ward," she asks me?

"No, I'm just visiting. I know a Mormon family at my children's school and they are really very sweet and interesting people and I wanted to check out the way you practice your faith."

All true. I'm priding myself on trying not to lie in the process of finding the right church or synagogue.

"Well, that's wonderful. Maybe you have some questions...I saw you taking a lot of notes over there..."

"Yes, well...."

"Oh, here....Elder Smith....this is Ruth and she's with us for the first time."

"Elder" Smith is not a minute over eighteen. He's got acne, a protruding Adam's apple, and a crew cut. He shakes my hand. "This is Elder Weston," he tells me. Another very tall lad of pubescence is standing before me, also with a fairly noticeable case of testosterone bursting over his face. Yet a third young man comes toward me. All three have encircled me, their ties in position and starched white shirts threatening to blind me. All are wearing very official-looking black name tags, with their names spelled out in white lettering. Each tag announces loudly and clearly that they are "Elders."

"Why don't we take a walk down the hallway?" Elder Smith says.

"Okay." I hear myself saying.

Yikes! I have no idea what I'm doing, and for a split second I think to run. But then I take a few deep breaths and remind myself that this is about exploration and I've vowed to learn as much as I can in my time here.

What's the worst that could happen...they tie me down to a chair and stick instruments through my eyes and into my brain, where they plant a microchip that programs me to become the perfect Mormon?

We're idling down the hallway now, me and the three Elder-boys. Elder Smith wants to chit chat.

"So where do you live?"

I tell him.

"We're pretty new here...we just got in from Salt Lake City a few days ago. We're missionaries."

"Oh..."

"Yup. I'm pretty stoked about it."

"What do you do?"

"Oh...we go from door to door and stuff like that."

He's "stoked" about *that*? I have a hard time believing that he's not somehow being sarcastic, the way my son was this morning when I asked him if he would be willing to take the trash out, and he leapt to the can and said, "Would I be?! *I'll* say! What is this, *Christmas!?*"

Going door to door....that's a tough beat for any one, even someone with his youth and resilience. I decide not to ask what it's like. I figure he'll just give me the pat answer that it's for the glory of God and anything done for the glory of God brings only joy...or some such thing. Maybe that's how he truly feels...these Mormons do seem pretty genuine in their faith. Still, I'd find it easier to believe if he told me that he absolutely hated experiencing all that rejection and that he sometimes felt like a damn fool doing it.

"It's kind of strange to think of you guys as 'Elders,' I smile. It's almost an oxymoron to call you one." He smiles back.

We're still meandering around hallways. I start to get nervous. What are they going to do with me? "Don't they have Sunday school classes now?" I ask.

"Yeah, that's where we're going...if I can find it," he chuckles.

We finally end up in another hallway, where the three "Elders" introduce me to two more local-born missionary "Elders," both of whom service my geographical area. I'm now really wishing I had lied about where I live. All five of these boy-men are standing around me in a circle, earnestly trying to engage me in conversation. If they're the ones who are going to be leading the class, there is no way I'm gonna make it through the experience. One of them will start to instruct me on what he thinks is important in matters of life and God, and I won't be able to restrain myself. I know that I'll interrupt him, and with a disingenuous smile on my face, say something like the following:

"Um....excuse me, Mr. *'Elder,'* (and I'll make quotations marks in the air when I say 'Elder')....I don't mean to belittle you or anything, but I have two sons your age and they're wonderful, bright lads, but they still need me to remind them to flush the toilet and to stop watching so much TV and to have more than chocolate chip cookie dough ice cream for dinner....so, I'm afraid that you have next to no credibility as an authority over *me* on how to live life. Now, if you'd like for *me* to share with you *my* philosophy of what's important, or to share with you what *I* think of the Bible, I'd be happy to. But we'll have to do it fairly quickly because I have to get to the grocery store to buy food for my sons who live in the house that my husband and I pay an adult-sized mortgage on....those being my sons who, as I may have mentioned already, are just about your ages."

Or something like that.

We make it into the classroom and it appears that none of the boy-men will be teaching the class. An attractive, blond, middle-aged woman is sitting in the instructor's chair, facing a small row of chairs arranged in a semi-circle. The four Elder-boys sit down facing her, then there's me, two other women and two other men. One of the men is overseeing a baby, lying on the floor in swaddling clothing.

She invites us to introduce ourselves one by one, and each person is given a very warm smile and friendly greetings from everyone in the room. It's my turn now:

"Hello...I'm Ruth Laker...I'm not a Mormon and have never worshiped here before...I've been wanting to see how a Mormon service is conducted....my son has a Mormon classmate and her family strikes me as such a nice one...and there was something very beautiful about the testimonials that we heard this morning...particularly from the children...so...anyway...I need to leave in about twenty minutes to meet my husband somewhere, so I'll have to sneak out during the class, I'm afraid."

That last part, while true, will hopefully give me protection in case they *were* going to implant anything in my brain. Now at least they know that there is someone who will be looking for me.

Everyone is beaming and tells me how glad they are that I've come.

One of the Elder-boys tells the teacher where I live.

"Well! I live right near you, Ruth...in the next township...I've been a member here for twenty-five years and I absolutely love it. It's been a true blessing for me to be a Mormon and to be a part of this ward!"

She seems entirely sincere.

"We were talking last time about the Creation story...how we know that God created the world in seven days...of course, no one knows exactly how long a "day" was, in God's time..."

Aaahhh. Is this their effort to blend science and Creationism? Their position might be something like: well, yes the planet went from fire to water to ice and back to water again, over millions and millions of years and that was the "first day," in "God's time."

Well, why not? Works for me.

"Please get out your Books of Mormon...we'll start with a reading from Nephi 1....."

An older woman student comes over to share her Book of Mormon with me. She flips it open to the requested page and Holly asks Elder-boy-Ben to read it aloud.

This class appears to be one of reading and then agreeing with whatever was just read. Holly, our teacher, has asked different people to take turns reading various passages that have to do with the alleged beginning of the world.

I am absolutely bewildered by this "Book of Mormon." It looks like a Bible in structure, and many of the things we're reading are similar to the Bible as I know it, but the names of the sections are totally unfamiliar: Enos, Jarom, Omni, Alma, Mosiah...it's as if someone created these names out of bits and pieces from Bible names. We'll take a little of Moses and combine it with some of Obadiah, and viola: Mosiah!

All the sections being read aloud are of the familiar Adam and Eve story. The woman who sat down to share her book of Mormon with me has totally dissected her book and made a serious study of it. Sections are highlighted in various colors; some have exclamation marks beside them. She's written little notes all over the margins.

I've always felt very uncomfortable reading other people's margin notes. There's something so personal about them. I have to admit that I'm curious about what she has written, but I keep averting my eyes away because in my mind, it would be kind of like seeing her step out of the shower.

"Bob, how would you like to read Nephi 1, verses 7 and 8 for us?"

The man overseeing the baby starts to read aloud. I glance over at the four Elder-boys seated beside me. Every one of them is holding his Book of Mormon in the same hand, and is bent over his book in exactly the same way. Each has his eyes locked to the page and appears to be in deep contemplation of the words being uttered. Truly, there is something eerie about it; like they're in the religious military or something, and must read the book in perfect formation.

"Ruth, do you feel comfortable reading something for us?"

"Sure..."

"How about if you read Nephi 2, verses 18-20."

The woman next to me has pointed to the exact spot where I need to start reading.

"And because he had fallen from heaven, and had become miserable forever, he sought also the misery of mankind. Wherefore, he said unto Eve, yea, even that old serpent, who is the devil, who is the father of all lies, wherefore he said: Partake of the forbidden fruit, and ye shall not die, but ye shall be as God, knowing good and evil.

And after Adam and Eve had partaken of the forbidden fruit they were driven out of the Garden of Eden, to till the earth. And they have brought forth children; yea, even the family of all the earth."

"Thank you," Holly says to me. "Now I think that Eve plays a very important role here...Eve knew what she was doing when she took the apple...she wanted to get the whole ball rolling...she wanted to be able to start having children and fulfill God's plan for us, which would ultimately culminate in His sending Jesus Christ. I don't think it's right for people to point a finger at Eve...I like to think of her as a 'mover and a shaker.'"

The Elder-boys are nodding their heads in agreement.

So why, I want to ask, if this was all part of God's divine plan, does the story have God blowing up at Adam and Eve and throwing them out of the Garden? If God knew that would happen, if indeed God *made* it all happen, then why get upset about what He Himself did?

As more people read, I find myself starting to feel restless and bored. Thankfully, during introductions, I built in that escape valve.

I whisper to the woman next to me, "Do you know the time?"

She shows me her watch. I start to lean over to collect my purse and my new Hello Kitty travel coffee mug, when she hands me a piece of paper with her name, address and phone number on it. "Just in case you have any questions," she looks at me knowingly. I get the feeling that she's thinking that I won't be able to resist the call of Joseph Smith and the pull of the Book of Mormon.

"Oh...do you have to leave now?" the teacher asks.

"Yes, I do, but I thank you so much for having me."

"Do you have a copy of the Book of Mormon?" she asks.

"No, but I'd like to look at one." Again, that's true.

"Here, you can have mine," the gentleman on the end of the semi-circle offers.

"How about that! He's being baptized today and he's giving away his Book of Mormon! Now that's what you call a dedicated disciple!" the teacher praises the man.

I walk over to him and take the book. I shake his hand and congratulate him on his baptism. As I head out the door, everyone smiles and thanks me for coming.

"Come back!" the teacher calls to me.

I close the door. Phfew! I made it! I didn't get processed or programmed or prayed upon. No one asked me to give my testimony and I won't be missionized by the man-boys. I'll just duck through a few hallways and I'm home free!

"Ruth!" I hear someone call from behind me.

Shoot! I turn to see Elder Jason jogging toward me. "Do you mind if I take your phone number?" He holds out one hand like a piece of paper, and demonstrates how he would write my number down using an "air" pencil in the other hand.

"Well, I'm thinking of coming back next week, so why don't we talk some more then...I've really got to run right now."

"Oh, you are? Okay, see you later..." Jason turns somewhat awkwardly and starts back to the room. I feel bad...I've broken my pledge and lied. I wasn't thinking of coming back next week. I know it, and I think Jason knows it too. That nice kid came running after me and reached out to me and I lied right to his face. Why couldn't I just have said: "Jason, I'm not sure if Mormonism is for me. I need some time to reflect on it. I thank you for your interest though. You take care."

I walk to my car, not feeling quite so smug anymore about my "escape."

When I get home, my husband is waiting for me. We've got a painting date and he's already decked out in his "painting clothes," which look like something a male stripper might wear as part of the "tease" aspect of his show; gaping holes and tears expose flesh in all sorts of interesting places. I change my clothes and join him in prepping walls and mixing paints. We start to talk about my experience that morning.

"Well, I don't know if this can really be determined in one visit, but I have to say that I think the Mormons win the prize for most deeply religious....and they seem like genuinely nice people too."

215

"Oh yeah...I knew some Mormons in college and this one guy, Jake Masterson, he was a truly very good man. One of the nicest people I've ever known."

"I can't imagine that these boys who are the same ages as our guys would readily want to become missionaries."

"Well they have to...at least the guys. Everyone has to do two years of missionary service. This one guy I knew had to take a deferment on college because he wanted to do his two years early."

"Really...how interesting. Well one of my guys said he was really 'stoked' about it. They have their own Bible of sorts...the 'Book of Mormon,' which is kind of weird."

"Yeah, Joseph Smith apparently found these tablets in the west somewhere and says the books were given to him by a heavenly being...it's all pretty suspicious to me."

"How do you know all this stuff about Mormons?" I ask him.

"I guess I'm just more worldly than you, my dear."

"Well, would you ever consider becoming a Mormon? I mean, the people seem to be sincere and really walk the talk."

"Yeah, but there's a 'Stepford Wives' quality to a lot of the people. Some religions really put you in a straightjacket with their beliefs, and I think Mormons are definitely in that camp."

When he said that, I was reminded of an article I read on depression and how it was particularly high among Mormons. The author hypothesized that Mormons feel a great pressure to be positive and "together," and to put a happy face on everything, which causes them to mask the things that are really bothering them and never deal with them effectively.

As we are discussing all things Mormon, a friend stops by and we engage him in the discussion. I tell them about the teacher's view that Eve was a "mover and a shaker," and that she merely wanted to get God's divine ball rolling when she bit into the apple. "Doesn't that story make God seem totally controlling and manipulative?" I ask them.

"Well, maybe Adam wasn't in on it...." my husband theorizes.

"Yeah, maybe Eve and all women are divine like God, and men are the ones who need to be tested and made better in this world. She and God planned the whole thing to start Adam's instruction," our friend Frank adds.

"You know...that is brilliant..." I say to the two men. "That explains so much, doesn't it?"

"Yep. You women have already arrived spiritually, but you still have to suffer through living with us," Frank laughs.

Later that night, I decide to read some of the Book of Mormon. The introduction section is fascinating, and claims that the Book of Mormon is comparable to the Bible. It was supposedly written by "many ancient prophets by the spirit of prophecy and revelation," whatever that means. "Their words, written on gold plates, were quoted and abridged by a prophet-historian named Mormon." The intro goes on to inform us that the book offers accounts of two groups of people who came from Jerusalem, one of these groups ended up being the principal ancestors of the American Indians.

So this book is claiming that the Native Americans have Jewish roots? If that's true, then why wasn't Sitting Bull's name more along the lines of Don't Mind Me I'm Just Sitting Here In The Dark?

After the introduction, there is more phantasmagorical reading: the testimony of the Prophet Joseph Smith. Long story short: in 1823, Joe is visited by a messenger from God one evening while he lay in bed. The messenger returns three times, repeating to him that he must go to a certain spot and find some gold plates that "give the account of the former inhabitants of this continent, and the source from whence they sprang." He told Smith that God had work for him to do and that Smith's name would be used for both good and evil "among all nations." He shouldn't show the plates to any person, if he did, he would be "destroyed," and when the time was right, the messenger would have him show the plates to a specially chosen group of witnesses, all of whom just so happen to be buddies and relatives of Joseph Smith. These witnesses give a sworn testimony in the book that they've seen the plates, which were used to write the books of Mormon. (Apparently, Smith had to give the plates back to the celestial being in white–they were merely on loan--so unfortunately we can't do any kind of carbon dating.)

How convenient that during the years of western expansion into the territory of the American Indians, a white man would come forth with an account of their lineage, the implication being that they should follow their original birth lines and become Christians, I suppose. It would also make all those poor, lost Native American souls ripe for conversion into the great westward-moving religious movement being formed by one Joseph Smith.

The story, as I read it, seemed like it was written by someone who wanted to cover all the bases and make sure it could never be unproven. Of course, ultimately, all power and glory would have to be given to the chosen one who was visited by this personage in the white robe.

I'm getting the feeling that Joseph Smith was a clever con artist. And now, the descendants of that possibly audacious con man are taught to stand up in front of a congregation once a month and to say out loud that they believe that Joseph Smith was a "prophet" and that the book of Mormon is "true."

Well, I can rule this religion out for me. I have enough trouble with the credibility and messages of many parts of the Bible I already know.

In retrospect, my time with the Mormons felt very much like field trip to another, curious culture.

Because it was given to me as a sincere gift, I don't want to toss my Book of Mormon. Instead, I put it on my library shelf. It reminds me of time spent with people, who, although possibly collectively duped, are really very, very nice and decent.

Mormon

#	Dimension of Church Experience	Rating
1)	Is parking close and convenient?	5
2)	How beautiful is the worship space?	3
3)	How comfortable is the seating?	8
4)	How welcoming and friendly is the congregation?	10
5)	How enjoyable and uplifting are the musical aspects of the worship?	2
6)	Does the leader have a pleasant speaking voice and does he/she make sense to me?	2
7)	How clean are the bathrooms?	10
8)	Are the people in the pews interesting to stare at?	7
9)	How tolerant to many ways of seeing and doing things does this group appear to be?	4
10)	Would I feel good about how these people would spend my money?	2
11)	How close did I feel to God in this place?	8
12)	Did I smile more than once during the experience?	4
	Total	75

Westover Bible Fellowship Church

I ended up at the Bible Fellowship Church by accident. I was fully intending to go to the Tabernacle of Hope Church of God but it ended up being another congregation of less than ten, and I just couldn't do it again.

So now I'm riding around looking for an alternative church to check out. I drive to the periphery of the old town, and start to cruise by the new subdivisions and developments, occupying spaces that were once open and free rolling.

Suddenly I brake. I've just passed what seems like a newer church, surrounded by vans and SUVs. I turn my car around and head back. The sign comes into focus as I approach: Westover Bible Fellowship Church.

This is one of those churches that tells you what they're all about right up front, right in the name: we're communing around the Bible, folks. Not like some of the church names such as, Our Lady of Perpetual Agony, or High View Church of God, which are much more cryptic.

I park my car semi-illegally in the front, and head into the lobby. A serious-looking man in a vintage brown corduroy blazer appears to be patrolling the space.

"Excuse me, can you tell me what time the service started?" I ask him.

"Ten fifteen," he tells me. "But he's just started talking, so you haven't missed much."

He holds the door open for me and I duck in. The sanctuary is a long rectangular room with four sections of pews, divided by walkways in the shape of a cross. My eyes scan the room. There's a fairly substantial crowd, although it's not packed. I head toward the back and slide into the end of a pew.

"All of us are a wife, a child or a slave," I hear the minister say as I unwrap my scarf and pull off my coat. "For all of us, Jesus is our husband, so you are the wife, God is the father and master, so you are the child and the slave. All of us know what it is to be subordinate."

So, let me see...this pastor is saying that the subordinate category is comprised of wives, children and slaves? Okay...

"Now, if I am in the position of leader: if I am a husband, a parent or a master, then I have a responsibility to care for those who are under me. And if you are in the position of helper: wife, child or slave, you are in a position to help those over you."

I'm looking around for signs that I somehow ended up in a time warp and have inadvertently traveled backward to 1860. I've got to find the portal or doorway I came through, so I can get back to the new millennium in a pinch.

"In Epphesians 5 and 6 you can see the back and forth play between those roles. This morning we wanted to look at the particular roles of husband and wife–we call this 'Subordinate Wife and Subordinate Husband'–there is joint submission going on."

The minister is a small man in stature, wearing what appears to be some form of polyester, light-weight jacket and sporting large eyeglasses. I glance around at the congregation. This certainly isn't a fashion-conscious crowd like at Middleton Presbyterian or the Synagogues. A significant percentage of this group look to be rather rotund. Others include young couples snuggling together in the pews, and elderly folks, like the threesome right behind me who make the occasional supportive comment to the pastor as he talks.

"Let's look at the wife: In Epphesians, verses 22-24, and later in verse 33–these are the verses that talk about the wife. Hear the word:

"Wives, submit yourselves unto your own husbands, as unto the Lord. For the husband is the head of the wife, even as Christ is the head of the church: and he is the saviour of the body."

"So the wife should act to her husband as the church should act to God–the wife is called to be submissive or obedient. Now, these two words do not encompass all these is for the wife...she is also called to forgive, console, love and encourage. She should be helpful and respectful—to submit in action and words. We would equate this with obeying. If your husband asks you to do something, *you should do it*. You can question, discuss, but *you should do it*."

Tell that to the millions of women being beaten up by their boyfriends and husbands on a regular basis. If I'm not mistaken, blindly doing what others tell you to do generally creates monsters and dictators.

"You shouldn't have an attitude! Paul says we should value our husband...imagine a wife saying, 'THERE! I did what you wanted? Are you happy with *that?!*' We don't want that, do we?"

I think I'm starting to understand the mentality of the suicide bombers–without the suicide part. I have a curious urge to go up to the pulpit and wrap the Pastor in explosives.

"She should find out what pleases her husband and do it. The churches task is to find out what pleases God–when we tithe, we don't say, 'There! I hate to give but I have to'...that's not the way! Her motive is not because her husband says to do it. Her motive to obey is not contingent on his performance. It is contingent on, if you love God, and want to obey *Him*. God speaks to wives *through* husbands. You don't say, 'well, what if I have a husband who...' or 'well I will, if my husband does...' Your responsibility as a wife is not contingent on your husband's performance! You obey because it is God's will for you!"

Okay. I *know* what's going on here! Come on out you Candid Camera people! You crazy-let's-create-a-twilight-zone-kind-of-setting-and-put-normal-people-into-it-to-freak-them-out folks! I've seen your show...come one out.........*please*...

"So here are some questions you wives might ask: How can I be someone who shows respect and deference, who supports and encourages my husband? How am I disrespectful? How am I manipulative, lazy, head strong? Where do I need to respect and ask for forgiveness?"

While he's at it, the pastor might add a few more questions to that list that seem to fit the tone and the theme: How can I get my hands on one of those outfits like Barbara Eden used to wear in *I Dream of Genie*, put it on and greet my husband at the door with a big hug and a "Hello Master!?" Better yet, how can I find one of those collars with the built in shocking device so my husband can just zap me, particularly if I'm too 'lazy or headstrong?'

"Now, one thing we know is that Paul doesn't deal with exceptions. I once counseled a wife whose husband wanted her to be exposed to pornography during love-making. In those situations, she says, 'I am sorry, that is when I am called to obey God over you.'"

"Amen..." I hear behind me.

"But Paul is not really talking about exceptions," the Pastor quickly interjects. "Sometimes a wife doesn't want to submit because she is being selfish."

The Pastor, while speaking the part of the woman, made his voice incredibly small and soft. I guess if the woman does need to defy the man, she must do it in a very tiny voice.

What I want to know here is, what happened to "God speaks to wives *through* husbands?" Everything this man has said thus far indicates that God and husbands are virtually indistinguishable. If a husband wants to see pornography, then based on this man's sermon, we have to assume that it is really God's wish that the pornography be seen. *Where does God stop and a husband begin?*

"Now we come to the subordinate husband. 'Husbands, love your wives as you love the church.' His task is clear: to care for his wife. He is responsible to love his wife as Christ loves the church. The church doesn't always obey Christ or respect Christ and yet Christ continues to love. Christ continues to love even when the church doesn't obey, and that is what husbands are called to do. Verse 28: 'You should love your wives as your own bodies.' This doesn't mean that you give your wife everything she wants or asks for. When I wake up, my body asks for coffee, twinkies, cheesesteaks. I eat from the three major food groups: salt, fat and sugar."

The congregation laughs.

"Husbands know that there are some things the body shouldn't have...you need to understand what your wife *really* needs. If you are a husband and you are not really caring for your wife, chances are she is anxious and trying to do it herself because you aren't doing it. You've got to be Christ-like and exercise care over your wife. For not a moment goes by that Christ is not caring for your life."

Okay. I'm through with the jokes. This entire scene: this church, these people, this man in the pulpit--this is all a very, very scary thing. And when I get scared, I get angry. I'm feeling this very strong urge to yell out loud: THIS IS THE BIGGEST CROCK OF CRAP I'VE EVER HEARD IN MY LIFE AND I CAN'T BELIEVE THAT YOU PEOPLE WHO HAVE CERTAINLY RECEIVED SOME FORM OF EDUCATION IN YOUR LIFETIMES, WHO CAN SUSTAIN JOBS THAT ALLOW YOU TO PURCHASE MODERATE TO HIGH PRICED SUVS AND VANS, ARE SITTING HERE TAKING THIS IN AS SOME SORT OF TRUTH!! IT WAS WRITTEN OVER 2000 YEARS AGO BY A BUNCH OF SPINDOCTORS WHO WANTED TO MAKE SURE THEY MAINTAINED THEIR POWER!

Well...maybe they're just leasing the vans and SUVs.

An amazing thing happens to me after that mental release: I have an epiphany. A serious epiphany that fills me with a pleasant sort of peace: If I want to grow as a spiritual being...indeed, if I want to grow as a Christian, then this is the chance of a lifetime. I don't meet too many people like this pastor on a day-to-day basis. If I can sit down with him, if I can have an actual conversation-a *dialogue* with him–me being me and him being him–if I can do that without telling him off or trying to throw his body off a roof somewhere, if I can feel love for him as another human being and find worth in him as he is, then I will have come a long way indeed. This is a wonderful opportunity for me.

But am I up to the challenge?

When the sermon is over, we sing a hymn and I stand up and collect my things. Some people behind me call to me that I've left my keys on the pew. As I approach the Pastor at the door where everyone is exiting, I reach out my hand.

"Hello, nice to have you," he says kindly.

"Hi, thanks. You know, your sermon really sparked some questions for me. Could I call you and set up an appointment?" I make an air phone with my hand, and hold it to my ear to demonstrate.

"Yes, why don't you give me a call." He too, holds up his hand to his ear.

Imagine what we could do with two cans and some string.

I call to set up an appointment with the pastor of Westover Bible Fellowship—one "Matt Sikes." I tell him I have some questions about his sermon on the roles of husband and wife and that I'm hoping he'll be able to clarify some things. He is very pleasant on the telephone and more than willing to meet with me.

A lot of prayer and meditation was necessary on my part to get ready for this meeting. I know that if I'm not careful, I'll just dismiss this gentleman early on, assume that I know what he's all about and not really try to meet him person to person, heart to heart. This isn't going to be easy, but I'm determined not to get defensive, to judge him, confront him in an unkind or abrasive way, to get angry or tell him he's an idiot. Depending on how he presents himself, it's possible that I could lose my cool and do any of the above.

The lights are all out in the hallway of the church, but I can see a secretary in a lighted office to the left, and next to her window is an open door. Matt is already on his feet and all the way to the doorway with his hand extended to greet me.

"Hi Ruth," he says pleasantly.

"Hi Matt, thanks so much for taking the time to talk with me." I follow him into his office and sit on a newish mahogany chair—one of four around a small round table. Pastor Matt sits across from me.

"I'm happy to do it. Now do you live in the area?" he asks me.

I tell him where I live and he is able to place it in his mind. "It's really nice over there on that side of the highway," he reflects.

"Yes, we love it, but unfortunately the developers are starting to creep in. We're trying to hold them off but it's not easy."

"Yes, I don't think anyone is able to avoid that these days."

"Well Matt, I had some questions after hearing your sermon on the 'Subordinate Wife and Subordinate Husband,' and I figured maybe you could help me out."

"Can I ask what your religious tradition is?" he asks. "It will help me to frame my answer."

"Well, I was raised Presbyterian. I consider myself a Christian, but I don't think Christ's teachings are the only ones with merit."

"Okay. That is helpful. Let me get a sheet of paper, because it helps me to say what I want to say more clearly." Matt hops up from his chair and gets a yellow legal pad. He sits back down across from me, uncaps his pen and writes a word across the top of his paper, then draws a neat line under it. I try to read the word upside down, but can't make it out. He looks up at me, pen poised in hand, ready to help.

"I'm a licensed psychologist and I've worked with a lot of people who are leading challenging lives and in particular, with women and children who are abused my husbands, stepfathers and boyfriends. I was concerned about this idea of submitting themselves to men, and I wondered what you would suggest, say, if a woman discovers that her husband is sexually abusing their daughter."

"Yeowsa!" Matt exclaims. He looks stunned. "Now that is...that is something different...that is clearly going against God's laws."

"So what would you advise to a woman in that situation?"

"Now...we have to see the situation in its context of course...but what I would say is that we need to get the man to deal with...the underlying difficulty...." Clearly Matt has been thrown for a loop, although I honestly didn't mean to surprise him. His words are coming out very slowly and he seems to be searching for what to say. I just figured all ministers were familiar with the realm of familial experiences, and sexual abuse of children is not an uncommon thing within families, unfortunately.

Matt continues on somewhat aimlessly. "He's not following God's laws as told to us in the Bible...we'd have to...." Matt uncaps and caps his pen over and over, but he's not writing anything. "We'd have to...obviously this has to be looked at...in a deeper context...we'd have to...tell the man that he cannot be selfish in this way...and I would expect the wife to take responsibility here...to...." He goes silent.

"Aren't you mandated by law to call Child Protective Services if something like that comes out?" I ask him.

"...yeeaas, I think I probably am..."

"So you've never had to deal with a scenario like this before, I'm taking it."

"Well, noooo....I have had children come to me and tell me that they think their parents are being excessive in their punishment, but I don't feel I need to call anyone in a case like that. I ask the parents to come in and we try to find out what the truth *really* is....but in the case of the husband who is having sexual relations with a stepdaughter or something like that...they would have to be confronted by the wife..."

"Who do you mean when you say 'they?'" I ask him nicely.

"Well, if a teenager comes forward and says that she is having sex--"

"It would most likely be a child under ten," I interject.

Matt looks at me blankly.

"Most child sexual abuse occurs with children under the age of ten–at least, that's when it usually starts. The children are much more vulnerable and less likely to resist or talk about it," I clarify.

"Oh....well....okay...if a child comes to her mom and says, 'Daddy touched me in a bad way,' the mother would have to step in and take some responsibility to tell him to stop it..."

For the next minute or so, Matt continues to seem totally lost: he looks off into space, fidgets with his pen, starts sentences and then stops them, shifts around in his chair-- but then he finds himself again. He sits up in his chair and addresses me with renewed authority. "You see, you see Ruth, what is really going on here is that the man is spiritually lost– he's selfish and he isn't following God's laws as told to us in the Bible."

"Yes, but I have to tell you Matt, I've worked with men who *used the Bible* as an excuse for their sexually abusive behavior. I was involved in a few court cases where the fathers were quoting scripture as an explanation for what they were doing. When my colleagues and I went and read what they were quoting, we could see how someone could possibly interpret the passage to mean that they could do that type of thing...I mean the Bible was written a long time ago when women and children were pretty much viewed as nothing but property."

Matt was shaking his head in vigorous agreement until I brought up that the Bible was written a long time ago. He tilts his head in a cautionary way. "Well, we have to be careful here Ruth...anyone can twist the words in the Bible to do their own evil, but the Bible still has a truth and a meaning that we have to recognize."

I decide not to challenge him on the bedrock of his beliefs. At least not just yet. "Well, can we talk about some of the specifics of your sermon on the 'Subordinate Husband and Subordinate Wife?" I ask, again nicely. So far, I've been trying to send loving vibes across the table in his direction, primarily to mask the part of me that might want to drive my car through the wall of his office.

"Sure!" Matt uncaps his pen and writes something else on another line on his paper. Thus far, the only things he has put on the paper are a series of lines that form "T's" and boxes, but have nothing within or around them. He makes his pen ready yet again.

"Several times in your sermon, you said that if a husband asks a wife to do something, 'she should do it'..." Matt nods his head, somewhat mechanically it seems. "I'm sure that some day–maybe even soon–a woman will become President of the United States. Now, what happens if she tells her husband that she is planning to introduce legislation that will reverse tax cuts for the wealthy, and her husband, being a businessman, tells her he doesn't want her to do this. What would you suggest she do in such a situation...."

Matt looks off in the distance. He seems to be pondering the imponderable. Again I feel as though I've thrown him a curveball, but I had no intention of trying to stump him. "Well...this is something I'd have to think about more deeply....I'm unguarded though and that's how I want to be...let's see....yeah...if a woman were a *surgeon*...and her husband told her he wanted her to *cut* a patient a certain way...should-she-do-what-he-says....I'm not sure...if she's....President and her advisors are telling her something she needs to do, and then her husband tells her to do something else..."

Good Lord. I've been trying to withhold judgment, but the fact that this man is even considering that a non-surgeon husband would tell his wife how to cut a patient open is beyond strange. And clearly, he seems to be having difficulty with the basic premise here: that a woman could become President of the United States. I wonder if he's ever imaged a woman in that role. It seems that, if one were to slip through, in his mind, she'd have to be told what to do by either advisors or her husband.

Matt appears to continue to go back and forth from the world of sitting with me, to the world of entering his mind and trying to think of his answers.

"Well, let's say that Hillary Clinton gets in..." he says with a slight grimace on his face, "and abortion has been outlawed. Let's say that she wants to reverse that decision, which would be immoral...in that case, if her husband were to tell her not to do it, well then, I think she'd have to listen..."

Does this man remember who Hillary Clinton's husband is? I'm not sure he'd be anyone's idea of a beacon of morality. Bill would have to have some nerve to tell Hillary how to act when it's her turn to be President. I'm not sure what to say to Pastor Matt. His way of thinking and reasoning is challenging to follow. Who decides just what is and isn't immoral? Husbands? Husbands like Bill Clinton? Jim Bakker? O.J. Simpson?

"Well, since Hillary's husband is known for being in favor of a woman's right to choose, I'm not sure your example works," I say with a smile. I decide to say that rather than, "Well, since Hillary's husband was caught with a very young and impressionable employee's lips wrapped around his penis, I'm not sure your example works."

"Right, well that's true," he agrees.

I think it's time for me to start being more direct with Matt–in a nice kind of way.

"I guess I just don't see that husbands should be telling wives what to do," I say gently but matter-of-factly. "It seems to me that it should be a mutual kind of thing and one of discussions...it is for me and my husband. He would never think to tell me what to do...in fact," I smile and chuckle, "I wanted him to come with me to meet you and get your perspective on things, and he said he didn't want to. After I described your sermon to him, he felt as though he would be in disagreement with you about a lot of things."

Matt jumps in. "Yeah, well I can understand how he feels. I recently wanted to see how things went in a more liberal church, so I decided to go to a Free Press Church....Morrison Free Press, I think it was..."

"I've never heard of a 'Free Press Church,'" I say.

"Free Presbyterian," he clarifies. "That's the way we refer to it...so I go and they have a woman minister-which I don't agree with-and she goes to give her sermon and the topic is Ephesians 5 and 6, and I'm thinking this is great! I get to be in a liberal church with a woman minister and hear her interpretation of Ephesians 5 and 6. So the first thing she says is that Paul tells us that husbands must 'love their wives as Christ loves the church,' and 'wives love your husband as you love your God,' then in the next breath she says that 'this is not the word of God---these words may have been inspired by God, but that was a long time ago. Now things are different and we must ask ourselves different questions.' I mean, she totally discounted the Bible and Paul's words as just some aspect of his *agenda* or his *issues.*"

Matt has recounted all of this in a rather sneering manner. Clearly I touched a nerve when I told him that my husband didn't want to come and meet him. He was being so polite and friendly, then oh-so-swiftly turned on the proverbial dime. Should I tell him that I agree with everything that this imposter of a woman minister has said?

Hold on to yourself, Ruth. Remember your goal here: to find something to value about this man and his perspectives, and to avoid getting angry or defensive.

"It's true that she can't know exactly how Paul felt or what he meant," I say, trying to build bridges with him, "and neither can you or I."

Matt is holding up his hand, giving me the "what just a minute" finger, not to be confused with another finger he could be giving me.

"Oh yes, I think we can know. If I said to you, Paul says in Ephessians, 'husbands love your wives as you love the church,' and then I said that this means that men can abuse and mistreat and not take care of their wives, you could rightly disagree with me and tell me that that is *not* what Paul means."

"But I don't fully know what Paul means. Paul isn't here to tell any of us, so none of us know for sure. We can only try to piece things together and in the end, make our interpretations." I don't bother to get into the fact that Paul could have been someone of questionable character, motives, or psychological stability, and that it could be very strange indeed that some people are blindly heeding what this one man had to say 2000 years ago.

Matt is quick to respond: "The words are the words though, and they have a meaning. If we say that they are only part of some time long ago, then we have nothing to guide us...nothing that means anything."

"Well, the words were written by fallible people, but we don't have to throw the baby out with the bath water. We can decide which words we want to follow or use as a guide, and which words don't seem to work to create a healthy society. For example, Paul says, 'Husbands love your wives as Christ loves the church.' I'm afraid that in the minds of many men, that puts them on a stature with Christ and is a dangerous thing for them to think. If they think that they are more connected to God than women, or more holy, than they can get carried away with their power and do all sorts of abusive things. Look at many priests for goodness sake. And you said in your sermon that 'God talks to wives through husbands,' which I feel is also problematic. I mean, no offense Matt, but I know a lot of men whose behavior, if thought of as some type of message from God, would be enough to make all of us atheists."

Matt moves forward toward the edge of his chair, anxious to respond. "Yes, but I also feel that God talks to husbands through wives."

"Oh, well you didn't say that in your sermon."

"That's true...and maybe that's because I have sin and am imperfect in my messages. It is absolutely the case that in marriages, wives can advise husbands. In my own marriage...you could ask my wife...I often ask her, 'Honey, what do you think?' and it might be in relation to the kids or money. We take each other's viewpoint into account all the time."

"Well, that's nice to hear," I smile.

"But–but–there can be no mistaking that the man needs to be in the leadership position. He has to assume that responsibility." He has held his finger up at me again, in a quasi-patronizing gesture.

I'm looking at Matt and interestingly enough, I don't have any desire to try to set him straight here. Normally, I would have gone on at length about the dangers of homogenizing men and women as though they have no within group differences. I'd suggest that in some marriages the temperament and skills of the wife might be those of a natural leader, while in others, the man might be more suited for it. Instead, I decide to try to build more bridges.

"You know, I think I'm appreciating what you've just said in a new way, Matt. I think some people view the conservative Christian perspectives as coming out a place of a male desire to maintain dominance and control. But I can see that someone like yourself takes his job very seriously as the head of the household, and I'm sure you don't want men to let their families down...that's a good thing."

Matt nods his head.. "Christian marriage is ideally one of mutual service...that's how I'd say it, Ruth. The man should assume the position, 'How can I serve you?' 'What can I do for you?'"

"I like the sound of that."

He smiles at me.

What the heck, I'll go a little further here. "Matt, since women initiate the bulk of divorce, do you think that it's possible that all this divorce is part of our development as human beings? That somehow we have to develop a new model for marriage–perhaps to overhaul the old ways?"

"I don't think an 'overhaul' is necessary...many people think that we'll come out on the other side of all this divorce with something new, but Christian marriage works fine...I don't want to give you a long lesson here...we just have to get back to the basics."

I think about all the older couples I know...my grandparents and great-grandparents–the grandparents of friends...my husbands grandparents--all of whom were church-going people. Most of them weren't particularly nice to each other. It was common for one of the partners to abuse and dominate the other. Generally it was the man, but my maternal grandmother dominated my grandfather mercilessly.

Visiting a friend's devout, Catholic grandparents on Christmas Day (he was ninety-eight and she was ninety-five), the pattern of their "Christian marriage" was still in place even after seventy-five years. At one point, she complained that he was having a shot of vodka, and he hurled the shot glass at her across the kitchen.

Ah yes, back to the basics.

"Well Matt, I thank you so much for your time...it's been good to hear more about how you see things." I reach over for my purse and keys.

Matt doesn't seem quite ready to wrap up our conversation. "Ruth, I will admit that I've bought the conservative position—I'll admit that. And maybe you could admit that you've bought the liberal position too. Maybe, as I keep myself open, you can keep yourself open to a more conservative viewpoint too."

Oh, he was doing so well and then he had to go and talk about "giving me a lesson," and suggesting that I keep myself "open" like him.

"Matt, I'm the one who came to your office to talk with you, didn't I?" I smile again.

"That's true you did."

"I'm open to all perspectives, not just yours. That's the way any thoughtful, reflective person should be, in my view."

"I'd like to give you a book," Matt says, ignoring my last comment. He heads to his bookshelf and hands me a small paperback, of which he has several copies, lined up neatly in a row. "This is a book written by a journalist who was once a very liberal person and who came to see Jesus and his teachings in a totally different way."

I'm getting turned off by his last-minute efforts to wrap me up in conservative tinfoil before I head out the door. Couldn't he just tell me that he's enjoyed hearing someone else's perspectives? Does he have to try to convert me as I'm turning to go?

Well, again, I remind myself to go easy on him. Evangelism seems to be the passion of many who follow Christ. They truly believe they've found the answer, and obviously on some level it is making them happy and giving structure to their lives—they want to share that good feeling with others. I guess I can't fault them for that.

Well, I can, but I won't.

I take the book from him and say a simple, "thanks." I give him a warm smile.

As I walk out the door, I hear him call, "Tell your husband I missed him!"

I laugh.

Well, that went pretty well; all that preemptive prayer must have helped.

Did I find any common ground with this man? I guess we'd both agree that husbands need to be responsible in their marriages, but then I'd add that wives need to be as well. I'd say that they need to be as interchangeable as they can be on many tasks: making money, raising children, cooking and mowing the lawn, making decisions, because that, in my mind, doesn't leave either in the dark if the other one is suddenly not around, and it doesn't box them into certain roles for life.

We agree that Hillary Clinton could become the first woman president, although I think we'd differ on Bill's advisory role. And I'm not so sure Pastor Matt would *like* having Hillary as his President. I'd be okay with it. But then again, I'm so anxious to see a woman in the White House during my lifetime that I'd settle for Roseanne Barr or Pamela Sue Anderson.

What did I find to like about Pastor Matt? I like the fact that he sat there with me for sixty minutes and really tried to listen to me. He probably isn't used to middle-aged, progressive professional women walking in off the street and questioning him about sexual abuse of girls and women as presidents and yet he really hung in there with me. I have to give him a lot of credit for that.

Something Pastor Matt said was very telling about him and probably lots of people who take conservative religious perspectives: "If we say that they [the words of the Bible] are only part of some time long ago, then we have nothing to guide us...nothing that means anything."

We live in turbulent times, and Pastor Matt, like most of us, probably feels overwhelmed by life. The Bible and the certainty with which he holds his beliefs are obviously a great comfort to him.

Nevertheless, from my perspective, we owe it to our children to teach them to question all perspectives, to think reflectively for themselves, and then to decide what to believe. If we lock ourselves into a rigid perspective, it's inherently simplistic. If we blindly follow only one book or one person then we reject all other wisdom. In the case of following the Bible in a literal sense, we reject the present and the future because we are trying to simulate something from the past. Yes, we need some type of grounding–I would suggest being grounded in love and true tolerance for many viewpoints. But in the end, we all have to be willing to tolerate ambiguity and change.

Change, after all, is the only thing that is certain in this world.

Westover Bible Fellowship Church

#	Dimension of Church Experience	Rating
1)	Is parking close and convenient?	7
2)	How beautiful is the worship space?	1
3)	How comfortable is the seating?	4
4)	How welcoming and friendly is the congregation?	6
5)	How enjoyable and uplifting are the musical aspects of the worship?	2
6)	Does the leader have a pleasant speaking voice and does he/she make sense to me?	0
7)	How clean are the bathrooms?	7
8)	Are the people in the pews interesting to stare at?	7
9)	How tolerant to many ways of seeing and doing things does this group appear to be?	0
10)	Would I feel good about how these people would spend my money?	0
11)	How close did I feel to God in this place?	0
12)	Did I smile more than once during the experience?	0
	Total	34

Unitarian Universalist

My husband likes to tell the following joke about Unitarians, which he attributes to Adlai Stevenson: There was a Unitarian at the Pearly gates, standing in front of St. Peter. St. Peter seemed a bit surprised and said, "What are you doing here?" The Unitarian said, "Well, can't Unitarians get into heaven?" St. Peter said, "Yes, of course, but remember back at fork in the road where there was the one sign that said 'Heaven,' and the other sign that read, 'Discussion Group About Heaven?' Well, so far we haven't gotten any Unitarians here."

A friend of mine had actually suggested that we go to a UU church together. He and I had been attending the same church prior to my research for this book and we were both feeling that we needed to be stretched more. He went UU once before me and seemed to be glowing from the experience.

I agreed to go, but I had some of the same kinds of reservations that I had before going to the Quakers: Would there be the whistles and bells? Stained glass? Casseroles? And there was one more concern that I didn't have with the Quakers: Would there be a God?

My buddy Steve and I decided to meet at the church. Rosewood Unitarian is located along the posh Main Line area of suburban Philadelphia; one has to drive right into the heart of Saab and cappuccino country to get there.

The church ends up being a house-like structure nestled among homes in an upper-middle class neighborhood. Parking lots are well-hidden by the winter vegetation, but I eventually find a spot not too far away, considering that it is only three minutes until the start of the service. A few people pass me by on their way out, but don't make eye contact.

Inside the door, a woman greets me with a bulletin and a "good morning." I'm glad for her big smile.

"Hi, I've never been here so if you could point me toward where the service is, I'd appreciate it."

"Oh, alright. Just go up these steps and it's straight back to your left."

I thank her and as I start to ascend the stairs, she calls, "It's 'Family Day,' so it's not really representative of a typical service!"

I thank her again and keep on trucking up the steps. Lots of people are funneling toward double doors, where more programs are being offered by greeters.

I slip into a chair near the back and scan the scene for my friend. The room is modern in design, with parts of the ceiling in glass so one can see the sky. The space seems cozy, but when I start to do the math, I realize that it is actually a fairly large room with at least 250 people sitting in new wooden chairs with padded seats and backs. The crowd seems to be skewed in the older direction, although there are numerous families and younger children as well. No sign of Steve, so I take off my coat and take in more of the room.

So far on my journey of discovery I have seen a number of things hanging on the wall in the front of the rooms or sanctuaries: there have been, of course, crosses and statues of Jesus, projection screens, stained glass windows, baptismal tubs, simple banners or words etched on the wall, blue foil stars, and now I can add to that list: Raggedy Anne and Raggedy Andy.

Yes, the only things hanging over the altar, if that's what they call it, are two very large Raggedy Anne and Andy dolls, surrounded by pink paper hearts stuck to the wall. The hearts are keeping with a Valentine's theme, which would make sense since it was a few days ago, but I can't for the life of me understand the significance of having these two huge rag dolls in the spot most often reserved for sacred images.

Well, at least it's not Barbie and Ken, or a couple of Tele-Tubbies. I see Steve out of the corner of my eye and motion for him. As he slides in next to me, he looks up at the Raggedy Anne and Andy and chuckles.

I'm thinking that if need be, I'll pray to the rag couple, but I will not under any circumstances endorse their socks to anyone.

We start singing the opening song, entitled: "Come Sing a Song With Me." It's not one that I've heard in the regular Protestant circuit. The words go thusly:

> *Come sing a song with me*
> *Come sing a song with me*
> *Come sing a song with me*
> *That I might know your mind*
> *And I'll bring you hope when hope is hard to find*
> *And I'll bring a song of love*
> *And a rose in the wintertime.*

The song also invites the listener to come dream a dream, to walk in the rain and to share a rose–all so that we might know the other's mind.

There appear to be three ministers at this church, one woman, one man and a student intern. All are sitting up front on an elevated area not unlike a small stage, facing the congregation. The male minister who

237

is dressed neatly in a suit and tie, stands with both an air of confidence and tremendous calm, an unbroken smile on his face. "I'd like to invite those who have a joy or sorrow to share to come forward at this time."

A man and woman and their young children come forward and take a lit candle from the minister, who I'm assuming is a fellow by the name of "Charles Scott," according to the bulletin. The man uses the candle to light one of seven unlit candles standing in a tapered candelabra that looks a bit like a menorah. "Good morning," he says. "I'm John Gallagher and this is my wife and family. We wanted to share that last week we delivered scarves to the homeless in downtown Philadelphia. It was a very gratifying experience and one we felt privileged to participate in."

The family moves away from the candelabra. A single woman comes forward and lights a second candle. "I'm Candace Greeley and I wanted to share that one of my patients died yesterday. She had a beautiful name–Cherub–and I'd like to ask that you keep her in your hearts."

Another woman shares that her mother is having difficulty with the fact that her grandmother, who is 101, is dying. Two elderly women from the congregation light candles for members who are in the hospital with serious illnesses.

Finally, a woman comes forward with a joy to share. "I'd like to share that becoming involved with this congregation has reignited my interest in singing. Next weekend I'll be performing at Carnegie Hall."

There are sounds of happiness and approval from the congregation. People start to clap. The woman walks back toward me and Steve and I give her a big smile.

The young woman, whom I'm assuming is the ministerial intern, rises, walks to the podium in front and speaks into the microphone. "Let's take a moment to reflect on all that we've heard." The room is perfectly quiet, even with the presence of children here and there. I look around and see that many people have their eyes shut.

"Now I'd like to invite you to participate in a Buddhist meditation with me. Relax in your chair...pay attention to your body and anything that might be uncomfortable...try to make adjustments so you can be as comfortable as possible..."

If I were to really do as this intern, Jeanne, is suggesting, I'd get naked and lie on the floor with a pillow and comforter.

"Relax and at the same time, keep your mind alert. Take a deep breath in....then out...then another breath in...and out....now think about love...love for yourself....think, 'may I love myself'....now think, 'may I be happy....really happy'......now think 'may I be free of fear...of anger...of sadness....may I be strong....healthy...happy....may I be at peace'....now think of someone else you love....think 'may you be happy....may you be free of fear...anger...sadness...may you be strong....healthy....happy....may you be at peace'....This is pretty cool and different–a minister leading a congregation through a Buddhist meditation. It's a bit rushed, but everyone in the room appears to be surrendering to the experience. As I glance around, each and every person is sitting with eyes closed, apparently giving their all to the meditation exercise.

"When you are ready, open your eyes and come back to the room... Each of you should have a pink heart attached to your bulletin. Now write the name of the person you thought of on your heart. We'll collect them and put them on the walls."

There is a great deal of hustle and bustle now as people fish around in coat pockets and purses, looking for pens. My friend is penless, so I let him have an extra of mine. We each write a name and the ushers come around and collect the hearts.

Two women start to sing a song in French. I look on my bulletin and see that it is "La vie en rose," by Paif and Louiguy. The tune is familiar–definitely something from a 60's light romantic movie. Their voices are incredibly rich and sultry...they sing with a sensuality that seems rather bold for church. It also presents an odd juxtaposition with all these Main Liners in their tweeds and wools, and yet everyone is smiling and watching approvingly. The members of the congregation seem to be drinking in the beauty of this fabulous music, just as they no doubt enjoy their fine wines and opera CDs.

Steve leans over toward me. "Didn't I hear this song in a Humphrey Bogart film?"

"I'm thinking a bit later than that...maybe Audrey Hepburn."

Now the three ministers are asking the children to come forward. Most of the children are already positioned near the front, so there isn't the usual stampede from all corners of the room. I miss that–the pounding of little feet and little bodies is so much fun to watch. Would that we adults could let ourselves go with such abandon. The ministerial trio tell the children and the adults that they are going to read a story entitled, *"Love You Forever,"* by Robert Munsch.

Oh dear. I know this story. I read it in a friend's bathroom and it made me cry. I had to stay in the bathroom for an extra ten minutes until my face returned to normal because it was a luncheon with lots of

happy people and I wasn't sure if my friend would appreciate my walking out of the bathroom with a tear-swollen face.
  The ministers have written a little song to go with the refrain:

I'll love your for always
I'll like you forever
As long as your living
My baby you'll be.

  One of them leads us in practicing the song, which we will sing together when she signals us. They begin reading:

A mother held her new baby and
very slowly rocked him back and forth,
back and forth, back and forth.
And while she held him, she sang:
I'll love you forever,
I'll like you for always,
As long as I'm living
my baby you'll be.

  The woman and the man take turns reading, while the intern calls out the part of an occasional "extra." The way these three work together is seamless and most pleasant to watch.
  As the story unfolds--the boy becoming a man and the mother becoming an old woman, the mother dying while the son holds her in his arms like a baby--I look around and see many people wiping their eyes. Luckily for me, that time in Theresa's bathroom must have inoculated me to some extent and I'm not feeling particularly sad.
  The offertory comes next and the French duo invite the children to help out. They pass around rhythmical instruments that appear to be ethnically diverse, i.e.: I don't know what most of them are. They explain to the children that the song is about the love that lives in a bird that lives in a tree.
  Once again the music is dazzling. Steve and I share a quiet look of amazement. Obviously these musicians are guests, or very talented members of the congregation who just happened to meet one evening at a potluck and realized that they both sang French cabaret-style music and played the guitars. Probably the former.
  The women sing a very spirited tune, while the children bang drums and ring bells, all of which sounds really good:

L'arbre est dans ses feuilles
Marilon marile
L'arbre est dans ses feuilles
Marilon don de.

How is the music normally done, I wonder? The one greeter told me that this wasn't a typical service. Do they have a choir? Do they have a music director?

The song ends with the children shaking their instruments in a frenzy. They've clearly enjoyed the experience with abandon. One woman asks the children to leave their instruments up front and they appear to do so obediently.

Reverend Scott comes to the podium and speaks into the microphone. "Here are some thoughts from children on just what love is: 'There are two kinds of love" our love and God's love...but God makes both kinds'... 'Love is when my grandfather paints my grandmother's toenails'... 'When someone loves you, the way they say your name is different–you know your name is safe in their mouth'... 'Love is when a girl puts on perfume and a boy puts on shaving cream and they go out and smell each other'..."

People have been chuckling at each of these, but the smelling one has gotten the biggest laugh by far.

"'Love is what's in the room at Christmas when you stop opening presents and listen'... 'Love if when your puppy licks your face even after you've left him all day long.'"

As other cute reflections about love are being shared, I glance at the bulletin to see what goes on at a Unitarian Church. These folks sure aren't slackers. Here is what is happening in just three weekdays at the church: Men's support group, AREC meditation, AREC Buddhism Adv., Everyday Spiritual Practices, Social Action Committee, Worship Advisory, Communications Council, New Church Task Force, Prana Yoga, Board of Trustees, Toddler Play Group, Women's Alliance Group, Children's Choir, Evening Book Discussion, Adult Choir, Open Studio, History Committee, Ski Spree and LATF Movie Night, a bus trip to Washington to march for women's rights.

Holy Berkenstocks, Batman! It's a bastion of liberal do-gooders!

It appears to be time for the sermon. The woman minister comes to the podium and speaks clearly into the microphone. "If Tina Turner were here, she'd ask, 'what's love got to do with it?' I first heard that song in an aerobics class. There I was, pregnant, bouncing up and down–gently–with other pregnant woman, and being forced to contemplate the meaning of those words...we know that without love, we cannot thrive in this world. Research is full of examples of those who have been unloved and have suffered or caused others to suffer as a result. Children who were abused quickly become adults who hate themselves. This continues unless the cycle stops-unless love is introduced to break the cycle."

She's got that right. Consider some of our most notorious once-abused children: Hitler, Stalin, Charles Manson.

"What does this mean for the children who are in this room? It means that you are worthy of love–your days should be filled with love...and you adults, too. When love of ourselves is in place, love of others will happen. And, love has the power to soften all of us. I have a family story to illustrate this."

Good. Family stories are good.

"When my son was two-years-old, he was at the dinner table with my father and spontaneously he said, 'I *love* you, Opa!'

My father didn't know how to respond, so he merely smiled at Sam. Here he was, this older German man, one who was raised to hide emotions, to brace himself against life, and he simply didn't know how to respond. It totally took him by surprise.

A few days later, my son again, was moved to say, 'I *love* you, Opa!' at the dinner table. This time, my father managed to say, 'Thank you, Sam.'

A third time, my son said, 'I *love* you, Opa!' And this time, his grandfather said back, "I love you too, Sam.'"

After that, my father started to tell my son that he loved him on a regular basis. When other grandchildren came along, he told them he loved them, too. Eventually, he took up wood carving, and carved wooden hearts with the names of all his grandchildren inside of them."

As I listen to her story, I reflect on my own family. My parents said they loved me, but I don't think my grandfather really did. He was more about giving little tidbits of wisdom from the hills of North Carolina, like, "Don't take no wooden nickels!" or "Don't let no grass grow under your feet!"

Our minister continues: "Love is a wide-ranging thing–we can apply love to any facet of our lives...even as we pay bills, we can feel love and gratitude for those things that sustain us. Of course, the greatest type of love is when we set aside our needs for others.

Love can be evident in everything that we do. How can we love in our daily lives? Take a joy ride. Feel the wind in your face. Run to greet someone. Take a nap and stretch before rising. Be loyal. Dig until you find something. Thrive on attention. Be silent and sit by others when others are sad. Avoid hitting when a simple growl will do. Right here in this room is the love of friends, love of lovers, parents and children, the love of French music. Feel the love in everything."

After the sermon, we sing another song and then the French singers regale us once more. Steve and I meander out to the lobby with the others. New people are supposed to take a red coffee cup, so others will be able to identify you.

I check out the information tables, and end up chatting with a former Catholic engineer who seems wicked smart. He tells me how much research he did before he chose the church, and tells me that it's a great place, but you have to make the effort to connect with others because the congregation can be a bit "Main Liney," and standoffish at times.

The woman who is in charge of new members comes over and introduces herself. She seems very nice and explains aspects of the UU faith. She was raised in it, unlike most people who come to it in later life. This particular congregation has over 700 people. We chat some more and then she heads toward more new people. Steve and I stand around with our red cups, looking like teenagers at the prom who came without dates.

No one else goes out of their way to talk with us, but I'm not discouraged. There is plenty of warm laughter and talk going on, in fact, the place is really abuzz. There is a freshness and thoughtfulness about this group that I like. And I'm thinking that they aren't obsessed with evangelizing or pulling us into the fold, which is refreshing for a change.

"Well Steve, I saw an announcement about an 'Ecofeminism' women's group that is meeting. I think I'm going to have to go. I've actually heard of that and I can't believe that there are other people in my time zone who are also aware of its existence."

"Yeah, you'll have to let me know how that goes," he chuckles.

On Wednesday night, the parking lots around the church are very dark, but the building looks inviting and warm with the lights on. The entire structure is really neat: part ski lodge, part mountain retreat. I find my way to the second floor and room 208, where I was told I would find the Ecofeminism study group.

In the room are five women: the minister and four women who appear to be between their 40s and 60s. I can tell right away that they are a lively, relaxed bunch; they're laughing and swapping stories. I shake a few hands and they welcome me warmly.

A large couch and several chairs are arranged around a coffee table. We sit down and they chit chat while waiting for any late stragglers. I glance back and notice a bowl of veggie chips and another of nuts on a table across the room. I know they're veggie chips because I had just bought a bag of those for the first time last week, and they were so good I inhaled them in one day. Now I've got a sudden urge to do the same thing to this bowl, but then that may not be the Unitarian way.

After about ten minutes of light conversation, the minister, Jeanne, suggests we get started. Jeanne, as I knew from reading the bulletin, is the intern minister. Her style befits a minister-in-training; she seems to be delicate in her handling of social interaction, and she's diplomatic.

A candle is lit in the center of the coffee table, and Jeanne invites us to "check in." I know this check in business from my days as a psychologist. We're all going to talk about how we feel at the moment and "share." How I've come to loathe so many words from my previous profession: "share," "process," "feedback," "boundaries," "appropriate," "check in." It's not that I mind talking about my feelings, or hearing anyone else talk about them, it's just that human interaction has become over-processed, like so many of our foods. Give me a little more spontaneity, a little less of the psychobabble.

Well, maybe this crowd will have escaped the influence of the past thirty-five years of psychology.

The first woman checks in: "I'm Meryl Fraley and I'm feeling angry and anxious tonight."

Maybe it's not too late to check out.

"I know I've got to just roll with it, but it's hard...I just have these angry feelings sitting in there and I have to make some difficult decisions...it makes me scared...but I'm dealing with it." This woman has crossed her legs up on the couch and is pulling on her shins as she talks. She continues in this vein, never really saying what it is that is making her angry or anxious. Surprisingly, no one asks.

The next woman speaks. "I'm Mary Henry...I'm glad to be here tonight. Most of you know I'm from England originally...my mother is over there and very sick...I've been flying back and forth and feeling very torn...I'm her only daughter which makes it even harder..."

Several of the women make noises of compassion and understanding.

"I've been putting off buying the plane ticket to go back, but I've got to do it soon....I just have so much to do here, too..." she looks at the group with an exasperated smile.

"I can really sympathize," a woman across the circle offers. "It's not easy having a parent who is sick even when they only live a few miles away. I can't imagine what it would be like across the ocean! I have to say though, that you really a model of composure under stress Mary, you really do impress me."

Mary looks away humbly and waves her hand dismissively. She shares a bit more of the details of her responsibilities here at home, then wraps it up: "But I'll manage and I thank you all for your support and you Carol, for your comments. It makes me feel better."

"No, thank *you*," Carol responds. "See, it comes back to me. You feeling better and telling me that you feel better makes me feel better."

And Carol telling Mary that her telling Carol that she felt better has in turn made Mary feel even MORE better...betterer...

Another younger woman, maybe in her late thirties, has entered while we've been sharing. Carol "checks in," sharing her enthusiasm about several things going on in her life then we turn toward an older woman with white hair and very smooth, shiny skin. She whispers, "We'll I'm here..."

Everyone groans sympathetically. "Are you sick?" Jeanne asks.

"I've got laryngitis," she whispers with a smile. "I've had it for over a week and the doctor says I just have to wait it out. Maybe being here tonight will loosen it up a bit."

Carol is shaking her head. "I've had it, and I can tell you Frances, the only thing that works is for you to be totally silent."

Frances gives a look of good-natured resistance. "I've had more phone calls since I got this, then I've ever had in my life!" she continues.

It's painful to listen to her trying to talk–making a sound not unlike one's car on a bitter cold morning when the engine doesn't want to turn over. Frances goes on to tell us about one phone call from a solicitor, going into more detail than might be necessary considering that the lining of her throat could very well turn to flame at any second.

Eventually it's just me and the young woman who arrived late who have yet to speak.

"You don't have to speak if you don't want to," Jeanne says to us.

"Oh, I don't mind," I offer. "I'm Ruth Laker and I'm glad to be here. I've been to two of your services. I'd like to find out more about UUism."

I talk a bit about my family and what I do. I can tell that the women are very interested in how I see things and, with the exception of the intern minister, they are all encouraging me to come to the church. It's nice to feel appreciated and to connect with a group of women who probably see eye to eye with me on many things.

The late-comer speaks next. "I'm Pat Mellon," she says. "I've only been to the church a few times, but I like the fact that everyone is so open. I feel very comfortable here. I'm going through a divorce right now, and it's a difficult time, so I'm a bit preoccupied with that."

Everyone makes sounds of support.

"I know how you feel," Carol offers. "I divorced twenty years ago and it wasn't easy. It's much better now though."

"I had to leave everything behind...the house, my dogs..." the young woman looks sad but she's trying to be brave too. I want to say some words of comfort and share from my own experience, but I don't think this is supposed to turn into group therapy, so I remain quiet.

"Well, thank you all for coming and for sharing," Jeanne says. "Tonight we're going to talk about 'Ecofeminist Theology.' How many of you have heard of this before?"

No one raises her hand.

"I've heard of Ecofeminist Psychology," I offer.

"Well, that's probably similar. Ecofeminism came out of the feminist and environmental movements of the 1970s." Jeanne goes on to share some of the history of the movement and the primary theory upon which it is based. She says that in her mind, "all of the exciting things that are happening in the world are in so called 'third world' countries." Women are the ones who often suffer directly because of the disruptions to the environment, and they are the ones who are now trying to fight for the integrity of the earth.

"There is data to support a very strong correlation between respect for the environment and respect for women," I interject. "In Scandinavian countries, in Germany, the Netherlands...these cultures have tremendous respect for the environment and they also highly value the roles women play as those who raise children and care for the family."

"Yeah, but that correlation doesn't hold up in here," Jeanne says. "We aren't very concerned about the environment."

Several women jump in and say that it does hold up here because we don't respect women in the United States either. I think about Ann Crittendon's book, *The Price of Motherhood: How the Most Important Job is the Least Valued*, as an illustration of just how far we still have to come in the U.S...not to mention the violence directed at women in so many spheres: our homes, on the streets, in the media.

A very stimulating conversation ensues. I'm impressed by how quickly these women jump in and wrap their minds around these issues, particularly since none of them had ever heard of the specific topic prior to tonight. They are a quick, fearless and mentally agile group.

Eventually, Jeanne tells us that we're not going to just sit and discuss things–she's got a task for us to do tonight as well. "I've got some environmental issues that different women have been confronting and I want you to break into groups and find a way to act them out."

Oh man. This has absolutely no appeal to me. I'm not in a regular acting mood, let alone an Ecofeminist acting mood. I think this ministerial intern may have just laid a big goose egg. I bet I'm not the only one who doesn't want to dramatize environmental issues.

Jeanne hands out three packets of information to the six of us. I really can't bear the thought of having to be creative on demand. I've been paired with the woman with no voice, so the burden on me is even greater. How in the heck am I supposed to act something out with a partner who can't speak? Is this going to be Erin Brockavich in mime or something?

The other four women bound up out of their chairs and head out to the hallway. Frances and I are left to sit and read our environmental scenario. It's about the damming of the Narmada River in India, which will decimate the lives of over a million people if carried out. Most of the people are tribal and their lives are considered to be of little value in the bigger picture of the government and the business interests who want the water diverted. As small dams are being built, the people have protested in neck deep water, refusing to leave their lands. There really isn't anywhere for them to go. As the author of the article writes, "the residents of the Narmada Valley are expected to vanish, like vermin, into the crevices of the city slums or resettlement colonies. Become a statistic. Join the 350 million Indians living in poverty."

Once again I am hit with just how privileged the lives of Americans are. Instead of being grateful though, tonight I'm disgusted. I'm sick of thinking, thank you God, for letting me live in this country. Tonight I'm thinking, why can't the rest of the world get their act together? Why is everyone so greedy? Why are there so many men with guns? Why can't we see that overpopulation is causing most of the environmental problems? What's wrong with people?

I guess I'm having an ecopsychologically-induced silent rant.

As we sit and read, I can hear the other four women in the hallway: laughing, sliding things around, thumping and bumping and talking enthusiastically. I guess I was wrong about their level of interest in the task. Frances and I are sitting absolutely still, flipping through our papers. I've finished reading mine, but I keep leafing back through the handout to avoid having to say anything to her. Finally, the silence is exhausted.

"Well, I guess you don't want a speaking part," I smile at Frances.

She smiles back. "No," she whispers.

"I'm really not feeling very creative tonight," I say.

"Me either," she whispers.

We sit in silence for another ten seconds or so. Ten seconds is a long time when you think you should be saying something. A *really* long time...

"How about if I just read the poem that's included with the materials?" I suggest.

"Sounds good," Frances whispers.

We both sigh in relief. I haven't felt so on the spot in a long time–this was like an acting ambush.

Jeanne calls the other two groups back in.

"Who would like to go first?" she asks.

Mary and Meryl volunteer without hesitation. They pull an art easel into the room. Meryl starts to walk about ominously, moving her arms as though she is whacking things down and making gnashing and smashing noises. Mary throws herself down by the easel and wraps her arms around it, looking at Meryl with a terrified expression and shaking her head no, over and over again.

They stand up and smile. Everyone claps.

Well, what it lacked in length it made up for in intensity. What was really amazing about that performance was how naturally and effortlessly the two women got into the role play; as though they role play environmental problems every day.

The other group volunteers next. Carol and Pat sit down at a long table and begin to act out a TV news program which has a representative from the company responsible for Love Canal debating a woman who represents the homeowners and families who were made sick by the toxic waste. Carol is particularly appealing as the insensitive, self-absorbed company woman, who pretends to care but clearly doesn't. She finally ends the scene by saying to Pat, "Well, all I tell you is 'shit happens.'" She bursts into laughter, as do we all.

They come back to the circle, laughing and sharing insights with the group about their roles. I swallow hard. I really haven't done the least bit of preparing, nor do I think I can match the improvisational excellence I have just witnessed from the four other women.

Suddenly, I have an idea.

As the women turn toward me and Frances, I stand up. "We decided to give Frances the night off since she can't speak. I'm going to read a poem that was written by a woman affected by the environmental situation in her country. I'd like to turn the lights out and just have the candle light if you don't mind...that way you will simply hear a disembodied voice and you can focus on the words more.

Everyone nods their heads gamely. I walk to the back, and turn out the lights. A few people gasp because it is so dark. Then our eyes adjust to see the single flame on the coffee table. I move to stand by the narrow window in the door for some dim reading light. I suggest that they take a few deep breaths before I begin.

> *As I build this dam*
> *I bury my life*
> *The dawn breaks*
> *There is no flour in the grinding stone*
>
> *I collect yesterday's husks for today's meal*
> *The sun rises*
> *And my spirit sinks*
> *Hiding my baby under a basket*
> *And hiding my tears*
> *I go to build the dam*
>
> *The dam is ready*
> *It feeds their sugarcane fields*
> *Making the crop lush and juicy*
> *But I walk miles through forests*
> *In search of a drop of drinking water*
> *I water the vegetation with drops of my sweat*
> *As dry leaves fall and fill my parched yard*

Everything is silent after I finish reading. By turning off the lights, I was trying to take myself off the hook, to remove the pressure of having them stare at me while I read. Surprisingly, it made me forget about myself as well. My ego melted away and my voice carried the poem all by itself: quiet and steady in some places, rising in agitation in others. I'm not a poetry critic, but I think it wasn't half bad.

I turn the lights on and go back to the group.

Everyone sits quietly for another few seconds. "That was really powerful to read it that way," Jeanne offers.

Everyone agrees.

Frances, my partner, pats me on the arm approvingly.

Relief.

It's now 9:40 p.m. I still have a half hour drive home. Not being close to the church is an issue when you have a twelve-year-old who is waiting for you to say goodnight. Still, I've enjoyed the spontaneity and strength of these interesting women.

Jeanne suggests that we end with a moment of silence.

We all sit quietly...everyone has closed their eyes except for Jeanne. After a minute she speaks quietly. "We are grateful for this opportunity to be together and to share from our minds and hearts."

That's it. No "God" or "Lord" or "Amen." Jeanne's voice seemed to be directed at us, but also beyond us as well. She was leaving room for the presence of God or Spirit, but at the same time, she wasn't going to give that Presence a name. If it was there it was there, if it wasn't, it wasn't.

I find myself again uncertain about this approach-- this "intellectual honesty." And yet, I have to say that I admire it too. There is something brave and true about these people. They know that each of us must find our truth on our own and they won't coddle us in the process.

I realize at that moment that that is what so many of the religions I have participated in seem to offer to their followers: coddling. Coddling and certainty that they have all the answers. Well, most people probably want that. Life can produce enough anxiety without having to add existential drift to the mix.

I go back to the UU church for several services. It's interesting that the first time I came, the woman who greeted me told me that it was "Family Day," and that the service wasn't "typical."

What was "typical" for the UU's? The time I went and there was a musical theater-type performance of the poems and writings of

Bertolt Brecht, complete with cabaret music, canes and feathered boas? The time the stodgy, pedantic, Ph.D. in Geography presented an overview of where the UU faith stood in America, using several large graphs to illustrate? The time the service revolved around the children who acted out elements of Dr. Seuss' "The Lorax?" The time the gentleman who was a principle clarinetist with the Belgrade Philharmonic performed? The time it was "Health Awareness Sunday," and a woman who was both a psychiatrist and a lawyer presented on the power of faith to help in healing, and then invited us all to partake of massage, facials and organic cooking after the service?

After two months at the UU church, I had absolutely no sense of *anything* typical. And I have to say, that made it very stimulating.

Alas, in the end, I found something seriously missing at the UU church: God.

I came to find that other UUers were hungry for more connection with something Transcendent yet afraid to throw themselves into some type of faith that would go against their mighty intellects. It's understandable, particularly in this day and age of a dumbed-down revival of Christianity in our culture. They didn't want to go back to the churches in which they grew up, yet they weren't getting spiritual needs fulfilled here.

More than once, I saw that the weekly sermon was about what UU people believe. Social justice and humanitarianism were the things everyone agreed on. Those are good things. But Webster's primary definition of "religion," is the following: a) belief in a divine or superhuman power or powers to be obeyed and worshiped as the creator(s) and ruler(s) of the universe, and b) expression of such a belief in conduct and ritual. Unitarian Universalism is not really a religion from my perspective, at least not in the way we commonly use the word. It's a shared philosophy that, boiled down, might go something like this: we don't know if God exists or why we're here, but we do believe we should care about social justice and humanitarian causes and do things together to promote them.

If the UU Church were a community center, it would be one incredible place where I would definitely want to hang out on a regular basis. It didn't take long to go to a very deep place with the average person on just about any topic–except spirituality. I found great intellectual, but not spiritual fellowship in that environment. And for me, that's just not enough.

Unitarian Universalist

#	Dimension of Church Experience	Rating
1)	Is parking close and convenient?	6
2)	How beautiful is the worship space?	9
3)	How comfortable is the seating?	8
4)	How welcoming and friendly is the congregation?	2
5)	How enjoyable and uplifting were the musical aspects of the worship?	10
6)	Does the leader have a pleasant speaking voice and does he/she make sense to me?	5
7)	How clean are the bathrooms?	10
8)	How interesting are the people in the pews to stare at?	6
9)	How tolerant to many ways of seeing and doing things does this group appear to be?	8
10)	Would I feel comfortable with how this group would spend my money?	10
11)	How close to God did I feel in this space?	2
12)	Did I smile more than once during the experience?	10
	Total	86

THE REVEREND CORNELL ROLLE

THE VERY REVEREND RONALD BAIN

THE OUTRAGEOUSLY REVEREND GILBERT SANDS

Episcopal Church

The Church of the Ascension Cathedral, in a fairly well-known Bahamian town, is very old. At nearly three hundred fifty-years-old, it's one of the oldest buildings on the island.

I'm on a late winter, mother-daughter vacation with my twelve-year-old when we venture into this beautiful old structure on an early Sunday morning. My daughter has pointed out that the earliest service would be best to have as few intrusions as possible on our tanning time.

I realize that this church will contain many idiosyncrasies specific to the island, Bahamians, and their unique way of doing things. Still, I feel fairly confident that there is enough formality within the Episcopalian tradition to ensure that some of what we will experience will exist even within Episcopalian churches in the states. Both Americans and Bahamians share a common link: the influence of the British on many of our religious practices. In both countries, the Episcopalian churches were founded by Englishmen and women, and as with Catholics, many of those traditions have withstood the passage of time.

I know these things because my best friend from college and roommate of four years was raised Episcopalian and I had occasion to worship with her and her family over the years. Episcopalians do appear to love their traditions and as my friend has told me, most hold them dear.

After polling a few Episcopalian friends, here are adjectives you'd be unlikely to pair with the word *Episcopalian*: Experimental; informal; radical; fun-loving; bodacious.

On the other hand, here are the words and phrases they'd be likely to associate with the "E" word: Damn rich, stiff butts, friendly in a stiff-butted kind of way; smart; great dressers; but still stiff-butted.

Trying not to let any of these preconceived notions influence me too much, we walk along the gorgeous turquoise waters and through the town toward the island church. Given that we've been surrounded by tourists in flip-flops and sweat shorts with words like "Tulane," "Juicy," and "Staff" written across their butts, it is both notable and refreshing that the parishioners heading toward the door of the church are dressed in their finest frocks.

Inside the first set of doors is a small vestibule area. The walls have only a few things on them to break the stark whiteness of the paint.

There are three pictures of black men in robes, and across from them, a single white sheet has been posted with the menu for an upcoming church dinner. The three men have titles which suggest a hierarchical system of some type: one is "The Reverend Cornell Rolle," another is "The Very Reverend Ronald Bain," while the third is "The Most Reverend Gilbert Sands–Archbishop." I'm not sure what the distinctions mean and what we could expect to be different between a person who is "Very," versus "Most" Reverend, but I'm figuring that it must be something like the difference between 87, 89 and 93 octane at the gas pump. In addition, the "Most Reverend," gets to wear a big, fancy red headpiece that makes him look like the Pope when he's ready for a night on the town.

The congregation appears to be roughly two-thirds black Bahamian and one-third white and all of them, black and white, are dressed to the conservative nines: pearl necklaces and earrings, dark suits, tailored skirts and pumps. Several of the black women are wearing very smart-looking hats. One in particular catches my eye: it is a stunning mix of mauve, pink and cream colored orchids, made of a fine, mesh-like material.

My daughter and I take seats near the back. The organ is already going strong, pounding out *Fantasia and Fugue in G Minor BWV 542* by J.S. Bach. "BWV 542?" I've always wanted to test drive one of those.

The bulletin gives the list of jobs at this church: Archbishop; Suffragan Bishop; Dean and Rector and Vicar General; Priest Vicar; Dean's Warden; People's Warden; Sexton and Caretaker; Dean's Vergers; Archdeacons; Canons.

Maybe it's just me, but there seem to be some sadomasochistic overtones to these titles. I read somewhere the British are secretly very kinky in their sexual practices. I'd be mighty circumspect if I was asked to be "Sexton and Caretaker" of the "Dean's Rector." The "Dean's Warden" sounds very much like a dominance position, and I'm sure he gets to call the shots about when and where the Dean does his "Vergers."

On one page of the bulletin, the "confirmation candidates" are listed. I think I can tell who might be the black Bahamians, and who might be the white. Some of the names have color and pizazz: Natasha, Kerylle, Tenaj, Arielle, Robertha, Cherish, Tikira, Ianthe, Pandora. Others are decidedly more subdued: Alice, Jane, Margaret, Sandra, Karen, Astrid.

Two white men in black robes are lighting candles in the front of the church. It's a beautiful old structure–very grand. It almost seems out of place on an island, with so much marble and statuary. The three

255

massive stained glass windows in the front are the showpiece of the building, with intricate scenes that are difficult to decipher with so much color going on. Only the wooden ceiling seems to go with the feel of the native environs--like an upside down boat keel--but even that is incredibly rich and complex-looking.

"Everyone is bowing before they go in the pew," my daughter leans over and whispers.

"They're showing their reverence to God," I respond.

Several of the black men near us are kneeling and appear to be in deep prayer. I look down and see that they have not the traditional prayer benches but lots of little miniature ottomans upon which to rest your knees. Wow. They're all a rich cranberry red and there are dozens of them in every row. Each person gets his or her own little ottoman. And they're so gosh darn cute!

I decide to try one out.

Nice...very comfortable...easy on the knees. If I were a member here, I'd be tempted to steal four or five of these to sprinkle around my house. They could be used in the kid's room, as meditation cushions, around the coffee table for Sushi Night.

As I pull myself back up to the pew, my abdominal muscles contract painfully. Immediately, I know the source of the pain: the Reverse Recliner. My daughter and I had been developing our own swimming strokes in the hotel pool the day before and one of my contributions was the "Reverse Recliner." One pushes off from the wall on their back, then, keeping legs straight and together, you contract your body in and then out, as though you are sitting on a recliner and pushing it open. Unfortunately, it doesn't get you very far and leaves you with burning abdominal muscles the next day. Still, it was more efficient than the "Death Beetle," where you float on your back and flutter your toes and fingers pitifully.

A marble wall fresco near us has the following inscription: "Sacred to the Memory of William Thompson, Esquire. Born at Hampton in the County of Lancaster and the Kingdom of Great Britain but who passt the Greatest Portion of the last twenty four years of life in Georgia East Florida and these Islands where he died on the 9th day of December, 1796, Aged 45 Years."

Gosh. I hate to think about anyone dying at 45. Even a lawyer.

"THIS IS THE DAY THAT THE LORD HATH MADE. REJOICE AND BE GLAD IN IT," a man's voice with a rich Bahamian accent calls from the back of the church.

Another man's voice say's, "WE WILL SING INTROIT HYMN NUMBER 333."

As we start to sing, a veritable Mummer's parade walks down the center aisle. Everyone is wearing a long robe of some combination of white, black and or red. Two people are holding staffs with red glass candle holders swinging from the ends. Inside a flame dances wildly as they move. Five black men and one white man walk behind the candle holder duo, while a robed choir of about ten black people follows them.

The woman next to my daughter has helped her find the page in her hymnal. Kate is dutifully trying to sing when I finally start to focus on the hymn. It's almost impossible to figure out where we are because the organ is blaring over the voices of the congregation. It seems to be getting louder and louder as each verse passes. By the time we get to the final verse, I can see the words on the page, but I can barely hear the sound of my own voice singing them:

> *Take up Thy cross the Savior said*
> *If thou wouldn't my disciple be*
> *Deny thyself, the world forsake*
> *And humbly follow after me.*

It must be a heady thing to be able to play an instrument that can drown out hundreds of voices raised in song. Bagpipers could probably do it, but not singularly–only in groups.

One of the Reverend's–I'm not sure if he's the "Very" Reverend or the "Most Likely to Succeed" Reverend–leads us through responsive readings. I'm taken with his Bahamian accent, which is unlike most of the natives. It sounds more British than Bahamian, but there is still an African or Bahamian flavor of some kind. If I closed my eyes, I would know that it is a black man doing the speaking. Still, his pronunciations are decidedly Anglo: "We come a-gane..." and "The Holy Speed-it..."

Glancing up front I see that one microphone is being shared by several of the robed gentlemen, while the Archbishop has his own mic and his own pew near the altar. At this point, the Archbishop asks us to pray. He sings what they call "The Collects" in a chant-like way; almost all of it is sung on one note. "Gracious-Father-whose-blessed-Son-Jesus-Christ-came-down-from-heaven-to-be-the-true-bread-which-gives-life-to-the-world: Evermore-give-us-this-bread-that-he-may-live-in-us-and-we-in-him-who-lives-and-reigns-with-you-and-the-Holy-Spirit-one-God-now-and-for-ever."

Wow! He did that with only two breaths. I'd like to give it a try. It'd be great to be able to sustain a note for that long, while also imparting an important message. I could use it with my kids: "Please-unload-the-dishwasher-and-load-the-dirty-ones-and-make-sure-you-rinse-the-silverware-first-please-or-as-you-know-the-biggest-gunk-won't-come-off-thank-you-very-much."

A black woman with what sounds like a true Bahamian accent gives the Old Testament reading from Joshua. It's about things I really don't care for: unleavened cakes, fearing God and camping.

Another black man's voice comes over a speaker from somewhere and informs us that the choir will now sing the 34th Psalm. The tensome stand, while a young black man conducts the piano through the introduction. Gee, why didn't they use the deafening organ, I wonder?

The group begins to sing: *I will bless the Lord at all times; his praise shall ever be in my mouth. I will glory in the Lord; let the humble hear and rejoice.*

Interesting. The sound of this group is crisp and yet light and ethereal. The diction is perfect and they stand with total attention to the conductor. I guess I shouldn't stereotype, but this is unlike any black musicianship I've ever heard. Great black musicians in all traditions: jazz, soul, rap, R&B, opera, gospel–they all perform with a passionate strength and power. These blacks are singing like...well, like good Englishmen from 1796. They've been Anglicized...or some might even say, sanitized.

Some parts almost sound and look silly. Like when they do one of those chant-type things, saying many words rapidly while bouncing on the same note: The-angel-of-the-Lord-encompasses-those-who-fear-him...What looks silly is how the conductor is conducting not just every word, but every syllable–moving his hands up and down with each one. Because the motions are so small and rapid, he can't use his whole arm to conduct, only his hands. The effect is that of a young man, stricken with Parkinson's in his prime.

Now it's on to the "Epistle." This is read by a white woman with an American accent. As she reads from 2 Corinthians, I glance around and notice that several of the older blacks are reading the Epistle very closely in their bulletins. Some are mouthing along as the woman speaks. The general theme is how everything old becomes new through Christ.

It's time for the anthem: *Jesu Joy of Man's Desiring* by, who else, J.S.Bach. Again it's a piano playing the accompaniment. If you're going to do Bach, you've got to have the organ. Don't they have a mute button on that thing to tone it down?

My daughter smiles when she hears the opening strains of the music–it's fun for her to recognize classical pieces; now that she's been playing the viola for four years, she's starting to feel like a seasoned instrumentalist. Her smile starts to fade shortly after the piece gets going, and shortly thereafter her expression turns to one of general boredom. I have to admit that this is one fairly lifeless rendition of the Bach piece, and again, because it is being sung by black Bahamians, it seems even more so because of my high expectations. I feel like someone should break from the pew, shake a tambourine and yell "JESU! OUR JOY! WE DESIRE YOU! LORD YOU BRING US JOY LIKE WE NEVER HAD! HALLELUIA!"

A memory springs into mind: the last time I heard this song performed, it was by an old friend's son–a nine-year-old. He played it on, of all things, the *tuba*. At the time I thought it slightly plodding, but now I have to say that it would be a refreshing pick-me-up to have Harley here, his cheeks swollen like a puffer fish, his eyes bulging. He could stomp around the church blowing his tuba and we could strut around behind him in follow-the-leader fashion.

My daughter leans into me. "This song is not at all captivating."

Captivating–I love it when my kids use interesting vocabulary words.

Now the Mummer's parade comes to the top of the center aisle, careful not to break formation. They're getting ready for something. Ah, the Gospel reading. One of the robed black men holds a Bible in front of his face while the Archbishop begins the reading. It's the story of the prodigal son–sung on one note the entire way through. This is a long reading–a *really* long reading. I estimate about 500 words...all sung on one note...the same note, that is...over and over and over...yep...he's the proverbial one-note guy...just has the one...

Well, it is a good story. And the father is certainly more sensitive to his sons than say, God was, in that dreadful Cain and Abel business.

After the Gospel reading, a small group of latecomers are allowed to enter and take seats before the sermon commences. Two are clearly tourists wearing bright floral shirts, baseball caps and sporting backpacks. Do they ever look out of place in this scene.

"I would like to talk with you about forgiveness this morning." One of the black priests has taken to the pulpit, which is built up in the air, somewhat in the middle of the room. I've always liked those types of pulpits–one probably couldn't help but share lofty ideas, being nearly airborne in one of those babies.

"If there is one sin that keeps us out of the gates of heaven it is forgiveness. Some of us find it easy to do, but many of us struggle with it. The reading we heard this morning is difficult for us....it goes against what we understand. Why should the father forgive the son? He only wanted his inheritance and he squandered so much. Our first response is, 'that's not fair.' And clearly, the other son is upset and feels the same way.

If we look at it in a different light, we have all strayed from God in one way or another. God has given us everything. How many of us have prayed to win the Lotto?" (The priest raises his hand and chuckles that no one else has.) "How many of you wish a wealthy relative would pass and leave you a small fortune? Many of us pursue power and wealth because we want it now. We will do anything...even illegal things...because we want it now. There is nothing wrong with wanting to achieve in life, but many of us are impatient and feel that we must have more and more."

I'm not sure about Bahamians, but I think he just described ninety percent of the American population.

"God tells us that His forgiveness if for everyone. Those of us who are struggling need not worry...we are not losing anything by others benefiting because all that He has is already ours. What is for you, you will get. Many of us spend time looking at others. God reminds us that what is yours no one can take. It has nothing to do with our relationship or the covenant between you and me....I have enough that all can have everything that they need....I am all Powerful."

This sounds good, but I can't help but wonder about those in other countries who don't have enough food, and who are comparing themselves to us Americans. Do they have all that is theirs? By consuming a huge percentage of the earth's resources and maintaining such a highly extravagant lifestyle, we take plenty from others. Are they supposed to be content with spiritual sustenance alone?

"He also tells us that we are His...we were made for Him. But He gives us an opportunity to *choose* to be His. Some of us, because of the pressures of the world, don't make that choice...we say, 'I'll do it my way.' But some come to our senses."

Here again, it sounds good, but I'm not sure it covers all the bases. One thing that almost always seems to be missing from sermons about will and choice is a good old-fashioned psychodynamic analysis of the situation. Why is it that ministers so rarely talk about the things that keep people from being good, honest and loving souls? It seems so simplistic to say that some people "come to their senses," while others don't. The stark reality is that most of us *learn* our bad habits. We *learn* not to have humility and a belief in something Bigger. And most importantly from my perspective, we *learn* our unloving ways.

In order to be able to receive the grace of God, or to tap into the "still, small voice," we must come into adulthood with a certain amount of mental and emotional health. Those who don't may "choose" Christianity, but it is often a warped form of the faith and one that causes even more psychological damage.

I know that this minister and indeed most religious leaders are asking us to surrender ourselves to God...to marvel at the world that has been made for us...to love others as ourselves and to devote ourselves to service. But that's a tall order for the millions of people who have learned not to trust those in authority...who have been emotionally, physically or sexually abused...who are jaded by a run-away culture that can't slow down and take their needs into account in a caring and gentle way.

What I want is for some minister to tackle the complexities of why it is so hard for us to truly be people of faith–the complexities that aren't so easy to tackle, like our psychological and social development. Once we've seen the whole picture, *then* maybe we can start to make choices.

"How often we wrong God...we do the same thing over and over and over, and each time we say, 'God, forgive me.' And don't we believe we are forgiven? We become a new creation, as though we did nothing wrong before. At the human level, we have to forgive our brothers and sisters who have wronged us...we need to put whatever wrongs they have done into the sea of forgetfulness and start anew."

I just realize something very impressive: the minister has been giving his sermon without any notes at all. He must be the "Most Able to Think on His Feet Reverend."

He places his hand on his chest in a gesture that is very endearing. "But you and I know how hard it is...God says, 'I don't want you to do it on your own strength...I'll help you.' What causes us not to forgive is that we remember the hurt and find it difficult to forgive. I ask God to help me forget the pain...then I can more easily forgive. As we come together today, let us ask God to pour His Holy Spirit into us...to give us the strength and grace, the courage to forgive as He has forgiven us. We cannot be truly reconciled with God if we have things between each other. So let us pray that we can forgive so we can be partakers of

God. We cannot do it on our own strength. With blessings, I wish you in His name, Amen."

The Reverend crosses himself and climbs down.

Well, it got much better toward the end. He did finally get a bit more psychologically sophisticated when he talked about how memories of pain interfere with our ability to forgive. I still don't think it's enough to ask God to give us the strength to "forget the pain." I think the pain has to be grieved and purged through tears and with the help of someone who listens and understands–compassionately. It doesn't have to be the person who wronged us, it doesn't have to be a therapist or counselor...it could be anyone.

Here's a case in point: a friend's father is on his deathbed at the age of 94. He had a horrific childhood; he was physically abused by an alcoholic father and emotionally abused by both his father and his mother. His older brother was the favored one and was given the family farm, while he was turned out in the streets. His parents were sadistic, and needed someone to pound on to make themselves feel better. He had become their whipping post. This man never beat his own children–to some extent he was able to stop the cycle of abuse by not hurting them. On the other hand, he also had nothing to give them emotionally. He was often ruminating in his own head, and his wife and children knew that he was consumed by anxiety and pain, even though he refused to talk about it. This man is extremely religious and faithful–he went to church every Sunday and prays everyday. But he has never met the pain directly and dealt with it, and it has plagued him his whole life. He grew up when there was no such thing as therapy or *Oprah*, or anything to help him grieve and understand. Now, he lies on his deathbed, haunted by memories from his past–terrified of offending the nurses and worried that they won't take care of him if he asserts himself in any way.

What happens when the parents of the prodigal son are sadistic and manipulative? The story doesn't cover that aspect of things. Ask God for help, yes, but not to simply "forget" the pain. God has to direct us by putting us in touch with the people who can understand our pain and help us work through it.

There's my three cents.

We recite the Nicene Creed, have another responsive prayer, listen to the "Concluding Collects," and then we are asked to give the sign of peace to our neighbors.

All of a sudden there is great energy in the room as people greet each other with handshakes, some hugs and a few kisses. Unlike the Presbyterians who like to remain sessile like a plant and only greet those in their immediate physical sphere, these Episcopalians are milling about, moving from pew to pew. The organ starts to pound out something and many people return to their pews and sing along. It must be some standard way to end the sharing of the peace--everybody seems to know the words my heart.

A few people totally ignore the fact that the music has started, and continue to make the rounds, walking from pew to pew, sharing the peace with as many people as possible. I like that. It's understandable that in such a highly traditional service with so many formalities, people would want to bask in the freedom that comes from simply strolling around and connecting with their friends in a more intimate and spontaneous way.

When the song ends, everyone sits and the Archbishop stands at a microphone very near the people in the front rows.

"Good morning!" he says heartily. "Welcome everyone to the fourth Sunday in Lent. Those of you who have been observing a vigorous Lent, the church invites you to take a break after the service and join us in the garden for some refreshments and a chance to meet others. We have a couple here from Lerochi...we'd like to welcome them...and another couple from Madrid...."

The Archbishop waits as the different people stand up and receive polite applause from the congregation.

"Any other visitors this morning? Please stand and let us know who you are..."

"I'm Randal Wickson from Vancouver, Canada," a tall, handsome man stands and says in a commanding voice.

People clap.

"I'm Mary Ellen Petrowski from New York City," a woman offers.

Again, applause.

"BOB AND JUDY WILSON FROM GAW-GIA " a man calls from the back. He's one of the late-comers who is dressed in the loudest yellow and blue tropical-style shirt I've ever seen. People clap and chuckle. I'm not sure if the accent, the yelling or the shirt is triggering the giggles.

My daughter is looking at me expectantly, wondering if I'm going to stand and announce our presence. Not after Sponge Bob Wilson in the yellow shirt–our fellow American.

The Archbishop continues to make announcements. He has a beautiful speaking voice and is very skilled at talking from the top of his head. "I'd like to thank Mrs. Phelps, our accompanist on the piano...ah, there she is...thank you very much."

He goes on to talk about the upcoming church dinner, he offers birthday greetings to a few people, he shares his hopes for peace in Haiti, Iraq and the Middle East. In a world where, increasingly, there seems to be so much noise pollution: leaf blowers, thumping music, traffic, jet engines...his voice is so incredibly mellifluous and soothing. I could just close my eyes and listen to him speak for the longest time.

"On the 16th of next month, my wife and I will be leaving for three weeks in the Middle East. Please keep us in your prayers. I'd like to make an appeal for food items. We are continuing to put baskets together for the less fortunate. Also, I'd like to extend a warm welcome to Mrs. Allene Campbell...she's been away from us for awhile and now we're happy to have her back."

Directly across the aisle from us, an elderly black Bahamian woman stands slowly, dressed in a very fancy navy blue dress and matching hat. She seems somewhat shaky on her legs, and her voice is old and cracking, but she seems determined to stand and waves to the congregation. "Tank you," I hear her say quietly.

"I believe that concludes our announcements," the Archbishop says.

The organ begins gearing up for another blast-fest. People are starting to sing the "Offertory Hymn" while ushers with wicker baskets come around. This little of touch of wicker is a reminder that outside this building are beaches with gorgeous white sand, translucent jade-colored water that is so clean you can see to the bottom of the ocean, conch fritters and grouper sandwiches to be had, heated swimming pools and hot tubs and snorkeling and massage and...*so what they heck are we doing in here?*

It's been at least an hour and as I glance at the bulletin, it doesn't appear that things will end anytime soon. Still to come are the Offertory Prayer, Eucharistic Prayer, Lord's Prayer, Communion, Agnus Dei, Organ Communion, Communion Hymn No. 326, Communion Anthem, Jesu, Joyance of My Heart (harmony arranged by J. S. Bach), Recessional Hymn No. 296 and the Postlude: Fugue in G Minor BWV 578 by J.S. Bach.

I look over at my daughter and she is being so patient. Not many twelve-year-olds would want to sit in a stiff-butted church, or any church for that matter, while on a vacation island, the blessed sun shining outside and happy people splashing in the warm waters.

I lean over and whisper in her ear, "I think I've had enough church for today, how about you?"

She smiles gratefully.

We sneak out the back and within thirty minutes we've gotten fish and chips to go, run to our hotel room, changed and we're back on the beach.

God is so very present in the delicious food, the sound of the surf and the feel of the water, buoying us up and rocking us back and forth.

Well, I can't say that I was bowled over by the Episcopal experience. It all seemed to me like a British wannabee kind of thing. Don't get me wrong, I appreciate refinement and it was wonderful to see wealthy, educated blacks and whites worshiping together harmoniously. I just don't always care for the British approach to things, which can be reserved and not very warm. I'm afraid that in the states, it might be more of the same, without the accents.

Later that evening, we're downtown again. We've just purchased some Haagen-Daas, served to us by a three-hundred pound employee who had obviously been sampling the goods one too many times. Given that I've been here for nearly a week, running, swimming, snorkeling, walking, doing the Reverse Recliner, and still I seem to have gained a few pounds, it appears I could do without the Haagen-Daas myself.

As we round the corner near the Episcopal Church, we see the Archbishop and a few other men in robes, smiling and laughing with a group of people, while some teenagers climb aboard a van. One of the priests gets in with them–obviously a field trip is in the works. Where do you go when you're on an island that's 6x10 miles in size?

I walk over with my daughter and make my way to the Archbishop. He is talking with someone but makes room for me to join in as soon as he sees me.

"Don't let me interrupt," I say.

"That's all right. I'll see you later," the woman says who has been talking to him.

He turns to me and smiles.

"Hi, I was here this morning for the 9:00 o'clock service," I say.

"What's your name?" he asks me.

"Ruth Laker. We're here from Philadelphia."

"Philly! You must have been sad to see Veteran's Stadium go."

"Excuse me?"

"I saw the imploding of the stadium."

"Oh...yes...well, when you've gotta go, you've gotta go..." I have no idea what the man is talking about. I change the subject. "It looks like some type of excursion is going on this evening."

"Yes, the youth group is going to a concert."

"I see. I was really impressed by the Reverend's ability to speak this morning without any apparent notes." I say.

"That was Father Ebong. Yes, we sometimes do that."

"Well I've been to a lot of churches as part of some research I'm doing for a book, and I can tell you that there are a lot of ministers who simply can't preach, even with their sermons written out word for word."

He smiles. "I know, it's true."

"Well, please tell Father Ebong that we were impressed that he spoke spontaneously."

"I will. How much longer are you staying?" he asks.

"Just one more day," I say with a sad face.

"Have a safe trip home!"

We thank him and head off with our ice cream cones.

It must be strange to live on an island and have all these visitors who come to your land to walk around in flip flops and beach wraps. Who stick their heads into your house and stare and point and then walk off sucking on their slushies. Who may share a few words with you and then fly away and never come back.

In our case, I've been informed by my daughter that we *will* be coming back, and soon, although I don't think it has much to do with the one hour she spent with the Episcopalians.

Episcopalian

#	Dimension of Church Experience	Rating
1)	Is parking close and convenient?	7
2)	How beautiful is the worship space?	10
3)	How comfortable is the seating?	8
4)	How welcoming and friendly is the congregation?	7
5)	How enjoyable and uplifting were the musical aspects of the worship?	6
6)	Does the leader have a pleasant speaking voice and does he/she make sense to me?	7
7)	How clean are the bathrooms?	7
8)	How interesting are the people in the pews to stare at?	7
9)	How tolerant to many ways of seeing and doing things does this group appear to be?	8
10)	Would I feel comfortable with how this group would spend my money?	7
11)	How close to God did I feel in this space?	2
12)	Did I smile more than once during the experience?	3
	Total	79

moviechurch.com

A strange postcard came in the mail advertising a church that meets in the Royal Cinemas 28. It was very cleverly written, and read:

If You Join Us For Easter, Here's What You'll Find:

-People still depressed the Eagles didn't make it to the Super Bowl
-A place for everyone—Catholics, Protestants and Skeptics
-A church faithful to the Bible *and* relevant for the 21st century
-Fun and secure classes for kids simultaneous with each service
-Rockin' stuff for your teenagers
-Casual, relaxed atmosphere
-A live band playing seriously good music
-No perfect people allowed

I like the sound of the ad and I'm intrigued. It is beyond me how a church could ever base itself in a huge movie cineplex compound, but my husband informed me that Catholic mass is offered at a flea market that he likes to frequent, so I guess God can be found anywhere, even while we're waiting in line to buy Goobers and Raisinets. This church appears to go by two names: "moviechurch," and "The Christian Meadow Community Church."

As it turns out, the week that I'm free to go happens to be the BIG day in Christianity. Resurrection day. I'm not thrilled about the idea of spending Easter morning inside a dark movie theater, but it turns out to be raining and generally nasty outside, so it doesn't much matter from the weather standpoint.

Easter is my favorite holiday. It's not just that I like the resurrection story and the promise that it holds--it's great to feel spring in the air and to see everyone coming out of winter hibernation. It's also not been an easy holiday to commercialize, although yesterday I did see a person in a tacky bunny suit, standing on the street and waving in front of the Rite Aid. Everyone was waving back and pointing to him or her from their cars. As I rounded the corner in my car and passed, I don't know what made me do it, but I shook my fist angrily at the bunny and scowled. I wasn't angry at all...I just wanted do something other than what was expected of me under the circumstances.

The CMCC has three services, so I choose the second and drive over without my family, who are going to meet me at another church a bit later. Attending a "moviechurch" requires some reconnaissance.

The blending of American cinema and religion seems novel to me, although some might argue that we worship our entertainers and look to movies for information about how to live our lives. Then there is the whole phenomenon of Mel Gibson's *"Passion of Christ"* movie, which happens to coincide with this Easter. Here is a serious attempt to use cinema to infuse religion in the masses. Mel even had little mini-movies sent to churches all over the U.S. of A., where the narrator didn't hesitate to suggest that one invite a friend to the "neutral territory" of the movie theater, presumably for evangelical purposes. I didn't go see it because nearly every review I read trashed it. For an evangelistic outing, it's got to get at least three stars.

Well, one thing is for sure, when a church worships at a cinema, it's no longer "neutral territory." And as I drive my old faithful to the Royal Cinema 28 on a soggy Easter morning, I am presuming that it's not merely to be entertained.

I have no idea what to expect as my car climbs the slight hill leading to the Cineplex. The blue neon that usually highlights the perimeter of the huge mausoleum-like structure is not aglow–a tasteful touch, if one can speak of movie theaters and worship in terms of "taste" without being oxymoronic. Surprisingly, the parking lot is at least half full, which is saying something since the cinema parking space is roughly the size of Rhode Island.

As I make my way to the entrance, I see that everyone is going in through the "exit" hallway and not through the regular entrance way. There is a small sense of relief in this, because I was afraid that I might have to buy a ticket for worship service, and I didn't know what I'd say: "One for the 9:45 moviechurch?" or simply "One for Jesus, please?"

A boombox is situated on a table just outside the exit-entrance, blasting some Red Hot Chili Peppers. This is surprising. I mean, having rock music at church isn't radical, but I'd assume that it would be Christian rock of some sort. Does all music qualify for this "welcome" boombox? Would Rod Stewart's "Do You Think I'm Sexy?" be fair game? Madonna's "Like a Virgin?" Certainly they'd have to draw the line at the Nine Inch Nails, "I Want to F---You Like An Animal."

Inside, there are lots of greeters with white name tags. A woman named "Judy" asks if I need help, which is nice, since I'm sure I look disoriented. The concession area has been corded off, and without popcorn and a water I may not be able to focus.

"Is this your first time here?" she asks.

"Yes, can't you tell," I chuckle.

"We get lots of new people every week," she smiles.

"I have to ask–why are you meeting here in the movie theater?"

"Oh, we're building a new church. We've just grown so fast that we needed a larger space."

"*I* see," I say with more than a little relief.

"See, over here are the plans for the new buildings–it will be on nineteen acres near Morganville."

I nod and look at the layout of the new church. It is indeed impressive. I'm so happy to know that this isn't some new type of hybrid–worshiptainment–like infommercials became in the late 1980s, that I'm more than willing to look over the plans for the new facility.

Judy orients me toward various food tables–they've got punch, juice, coffee, tea, doughnut holes, lemon cake, muffins, cookies. I decide to pass on the breakfast sugars and head toward the actual theaters. Signs indicate which theater you belong in. One is for "children 4-8" another for "8-12" ....ah, here we go, "Adults."

Very loud rock music is coming from the room as I head into the entrance hallway. A man with a cool headset is waiting to greet me and hand me a Bible. I take it and look up into the theater room. The place is packed. There must be over 400 people in the space, standing and clapping to the music. I start to head up the wide steps, having some difficulty finding a seat.

There is something ironic about this moment only because just a week before I was walking up the same steps with my husband, taking our seats at the top of the room for the opening night of "*Hellboy.*"

I finally find a space at the far end of a row. I have to squeeze past a young couple in their early twenties–both with jeans and sneakers on. I'm suddenly feeling very matronly in my long Easter dress, off-white pumps and sweater. As I glance around, I notice that no one is in anything resembling holiday finery. I can't see one pastel hat, suit or tie–just a sea of people dressed like they're going....to the movies.

> *"I'm resting on a sure foundation*
> *It's You, It's You Lord,*
> *You're the rock of my salvation!"*

The ad didn't lie: there is an eight-person band in the front of the theater and they are pretty good, although I could do without the tinny sound of the two electric guitars. The crowd is not as into the music as one would be at a concert, but then they're not serving beer. Most people are standing awkwardly, trying to loosen up, but not sure how to do it. Others clap a bit. The young woman next to me is clapping, but doing it so absently that she isn't anywhere near in time with the beat of the music. The band consists of six males and two females. The females are in the traditional "back-up" singer position, while one male is on the lead mic. His voice is smooth and clear–a nice tenor in the Michael Bolton range, but he's not actually Michael Bolton which is a plus. When the song is over, the crowd claps politely. No one goes crazy or flicks their lighters.

The lead singer speaks with a soothing smile. "When I heard this next song it didn't connect with me cause it's about enemies and I thought, 'I don't have an enemy in the world!' But I realized that an enemy is anything that can get the best of us...our finances, traffic, anything could be an enemy if we let it." The band gears up and the singer lays into it:

> *"My hope is You*
> *Show me Your ways*
> *Guide me in truth*
> *In all of my days..."*

The guy in front of the electric keyboard is shaking a tambourine ala Tracy from the "Partridge Family." Unlike Tracy, he seems to just be going through the motions. He lacks the finesse she had at knowing how to draw tone out of her instrument - at times with immense power - then with a tender sweetness.

The song is over and the leader of the band takes us quickly into a word of prayer. "Father in heaven, we *do* need you. As this service goes on, reveal to us how we need you and help us to trust you to lead us where we need to go. Amen."

Another man comes to the microphone. "Now we're at the part of the service where we worship with finances. If you are moved to do so, please share your gifts with God."

As a small army of ushers come out, men and women, all dressed in khaki pants and jean shirts, a film starts to play on the screen. A teenage girl is looking in the refrigerator, when her parents and younger brother come up to her, dressed very formally and looking like smiling robots.

The girl peers at them suspiciously. "Why are you dressed up?"

"We're going to church, dear," the father says with a frozen smile on his face.

"Why are you going to church?" she asks, again, with suspicion in her voice.

"We don't need a reason to go to church," the mother says, also smiling strangely.

"Is it Christmas? Cause if it is, it snuck up on me and I don't have anything for any of you." the girl tells them.

"No, it's not Christmas," the father says with his unbroken smile.

"Is it Easter?" the girls asks.

The film ends abruptly and everyone laughs.

Immediately, signs are flashed up on the screen offering different information: the egg hunt at 12:45 today at a local park, the fact that there is no softball practice today, the IMPACT group of grades 6-8 won't be meeting this week, "Scrap it, Stamp it" for women will be meeting on Tuesday, an upcoming baptism class and another called "Starting Point." Cool recorded music is accompanying the announcements.

Wow. I was wrong. This *is* a strange new hybrid called "worshiptainment."

Once again our band is in place. They start to sing–this time with a flashy Power Point show going on behind them. Before there were pictures to accompany the songs, but now it's all about the words. The song is one of those existential-whammy-type pieces, the lyrics designed to snap us to attention about the brevity of our time on this earth.

> *Don't close your eyes to life,*
> *Yesterday is dead and over*
> *This is your life*
> *Are you who you want to be?*

All of the words are incorporated into the Power Point show. Some of them float down into the screen, others bounce away. Some disintegrate. A few words start small and grow and grow until they fill the entire screen with their ominous presence. Like when they sing, "Don't close your eyes to life." "Life" starts small and then grows and grows until it smacks you right in the face.

LIFE!!

Having been cursed with a precocious sense of the melancholy, I've been contemplating my death since I was about four, so the song isn't zinging me so much. While I'm sure many of the people in this theater might be blithely coasting through their lives, not thinking too much about the big picture or fretting over what's to come, I would not be among them. They can probably use this existential wake-up call. I, on the other hand, am a good candidate for medication.

The song is over. There is more polite clapping and the lights come on. A young man, who appears to be not more than thirty, comes to the microphone. He is tall, well-built and wearing a long-sleeved shirt and dress pants, without a tie. On his feet are some nice-looking tasseled loafers. He has a mop of dark brown hair, which is conservatively short on the sides and a bit longer on the top. It's swept across the top of his head to one side. I'm thinking that his hair must somehow symbolize the political and spiritual leanings of the group: as centrist as they can be– young and fun, but still serious about Christ and God. His face is large and has rather large features as well: big eyes, close set, a sturdy nose and full mouth.

"A philosopher and statistician named Susan Skolnick has devoted her life to the study of risks. She has written *The Book of Risks* and given how she describes it, we would have to conclude that many of us suffer from what she calls "risk lock." In other words, we're afraid to go anywhere or do anything."

As soon as this gentleman (presumably the pastor) starts talking, the screen behind him goes into action. When he mentions the book, a picture of it is flashed on the screen. The words "risk lock" appear, to further emphasize what he is talking about. This church appears to be, in large part, about audio-visual aids.

"Everything is risky. If you're afraid of taking risks, then my friends, you've chosen the wrong species. You could very easily become one of the 500,000 people who end up in the hospital every year because they fall out of bed. You could be one of the 600,000 who sustain injuries from the furniture in their dens. You could be one of the 20,000 people who need to visit the doctor after receiving serious paper cuts from handling their money!

Eileen Guder writes that, "you could do all the safe things," and he reads a huge list, "and then break your neck in the tub and it would serve you right!"

Everyone chuckles.

"Today we're kicking off a series called 'Living Your Best Life.' Now I want you to imagine something, if you would. I want you to imagine yourself when you were 10-15 years younger. If you're fifteen-years-old, that might be difficult, but try it. Now I want you to imagine that younger you sitting across a coffee table from the you who you are now. Ask yourself, 'what were your dreams?' 'Have you attained them?' See what the younger you has to say."

    I imagine myself at twenty-five. I'm not sure what I had was a "dream," but rather a "self-imposed mandate." I would become a psychologist and help people because that is what I was good at: sorting out people's emotional messes and being strong for others. I was naturally empathic and good at giving others structure.

    "God would say, 'I created you to do great things.' Have you done those things? Turn in your Bibles to Matthew, Chapter 14, verses 22-33. This is one of my favorite Bible stories. Jesus knew that he'd have to pull his disciples out of a place of safety. He sends them out in a boat–kind of pulls a trick on them–while he goes off to hang out on a mountain top and pray. Hear the word:

    "....and when he had sent the multitudes away, he went up into a mountain apart to pray: and when the evening was come, he was there alone. But the ship was now in the midst of the sea, a considerable distance from shore, buffeted by waves, for the wind was contrary. And in the fourth watch of the night, Jesus went unto them, walking on the sea."

    The pastor finishes the story, which ends with Peter walking out to Jesus, losing his faith, and then being rescued by him.

    "Hey, do something for me. Flip your program over and write these principles for me. There are three primary principles I want you to get from this verse: 1) You'll never stray so far that Jesus can't find you. Mae West, the famous actress of years back-some of you may remember her? She once said, 'I used to be Snow White, but I've drifted.' Many of us can probably relate to that. But consider the words of this scripture again.... 'considerable distance....buffeted by waves....the fourth watch.' The disciples were out in a boat far from anyone, the waves coming up and around them ominously...and it was the fourth watch....in the old system they'd have people who would watch for boats between different hours and the fourth watch was between 3 and 6 in the morning. No one wanted to be out at this time because you couldn't be seen and those who were on watch were never awake anyway! So this was a very unnerving situation for the disciples. But Jesus came to them nevertheless, and folks, he'll come to us too."

    I see that many people are taking notes. The bulletin, which interestingly enough, the pastor called a "program," is a big piece of paper folded over like an ad flyer, with pictures of funny people and a movie reel going all about it. There's a small space for notes on the back. It's not nearly as extensive as what we received at the Baptist Temple, but the concept seems to be the same–to get people involved with their pens and pencils.

"Here is the second principle: 2) If you want to walk on the water, you've got to get out of the boat. You know, for a long time, I think I misinterpreted this story. I always thought Peter was fearful and without faith, but Peter wasn't the guy with the least faith. Who had the least faith in this story?"

No one says anything.

Four hundred people sit totally mum.

As a former teacher, I know how painful this moment can be. I call out, "the guys who stayed in the boat!"

"Yes, the disciples who didn't even bother to get out of the boat and go to Jesus were the ones with the least faith! At least Peter GOT OUT OF THE BOAT! Many of us are stuck in the boat. For some of you, the boat is your job. I had a friend who was working for GM, making six figures, and he told me, 'Joe, every day I go into that job I die a little spiritual death...every day a little bit more....' So I asked him, 'Well, what is that you really want to do?' And he told me, 'I want to build decks.' And like a good friend I said, 'What are you crazy? You can't build decks! You make six figures! You'll be broke!' But then after I got that out of my system, I told him that he should build decks, that he should follow his passion and his dream. And you know what, he did start building decks and now he has a very successful business of his own."

I'm totally engaged in this man's sermon, or as they call it in the program, the "message." Sounds less pompous than "sermon." I love stories where the person just up and leaves a job or walks away from something that was confining them. I did it myself.

"I love this church...lots of people at this church quit their jobs...all the time!"

People chuckle.

"I'm serious! We have people constantly quitting their jobs because they want to change their lives–they want to do something amazing. We had one person who wanted to go to medical school, so she quit her job, and she and her entire family moved to the Caribbean so she could go to medical school."

I'd go to the Caribbean to work at McDonald's...one day a week.

"Another person quit his job and became one of our ministers...my friend Don MacCabe. Remember Don, when we were meeting back in our living rooms, and I told you you'd make a great pastor? And now here he is!"

People clap.

"Maybe your boat is your relationship. I've got a heart for singles....people who are single and around 30. They're getting the message from our culture, not God, that they've got to get married fast. They're willing to cut character corners, because, hey, it's better than being alone on a Saturday night. I want to say to you, 'No, it's not!' Don't just settle for anyone. There are people out there in relationships that they have no business being in...just because they think they have to have someone—anyone! Be in dialogue with God and that person will come to you, if and when it's time."

I think he's absolutely right. And besides, even when you're married, you often spend Saturday nights at home, lying in your bed reading a book on Zen meditation practices, while your husband is downstairs in his office watching *Ankle Biters*, a movie about dwarf vampires that knock people down and then suck blood out of their ankles.

But that's just a hypothetical.

"For those of us who are married, God says don't get out of the boat—unless you are being abused—but get out of the boat of mediocrity in your marriage."

Now here I don't know what to think. Does God really tell us that people can leave a marriage if they're being abused? Where is that in the Bible? I think that's the position modern day clergy have taken because they know that they would lose all credibility if they told women to stay with abusive men in this day and age. I mean, clergy used to tell women to suck it up all the time. Now, we've progressed. But is that because of some new revelation from the Bible, or just because we know it in our hearts to make sense? Why can't we just say that the Bible may not have addressed this issue, but we believe this as thinking, spiritually evolving people? Isn't it okay for us to be different than we were 2000 years ago? Isn't it okay to come to realizations that might not be in the bible, or may even go against something in the bible that we just know isn't good for us?

"Whatever it is that is your boat, God is asking you, 'When are you going to get out of that boat?!' It you don't act now, one day you'll be sitting in your recliner with shriveled hopes or dreams because you never got out of the boat! GROW OR DIE A SLOW EMOTIONAL AND SPIRITUAL DEATH!"

There's silence for a few seconds. It's a powerful, well-placed silence.

"Number three: The best person to follow is Jesus. Right now, it seems that everyone is into the religion of the month club. One minute it's Buddha, the next it's Mohammad...but when we're in deep trouble, we call to *Jesus*."

The minister goes on to tell a story about how his son cut his eye and how when they took him to the doctor, they were given the choice of having it done there, or going to a plastic surgeon. Without hesitation, he and his wife chose the plastic surgeon because we always want the experts. His point: we should choose Jesus because he's the expert.

"All those other guys...Krishna, Buddha...all great guys...very smart and also very *dead!* Jesus rose from the dead and lives on and he is the one we turn to in time of need. I want to ask you to make a commitment to come for the next four weeks–a commitment to God and a commitment to Jesus. We're going to cover more topics in our series. Next week we'll talk about how to break the stranglehold of stress, then how to develop more meaningful relationships, how to quit your job and find your calling and then we'll talk about how to raise positive kids in a negative world. We hope to see you again."

The lights dim and the pastor goes into prayer. "God, I know there are many people here who have incredible gifts. When you made them, you looked down and smiled. Help us all to understand what those gifts are and to use them to the best of our abilities. We thank you for this time to worship together. Amen."

The rock star guy comes back to the microphone and explains to us about how communion will be done. Apparently, they do this every week. The ushers come around with traditional-looking communion plates and little cups in their racks. The denim shirts and tan khakis being worn by all the ushers are familiar...*oh, ye-es*...my son wears the same outfit when he works at Blockbuster.

As they pass the bread and cups around, it would seem that they have a lot of mouths to feed. The pieces of bread are actually teeny, tiny cracker squares, bigger than your pinkie nail, but smaller than a chicklet. I'm taking my communion rather absently because I'm still digesting the pastor's sermon, which really was a substantial portion of the time–25 minutes, just like the program indicated it would be. Amazingly, that 25 minutes flew by; this gentleman was extremely entertaining, his message was basically well-crafted and made very relevant to the listeners, and the use of the audio-visual aids added and didn't detract, like they so often can.

The end of the sermon was, for me, a bit disappointing. I don't think he made his third point very well. To say that in times of trouble we call on Jesus and not those other guys who are all very "dead," seems a bit weak to me. I want to believe in the resurrection as much as the next person, but we do need to respect that a majority of people in the world believe in reincarnation, which can be thought of as a form of life after death. The Dali Lama himself provides compelling evidence that he has lived previous lives. Yes, I'll call on Jesus because I'm a westerner and was raised in a Christian tradition and believe in the goodness of his teachings, but I won't discount that there are other forms of wisdom and maybe even other truths as valid as those taught by Christ. God is God, but there can be many messengers and teachers.

The rock band reassembles and asks us to stand for one last song. This time one of the two women is singing the lead part. Her voice is amazing-loud and commanding like the best of the women rockers. Melissa Ethridge couldn't do better! After she has sung a stanza or two, the male singer says into the microphone, "Have a great week–we'll see you next Sunday!"

Everyone gets up and starts to leave. I'm appalled that they could walk out on the woman as she finally gets a chance to shine. How *convenient* that the guy led all the songs in the beginning of the worship time, and throws her the bone at the end when everyone is up and leaving. She should quit–get out of the boat--and start her own Christian rock band with six women and two men in back-up positions.

Everyone is exiting now and there is a bit of a bottle-neck where people are returning their pens or Bibles. The people in the denim shirts attempt to make eye contact and say good-bye to as many people as possible but it doesn't look easy. I find myself being swept up with the herd and can't really break free until I'm in the outer hallway of the theater. I see a man with a headset on and I walk over to him. I'm open to this worship experience, but have to make sure this isn't like that Independent Baptist Super Church, where women have to sit in the back of the bus because we've got breasts and a vagina.

"Hi," I say.

"Hi-yes, can I help you with something?"

"Yeah...I'm wondering how many ministers you have at this church."

"I think there are three...but I'm not really sure...you could ask Joe...he's somewhere out here...there he is...you can see his head sticking up over everyone..." he laughs.

I thank him and move toward the man who had given the message. He is indeed a head taller than everyone else, which reminds me of Dilbert's observation that tall people will always make it far, regardless of their competency levels.

I walk over near Joe as he chats with an elderly couple. The older man is doing all of the talking, and has Joe in a question-and-answer headlock. The minister's patience is impressive, particularly since he periodically has to tell his daughter, a girl who looks to be about five, is wearing a fairy-like Easter dress and climbing all over things, to stop doing this or that.

Finally, the couple moves on and Joe turns to me. I shake his hand and tell him my name. He greets me pleasantly.

"I've been to another really large church like this one–Mt. Zion Baptist–and they didn't allow women to be ministers or leaders in the church. You're not into that whole 'Timothy and Titus' thing when it comes to women, are you?"

"Well, that's a trick question. We believe that the Bible is *the* word of God, end of question, but the *New* Testament tells us that there should be no distinction based on gender or race or anything else so we don't have any problem with that."

That same New Testament also contains Timothy and Titus, which the Independent Baptists use to keep women away from the real power, but I decide not to make that point. "Do you have any women ministers?"

"Molly, please put that down..." His daughter is now lifting a floor lamp and hoisting it up and down so that it seems as though it might come smashing into us at any second. "Not at this time. Give us about a year and a half. We've been growing so fast, we can barely keep up."

"You have so many people here...it seems to me that having women leaders would be very important for balance."

"Well, we do have a woman in charge of education..."

"Is she an ordained minister?"

"No. But we don't want to take someone just to have someone....we have to wait for the right person, who has the right character and the right background...Molly, *please stop playing* with that lamp!"

"There are a lot of great women coming out of seminary now—about half of graduates are women, aren't they? And they're still not getting the jobs..."

"Well, I've got my eye on a few women...it is just a matter of time."

I tell Joe that I'm doing research for a book on how to pick a church, and that I've been amazed to see how discriminated against women still are in the religious world. It's the glass ceiling phenomenon, only it's more like a glass partition around the pulpit. Women can do lots of things: they can teach Sunday School, they can be Choir Directors, Youth Leaders, Education Coordinators, but they aren't given their rightful place in the pulpit, where they should be at least half of the time. I wrap up my own hallway sermonette by reminding Joe that women are 51% of the population.

"And among church-goers they're about 60%, isn't it?" he asks me.

"That sounds about right....well Joe, I won't keep you any longer..."

"How did you find out about us?"

"Your postcard. It was very clever. And I enjoyed your message."

"Well, it was really nice to meet you," he says. "Let me know if I can do anything for you." He maintains eye contact with me for a few seconds and doesn't appear to be in any rush.

I felt very comfortable talking with this young man. Maybe he's the real thing.

I exit and head toward my car. The boombox is greeting the next throng of worshipers with some *Matchbox Twenty*.

A thought strikes me as I turn the key on the door to my car: *this is the future of religious worship in our country.* Out with the old: the yellowed hymnals, the stuffy organ, stiff pews, choir robes and suits and ties, the "thou shalt not " sermons and the shaming. In with the new: rock bands and "messages;" audio-visual aids; slick presentations on big screens; work sheets and assignments that help us with our personal development; casual clothes; and ample smatterings of good-natured humor. There's a new generation of worshipers and for them, worship has been sorely in need of an overhaul. That's why churches with these tight productions, packaged in a casual, rockin' format are overflowing with people.

The whole self-development aspect of the program was so central that they didn't even bother to mention the resurrection or the fact that Easter is celebrated because of that, or the fact that it *was* Easter Day. Easter was an afterthought at this church. They had things to do; power point shows to launch, songs to perform, homework assignments to give. Prayer, too, was also almost an afterthought. I spend more time throwing my change into the tolls at the turnpike than they spent on those two prayers.

Still, I can see how it could draw many people in. Americans want things prepackaged and delivered in a straightforward fashion. We're not about the subtleties so much. I must concede though, that this church experience did stimulate my thinking and whether or not it was their goal, I was entertained.

I liked Joe--his funny, gentle style. He seemed to like telling a story and he was good at it. I only worry that a leader at such a big, self-made church has the potential to go bad, like Jim and Tammy Faye Bakker. I worry that this could be another PTL Club in the making. Maybe this guy is humble and open-minded now, but as the masses adore him and flock to this church, there is a real danger. Absolute power corrupts absolutely. I've seen it time and again with doctors, professors, ministers, athletes–anyone who is adored by others.

The things he said about hiring a woman struck me as cotton candy: it was all puffed up but when you bit into it, there really wasn't anything there. I've heard many a liberated, professional man offer reasons as to why they haven't hired or promoted women and in the end, it all boils down to the same thing: they're still cemented in a good 'ole boy mentality, only they don't realize it. They're good 'young boys, and they think they're too hip to be discriminating–but they are. If Joe really wanted a woman to be a part of the primary leadership of the church, she'd already be there.

There are plenty of good women out there. *Plenty*. And it's going to take smart, strong men to help bring them into their rightful places of leadership in our culture, including in our churches.

Well, I have hope for Joe. I'm going to ask him to read this book. And I'm going to encourage him to hire not one token woman minister, but three, to match the three men who are now leading the church. If the church keeps growing, they'll need them.

moviechurch.com

Yup. The future is here.

moviechurch.com

#	Dimension of Church Experience	Rating
1)	Is parking close and convenient?	5
2)	How beautiful is the worship space?	0
3)	How comfortable is the seating?	8
4)	How welcoming and friendly is the congregation?	3
5)	How enjoyable and uplifting were the musical aspects of the worship?	6
6)	Does the leader have a pleasant speaking voice and does he/she make sense to me?	9
7)	How clean are the bathrooms?	8
8)	How interesting are the people in the pews to stare at?	4
9)	How tolerant to many ways of seeing and doing things does this group appear to be?	7
10)	Would I feel comfortable with how this group would spend my money?	4
11)	How close to God did I feel in this space?	2
12)	Did I smile more than once during the experience?	4
	Total	60

AN IDEA WHOSE TIME HAS COME.

United Church of Christ

Racing to attend Claremont United Church of Christ, I am met with the most incredible spring day one could imagine and involuntarily, my body grinds to a halt. The sun is shining, the air is warm with just a hint of a soothing breeze, birds are singing and the sky is a gorgeous blue! Couldn't I find an open-air church somewhere? Nothing would be more uplifting than to worship outside on a day like this!

Well, duty calls, so I carry on, only at a gentler pace.

This particular UCC church would be of interest to cartographers, particularly those who might fly around in helicopters and look at things from an aerial view. The building is old, late 1700's old, and as time marched on, things crept in closer and closer to the church. The road was oddly formed over time, so that it comes directly at the building, sharply cuts to the right and then continues alongside it. To anyone standing in the front door of the church, it must seem as though cars are playing a game of chicken; plowing right toward the building, then pulling away at the last second.

Then there is the matter of the graveyard. The very BIG graveyard. The close-to-ten-acres- of-graveyard, which surround the church on the three sides not taken up by the road. In fact there is no regular yard for this church–no space for swing sets or basketball hoops or picnic tables. Graves have swallowed all the land. There are old graves within inches of the black-topped parking lot, graves within a few feet of the church building on three sides, graves as far as the eye can see behind the church.

Here at Claremont UCC, the dead rule.

Finally, there is the black-top. The little bit of land that was left for the living was totally paved over. It doesn't seem like paradise, but they put up a parking lot. This means that there is black-top right up to the front steps, and parking spaces have been created at lots of odd angles, crammed in along the road, the building, the graves and two huge trees. Standing on the small patch of blacktop, looking at the sea of graves, I am reminded of a National Geographic special I saw, where the hippos and crocodiles who shared a watering hole were crowded in closer and closer together as the water dried up in the drought.

The bells are tolling as I head toward the door, which is a really nice thing. I love the sound of church bells calling the faithful to worship. There is something both comforting and exciting about tolling church bells. They say: "The human species is a marvel!" "We will continue on like our forebearers!" "There is so much more to life than your day-to-day worries!" "Come and taste the Divine!"

When I was in Delft, Netherlands last year, the bells in the old church tower played songs, but not religious ones. They played things like "We All Live in a Yellow Submarine," and Rod Stewart's "Maggie." Although I appreciated the innovative spirit of the Dutch, somehow it wasn't quite the same as what I feel this morning hearing the more traditional bells.

I pass a couple with two young girls who are working to get everyone out of the car and into the building. One of the little girls, the one still buckled into her car seat, is singing with a precociously strong voice, using vibrato and wailing away like a contestant on *American Idol*:

> *"AND I-E-I, WILL ALWAYS LOVE*
> *YOU-E-OU,*
> *WILL ALWAYS LOVE YOU-E-OU-E-OU!"*

Inside, a greeter gives me a weak handshake and little eye contact. That's actually a good sign. It means that this isn't one of those really needy or evangelistically-crazed congregations. The folks in the pews seem like your standard cross-section of middle-class, white suburban worshipers at a modest-sized traditional church: sixty percent are gray-haired and seem to have been planted in their spots for some time; another twenty percent are in late middle-age, and the remaining twenty percent are families with young children. The church isn't packed, but it has a respectable number of people considering the graveyard and all. Maybe it's some type of portal to the afterlife, but they're backed up with old people because there's no more room in the cemetery. When one of the neighboring farms is sold off, half the congregation will suddenly disappear.

The minister walks up to the podium and starts to make announcements. Now here is someone who might be considered "tall, dark and handsome." Even under his robe, you can see that he has broad shoulders and a big frame, and his hair is jet black. A commanding baritone voice informs the flock of things like the approval for the plastering of parts of the church and upcoming new member classes.

"Are there any other announcements for the good of the community? Then let us listen to God through music."

Listen to God through music? Does this mean that hymns are now considered the word of God too? It's so hard to keep up…

The organ plays a prelude, candles are lit, the pastor leads us in the Call to Worship and then we sing the opening hymn, "Come You Faithful, Raise the Strain." The choir enters as the hymn is sung, eight women and two men, all of them over sixty.

We proceed on with the Call to Confession, the Prayer of Confession, the Assurance of Pardon, the Praise Response and the Affirmation of Faith–all of which are done with audience participation and while standing–a looooooong time. Even with the jogging I've been doing lately, my legs don't seem to like this one bit.

Next the pastor reads the "Epistle Lesson," which is from the book of Revelations. I finally educated myself about "Epistles" after forty years of hearing the word. It means "letter" for the others of you who snoozed through Sunday school or didn't schlep to church at all. It's not necessarily a pretty word. One could easily mistake it for "pissed off," or "thistle," if heard from a distance.

The Cherub Choir gets up to sing "I'm Happy When I Praise the Lord." I can't hear them because they are singing softly like young children tend to do, and obviously the aspiring Whitney who was out in the parking lot isn't part of the group. The song has something to do with being a little lamb. They act out wagging their tails, clapping their hands, stomping their feet. I can't help but stare at one little girl, no more than six, who is wearing a sparkling dress with spaghetti straps, which reveals a lot of skin, and huge, dangling earrings with big fake lavender stones in them.

Boy, I'm not getting into this at all. I didn't feel grouchy twenty minutes ago when I was outside in the fabulous sun and perfect weather, but now I'm sinking into a foul mood. There is simply nothing the least bit inspirational about this church or the people in it. Maybe I'm just not willing to give them a chance because everything pales in comparison to the weather outside. It has been so bloody rainy and now it's hard to be inside on such a glorious day. I'm going to try to be more positive.

"Could the children come forward..." the minister asks.

A dozen tots come bounding down the aisles. Beside me, a little girl of about five has been spread out on the pew, lying on her belly, humming and circling random letters in a word search. Her grandmother leans over and asks her if she wants to go to the front for the children's sermon. They girl shakes her head no and continues to hum. Her little white tights and black paten leather shoes are flapping back and forth in time to her own music.

"Good morning," the minister says to the children.

"GOOD MORNING!" they scream.

I jump in fear.

"How are you?"

"**FINE!**" they scream again in unison.

Good Lord in heaven. What has been *done* to these children?

"Before I talk with you this morning, I want to share with you a reading from John." The minister starts a reading which goes on for several minutes. He clearly has little appreciation for the verbal comprehension level of his audience or for their attention spans. In fact, I'm getting a picture of this minister as a painfully stiff, militant guy who has next to no imagination. It's a shame because he had such promising shoulders.

I can't really see the children, partly because of where I'm sitting, and partly because my eyes are drooping shut. After some time, it becomes clear to me that if there is even one child who is still listening to this Bible reading and truly taking it in, then they are probably not humanoid. The reading offers the rather gruesome invitation on Jesus' part to let Thomas stick his finger in his wound to see that it is truly him.

"How many of you see that microphone over there?" the minister asks the children.

They all raise their hands.

"See it has a microphone...and a stand...and a cord...and...and it's plugged in..." He has been showing all the features of the microphone to the children. "Now, how many of you think that I'm wearing a microphone?"

All the children raise their hands.

That may not be how he wanted them to respond; he seems suddenly lost.

"Well, what about a phone? How many of you think I have a phone on my body?"

Again, they all raise their hands.

Again, the minister seems a bit taken aback.

"Yes, well, I do have a microphone and a cell phone...let me get it out here...I turned it off so it wouldn't bother us...it's in here somewhere...here it is...caught on my sleeve..."

The decision of the little girl next to me to forgo the "Moment For All Ages," as it's called in the bulletin, was wise indeed.

"We can't see the microphone and the cell phone, but I do have them...and sometimes we need to see to believe...we are blessed because we can see Jesus in each other and in the beauty of the earth. Let us pray..."

If there were newspaper reviewers for sermons this kind of thing wouldn't need to happen.

The children are dismissed by the Commandant, and head out the back, presumably to enjoy the delicious feel of freedom. Oh, how I wish I could go with them...

The choir stands and the organ begins to play. The conductor raises her arms and then...oh heavens! It's a nightmare of sounds–a horrid, swirling collection of screeches and bellows–as though eight cats and dogs have met in a back alley somewhere and just finished off several bottles of Boone's Farm. This is without a doubt *the worst church choir* I have ever heard in my life! No one is in tune, people aren't sure of their parts, random sounds are coming from all directions...If Simon Cowell were here he'd use only one word to describe it: ghastly.

The torture ends and we hear the strong voice of the Captain at the microphone–the microphone that everyone can see. "Oh Lord, we gather together on this beautiful spring day to worship you...open our hearts...our eyes...our ears and our souls."

There's one I've never heard: "open our souls."

It's sermon time. The minister is standing at the top of the middle aisle and adjusting the microphone on this robe–the microphone we're not supposed to know is there. He starts to walk slowly down the aisle. "Hey Cleopis...how much further to the tomb? I'm so tired of walking...there's a person over there...yeah, you can walk with us....excuse me? Cleopis, you explain to this guy what happened...(as an aside to the congregation) I can't believe this guy...he didn't hear about the crucifixion?...where's he been?...behind a rock or something?"

The minister has, by now, trudged slowly down the center aisle. He deserves points for doing something besides standing behind the pulpit, but he's not a natural born actor.

"Hey Cleopis...maybe...maybe he knows more than we think...he's...he's talking about everything that...that Jesus said...he has all this knowledge...hey, let's invite him to stay with us...the inn...the inn is just ahead..."

The pastor has now ploddingly circled the church for the second time and because I'm sitting in the back row, he's coming around right behind me.

I fantasize about all the funny things one could do as a parishioner at this point. You could jump up and follow him, the way Groucho Marx used to walk around behind people. You could write a small sign and hold it up so that only he could see as he passed–it might say something like: "DON'T LOOK UP!" And yes, it would be very juvenile, but you could gingerly tape a sign to his back as he passed by, one that said "Honk if you love Jesus..."

Well, it's official. Nothing excites me about this church–nothing. I'm starting to think that I might be more stimulated outside in the graveyard.

Hey, that's not a bad idea. It's a beautiful day...

The minister has reached what I expect is the climax of his sermon, which is delivered in an unfortunately anticlimactic manner: "...look, he's breaking the bread just like Jesus did....it *is* Jesus, Cleopis..."

I'm outta here.

Wow. Walking out the door of that church into the sunshine is amazing. It's last-day-of-school amazing. It's last-day-of-time-served amazing. It's leaving the DMV amazing.

The sunshine couldn't be more intoxicating. Something just feels so pure about the sun today–everything is really crisp and clear. It's probably because the temperature is perfect and now there's no wind. It's just me and the sun in total harmony.

It's easy to get started looking at the graves. One has only to step off the blacktop in any direction and there they are. The ones closest to the church appear to be mighty old.

MARY AND JACOB HOOK

Jacob was born just inside the 18th century: 1799. He died in 1854. Mary was a bit younger–born 1803 and died 1887. She lived a good long time without her man. I wonder how she felt about it. Maybe she was terribly lonely and never felt the same without him. Maybe she was glad to be rid of the bastard and danced on his grave. We'll never know...

And what's with that name–Jacob Hook? How many people do you know with the last name "Hook?" No one has the last name "Hook." They all died out with the Captain, I guess.

Other names also seem to have faded over the years: Custer, Grepps, Worman. I've yet to meet any of their ancestors. A few seem to have carried on: Shuler, Hawk, Greer.

As I move away from the church, the graves become newer and the names more familiar: Miller, Roberts, Sheeder. Very few graves have anything but the names and dates of the deceased on them.

Well, at least the dead and the living are consistently boring around here.

I scan the graveyard as a whole–trying to get the "graveyard gestalt," if you will. Only two things grab my eye in the larger picture: there are ten stone phalluses as tombstones and there is one grave off in the distance which looks totally bizarre and out of place.

Time to investigate.

Approaching the oddball grave, I notice that it has an arched stone–kind of like a cross between the Stonehenge figures and a Chinese letter. There are bright plastic flowers all about it, a swan, some little baskets with faded floral remains. Ah, this might explain it: NUCCI. Probably a south Philly Italian who migrated out to the country.

It's a shame really. Why can't graveyards be more...lively? What we need are people to do graveyard makeovers. I sit down against a tombstone and pull out my pad. After about twenty minutes of scratching, a crude poem is rendered which attempts to address this problem.

Graveyard Makeover

The makeover craze has infected our land.
Gay men are transforming us left and right hand!
Overlooked but in much dire need of a lift
Are the graveyards and all the poor souls who've been stiffed!

Little Tim Fester died when he was eight.
His tombstone, quite frankly, is not looking great.
A mechanical pony ride over his plot.
Kids could ride just by putting a dime in the slot!

The Baumgartner twins came and went the same day,
Grace always worked hard, Ruthie did play.
We'll plant a small garden with lounge chairs for reading.
Ruth's ghost can come back and do all of the weeding!

One little tombstone says only "Asleep,"
Poor fellow, his relatives must have been cheap.
We'll dig up the grave and we'll run an ID,
Then the name we'll display on a neon marquee!

The Dinwiddie family has quite a large plot
But their tombstones quite frankly aren't looking so hot.
Does death only come in this one shade of gray?
We'll paint them all jewel tones then use glitter spray!

When I die make sure I stay up with the trends
I want to impress all my new graveyard friends!
Just in case my ancestors will not fit the bill
A makeover budget's been placed in my will.

There might too many exclamation marks in the poem, but I think it goes with the whole makeover flavor.

Well, I think it's time to mosey on.

No church could compete with a day like today. God's handiwork is out here, not in there.

United Church of Christ

#	Dimension of Church Experience	Rating
1)	Is parking close and convenient?	8
2)	How beautiful is the worship space?	7
3)	How comfortable is the seating?	6
4)	How welcoming and friendly is the congregation?	3
5)	How enjoyable and uplifting were the musical aspects of the worship?	0
6)	Does the leader have a pleasant speaking voice and does he/she make sense to me?	1
7)	How clean are the bathrooms?	8
8)	How interesting are the people in the pews to stare at?	2
9)	How tolerant to many ways of seeing and doing things does this group appear to be?	5
10)	Would I feel comfortable with how this group would spend my money?	3
11)	How close to God did I feel in this space?	1
12)	Did I smile more than once during the experience?	0
	Total	44

Chapel on the Hill

A very sweet friend of mine, Ilsa, suggested that we might go to one more church before I wrapped up my search. She knew that thus far on my quest, women hadn't figured very prominently in the religious scene and she had heard of a church that was led by a woman who seemed to have a rather unusual style. Although she hadn't met her directly, she had heard a wedding described at which this minister officiated, and she remembered that it had something to do with Hawaii and bare feet.

Ilsa and I drive over to the Chapel on the Hill which, true to it's name, is a chapel situated on a slight hill. It looks old and quaint from the outside and nothing concerns me in particular except that there is only one car parked near the church. The lights are on, but it's not a bustling place.

Well, we're fifteen minutes early. I warn my friend that we might want to stay in the car until we see some other people coming. If no one else does show up, we can always peel out at the last minute and no one would be the wiser.

Ilsa and I share a bit of benevolent gossip, and as we are so engaged, five other cars pull in. It may not be a quorum, but at least we won't be the only ones. Gamely, we head into the church at 10:01. The front steps are painted a bright sky blue which is a refreshing deviation from the bleak color of concrete.

Stepping into the building, I am taken back to my Great Aunt Romaine's living room: each of the chapel windows has a deep sill on which are sitting such things as fancy dolls in shiny gowns and hats; teddy bears with parasols; candlesticks and lots and lots of glass votive candle holders; angel statues; pictures of Jesus; pictures of Hawaii; and enough dried flowers to make a barrel of potpourri. There are many pictures spread over the front wall, two-thirds of which are images of Jesus. A few feature Mary and her infant babe, and then there is a bright pink and purple rendering of the Hawaiian surf. Angels also play an important role in the wall art.

The altar table is covered by what looks like an antique pink tablecloth with lace edges. Pink seems to figure prominently in this church. The organ has been pushed up against a far corner in the front, at such an angle that it is obviously not going to be used. A severe-looking wooden "throne," which was probably once the minister's chair, has a plastic garland of white flowers wrapped up and down its frame with a large lace doily carefully draped over the back.

Seated in the pews are six people; one very old man in the front, an elderly woman; two middle-aged women and a young mother with a baby. Ilsa and I take seats on the right near the back, which isn't that far away in such a small space. At the front of the room, seated to the left of the altar, is a woman well into middle-age, who is attractive in a real estate kind of way. She's wearing a smart, gossamer blouse and skirt with a lovely tan, yellow and peach print. Her shoes are a beige pump that match very nicely. Her hair is dyed a definite blond and she has what looks suspiciously like a hairpiece clipped to the back of her head which gives her the full ponytail effect.

One of the women places a CD into a player at the foot of the altar.

Jesus, sweet Jesus,
How I love that wonderful name
Jesus, sweet Jesus,
He's worthy of his praises and his
name

When I was a teenager, I remember driving with my mother to a mall or the grocery store, and she would play this radio muzak which was so mindless, so vapid, so devoid of anything resembling passion or vibrancy or life, that I would almost cry out for her to turn it off. Somehow I never did, I suppose because I knew that it gave her pleasure.

Hearing the song coming from this CD player, I'm taken back to those moments in the car with my mom.

The woman with the blond hair is now coming toward us. She reaches into a bookcase alongside our pew and hands us each a flyer. Silently, she turns and walks back up front. Resuming her seat, she assumes a look of deep meditation: closing her eyes and lifting her face toward the light from the window.

I glance down at the pamphlet, which features a color photo of the blond woman–apparently in Hawaii, judging by the water and sky. Her hair is poofy on top, but has lots of little braids cascading over her shoulders, which seems more Caribbean than Hawaiian, but then, I'm not steeped in island styles and customs.   The pamphlet says the following:

The Reverend Debbie Lee Green
Aloha....
The Chapel on the Hill
Non-Denominational Church   In Jesus of Love

The Reverend Debbie Lee has bullets listed below her picture, which tell of her myriad of services: hands-on-healing (in the Name of Jesus of Love); Tapes of God's teachings; positive affirmations and encouragement and wedding services to name a few.

Inside the pamphlet, a story is printed. It would appear to tell the story of Reverend Debbie Lee, judging by the bits and pieces of sentences my eyes scan: "Reverend Debbie Lee Green is religiously devoted to helping all of God's children..." "Reverend Green was sensitive to God's words at an early age, but was unaware of the significance until adulthood..." "Reverend Green teaches the true meaning of ALOHA..." "In 1984, she first recognized she was an instrument for God..." "Reverend Green heard God say to her, 'you can help her...'" "Reverend Green walked into her grandmother's room and raised her hands in the air and said, 'Take all my love and energy and put it into this woman!'" "Reverend Green laid her hands on her and they became hot, but she did not understand what had occurred." "Reverend Green has had many wonderful and miraculous healings...." The pamphlet also tell us that Reverend Green was an abused child and entered into an abusive marriage, but by going within herself, she found her truth and beauty.

The pamphlet indicates she studied for the ministry from 1986 to 1992 and became an ordained minister on October 10, 1992. We are told that she worked at the Pennsylvania Department of Corrections which paved the way for her to be the minister she is today.

It's curious that she would mention the PA Department of Corrections by name, but not the place where she studied the ministry. It's also curious that her grandmother, on whom she performed her ground-breaking miracle, died the year before she became ordained and printed her nifty pamphlets. It's even more curious that the literature that she hands us to read about the "church," is almost entirely about Reverend Green.

"Please stand for the Lord's prayer," Reverend Green says in a business-like fashion. She reaches over and presses a button on what appears to be a 70's era tape recorder. The faded sounds of a well-worn tape start to play a barely audible accompaniment. The Reverend starts to sing in a full-bodied, deep alto-moving-toward-tenor:

Our Faaather who are in heaaaven,
Halloweeeed be they na-ame

Her voice is so bold that the contrast between it and the taped music is kind of like a muscle-car engine in a rusty little Volkswagen beetle. I start to join in–meekly–but there really isn't room for any other voice in the airspace. Reverend Green's has boldly filled it all up.

When she finishes, Ilsa and I look around...not quite sure what to do...when others sit down, we join them.

"Today's lecture is based on experiences I had this week...again with my experiences...I was going to see my mother...you know when you have to do something that you don't really feel like you want to do but you know you should do it so you push yourself through it...so I took her on some errands and then I was in this store shopping...Mom wasn't too happy that I left her out in the car...and this boy wanted to buy a baseball cap, and his father said to him, 'why do you want a baseball hat...you're no good at that anyway...'"

Three of the four women gasp and shake their heads in amazement.

"...and you know, the Holy Spirit was really working through me....I didn't have to go up to the Dad...I didn't have to say, 'Hello, I'm the Reverend Debbie Lee Green...' I just walked up to the boy and said, 'I really like your baseball shirt...' and 'is that your favorite team?'...and believe me, for me to talk baseball with anyone is a *miracle* because I know nothing about it..."

Reverend Green emits a very husky laugh.

"...and you know what? That child's entire disposition changed...I allowed God to use me as a buh-lessing at that moment, and that boy went from having a frown to a big smile on his face. He was down and I helped to bring him up. We are a buh-lessing and we need to start acting like a buh-lessing....his smile counteracted all the dark stuff that was there..."

I'm tempted to raise my hand at this point in the lecture and ask, "Could you elaborate on 'the *dark stuff*?'"

"Now when I say 'buh-lessing,' you immediately think of money...God send me money..." Debbie Lee lifts her hands and makes her fingers "rain down" as though money is falling from the sky.

I react to her presumptuous statement with slight indignation...how does she know what I think about when someone says "buh-lessing?" Then again, if God did want to send me money, that would be okie doke.

"A buh-lessing is that you got up today!"

"Amen," one of the women responds.

"A buh-lessing is that you have your health ! A buh-LESSing is that you have a job!   A buh-LESSing is that you have a car and a place to live!"

Well, my car is fourteen-years-old and has no air conditioning, but I have been blessed with three great children, the most loving, supportive husband I could imagine, a pretty nice house with only six more years on the mortgage, consistently excellent blood pressure numbers and high arches. My nails also grow fairly quickly and aren't prone to splitting or chipping.

"Maybe this boy was being mentally and physically abused and I know about that...I was mentally, physically...in every way abused..."

I'm not sure what to make of this. Back in the Bahamas I was criticizing the Reverend for not talking about the psychological factors that shape us and have a big impact on our openness to thinking transcendently. Here is a woman who seems more than willing to tackle psychological issues, but it's making me uncomfortable.

"One of my favorite Bible verses is 1st Corinthians, chapter 13. Let's go to that please."

Ilsa starts to reach for a Bible and then seems to lose her interest in looking it up. She opts just to listen.

"Love is patient...love is kind...love is never boastful..." Reverend Green reads the familiar verse in its entirety. "All of us have a beautiful spirit in us...some people are fault-finders...if you don't have something nice to say, don't say anything. I coulda took authority with this man...I coulda said, 'I'm the Reverend Debbie Lee Green,' but I didn't. I simply reached out to the little boy with kind words and I made his day. You shoulda seen him when he left...wavin' to me..."

Reverend Green scans her notes.

"Another thing...I had another adventure...I did all these things with my mother and I stopped at Home Depot...I was lookin' for plants...I basically have no green thumb but I want to keep trying and so I found this one plant and it didn't have one of those tags in it that tells the name and explains how to take care of it...so I find this woman who works in the store and I ask her, 'Do you know what kind of plant this is?' and you know what she said to me? She said, 'No, but I had one and it died.' Now, was it an accident that I met this woman?"

The two women near the front shake their heads an emphatic "no!"

"My mom's in the car...she's unhappy for an hour while I'm in the store...and this woman starts to tell me all her problems...I didn't go up to her and say 'I'm Reverend Debbie Lee Green'...but she told me everything that was troubling her and I said, 'through your adversity you shall gain strength'...and you know, her whole face changed...she felt better about herself....I gave her buh-lessings..."

I'm picturing a row of three cars parked outside the Home Depot: in one is a German Shepard, in another, a cocker spaniel and in the third, Reverend Debbie Lee's mother. All three have their noses pressed up into the open crack, sniffing the air in slight desperation.

"I was coming home just late last night...it was 10:30....coming from my mother's...it's a two hour drive...and this little boy is out on the road, without lights on his bike, and I'm thinkin: where is his mother? And I *buh-lllessed* him...I sent my blessings out to him because you don't know what he was doing out there late at night and there is so much trouble in the world and things that could go wrong...so I sent out my love and offered it like a shield...it was a buh-lessing and I shared it with him even though he was a complete stranger...we're all God's children after all, right?"

For the first time in my search for the right church, I'm experiencing a strange mix of both pity and admiration for the minister.

Debbie Lee shares yet another story about a shopping trip, where she and another woman reached for the same outfit, and she told the other woman, "No...please! *You* take it. I want *you* to have it!" This was told to illustrate just how we can be generous with our blessings to other people.

At some point, the Reverend mentions that she doesn't have children and isn't married. From the assortment of personal stories she shares, it would seem that a great deal of her time is spent driving to various stores, speaking to strangers in an effort to be a blessing to them, and then returning to her angry mother who has been left in the car. Reverend Green doesn't bother with things like analyses of great thinkers or writers in the Christian faith–not even of Christ himself, except to mention that he is about love and buh-lessings.

The sermon doesn't really end per se--it just seems to kind of peter out. When it dawns on Reverend Green that the sermon is over, she makes a quick segway into the next activity. "Let's stand up now and praise the Lord in song!"

One of the other women is operating a CD player which is directly under the altar table. Some boppy pop Christian tune starts to thump and Reverend Green and the two women near the front begin to clap and do aerobic-style movements to the music. What is truly amazing is how intense they are about it from the get go. It's as if they have an "On" switch. There's no warming up to it–they hear the first beat of the music and away they go.

The elderly gentleman is standing next to the Reverend doing his own brand of dancing. Although it's a rather crude way to describe it, he seems to be "getting off" on watching Reverend Green as she gyrates her body next to him. Somewhere, mid-song, she spontaneously grabs his head like it's a melon and plants her lips on the top of his bald skull. He blushes like a schoolboy while Debbie Lee goes right on with her aerobics for God.

I'm not sure who looks more absurd: Debbie Lee and the Leettes, waving their arms and shaking their hips like cheerleaders run amok, or me and Ilsa–bending only slightly at the knees and lamely clapping our hands.

After three songs of what feels to me like forced euphoria, Reverend Green instructs us to sit back down. She sings one more song as a send-off. Again, her mighty tenor voice bores straight into our bodies–it won't be dismissed. There's something amazing and sad about listening to her sing. I imagine a foghorn bellowing in the darkness– thinking that its call will protect others or help them find their way...not realizing that it's really calling out because *it* is lonely and lost.

Debbie Lee sends us off with the words: "GO AND BE A BUH-LESSING UNTO THE LORD!"

Here she comes. We step out into the aisle alongside our pew.

"Hi, I'm Reverend Debbie Lee Green," she shakes our hands.

I think she likes saying that she's a Reverend.

We introduce ourselves.

"How did you find out about us?" she asks as she pulls herself in and up to sit atop the pew that was in front of us. She kicks her shoes off and puts her stockinged feet on the seat of the pew where we had just been sitting.

"Well, Ilsa knows some friends that you married..."

"Oh, I do *soooo* many weddings!" the Reverend marvels.

"Mary and Jake Lippscomb?" Ilsa prompts her.

"Oh yeah! How are they doing.....did she have her baby yet?"

"Yes, she did–a little girl."

"Oh, how great for them! It's hard for me to keep up with everyone...I do *so* many weddings all the time!"

Not to mention driving her mom around...

"We're going through a bit of a "cleaning out" time in our church....we used to be full but we had so many gays, to be honest with you....not that I have any problem with someone loving another person like that...but they wanted me to perform marriages in the church and I wouldn't do it....I just don't believe in that....that's not what the Bible tells us...."

We nod our heads, not knowing what else to do.

"I mean, it got so bad that I had to tell them to go away! Can you imagine having to tell people they can't come back to your church? But I did. Now we're going to get to start all over, and you two have been a buh-lessing to be here today. You're a breath of fresh air and I can tell that you're being here is a bleessing for me."

Oh dear. A quick topic change is imperative.

"It must be a challenge to be a woman pastor in what still seems to be primarily a man's profession. I visited your neighbor down the road at Westover Bible Fellowship and he made it clear that he didn't think women should be preachers."

"Oh yeah...none of them like me...." Debbie Lee lets out a gutteral laugh. "I don't care though....you know what? They're just gonna have to get used to me cause I'm not goin' away. It's easier for me to do my ministry when I go out and help people in other places though...it's been harder to keep people in the church."

"How long have you been here?" I ask.

"Ten years."

Wow. Ten years and she's got five people in her congregation. That's two years to bring each person in. Talk about your individual attention.

"But I'm not worried...." Debbie Lee continues on. "The good Lord has put me here for a reason and I'll keep on doing what I do as long as He wants me to do it."

It's amazing how many people in the religious field think that God has called them to it. What about the men driving the garbage trucks? The people who take your change at the toll booth? The burger flippers? Vanna White? Were they called by God? Come to think of it, don't many murderers claim that God instructed them to do it?

We say our goodbyes to Debbie Lee. As we leave, she hands us a song that she wrote. It's called "For the Sake of the Children," and is printed on some computer paper with images of five little multicultural children across the top of the page.

Ilsa and I walk out. When we get closer to the car, I ask her what she thought of the experience.

"Well, I liked the basic message in her sermon," Ilsa says as she pulls on her seatbelt. "We can be blessings to each other, if we try to be."

Oh Ilsa. Sweet, sweet, Ilsa.

"What did you think?" she asks me.

I try to rein in my critical tendencies and be a bit more charitable like Ilsa. "Well, if she had said 'buh-lessing' one more time, I was going to run to the side wall and start banging my head."

Ilsa laughs. "Yeah, she did seem to like that word."

"I guess I felt sorry for her. I feel like she's someone who's in pain...who wants to heal herself through trying to heal others. Unfortunately, you can't help make others whole if you're not whole yourself. That may be why she's having so much difficulty."

When I get home I read the words of Reverend Green's song. It's a disjointed, rambling composition, which includes some rather curious sentiments: "I have seen cultures suffer and die", "I saw my future trapped in an unloved box...", "Our children of the future need our help to set them free."

Still, despite what seem like serious problems with Debbie Lee's potential to attract a big following, you had to give her credit for hanging in there. While the male minister down the street, who surely has his own issues, is preaching that women need to be obedient to men, Debbie Lee is less than a half mile away–boldly sharing her experiences, bellowing her songs and gyrating her hips.

Chapel on the Hill

#	Dimension of Church Experience	Rating
1)	Is parking close and convenient?	8
2)	How beautiful is the worship space?	3
3)	How comfortable is the seating?	6
4)	How welcoming and friendly is the congregation?	1
5)	How enjoyable and uplifting were the musical aspects of the worship?	0
6)	Does the leader have a pleasant speaking voice and does he/she make sense to me?	1
7)	How clean are the bathrooms?	5
8)	How interesting are the people in the pews to stare at?	4
9)	How tolerant to many ways of seeing and doing things does this group appear to be?	3
10)	Would I feel comfortable with how this group would spend my money?	1
11)	How close to God did I feel in this space?	1
12)	Did I smile more than once during the experience?	8
	Total	41

Conclusion

It started back in June and now it's near the end of May. Twelve months spent going to different churches and synagogues. Twenty-one religious denominations, twenty-six churches and synagogues–many visited multiple times. What an odyssey! Before I share with you, gentle reader, what I have concluded about the church or synagogue that's right for me, I need to reflect on the experience as a whole.

Heading out the door on any given Sunday, I never knew what I was going to experience. In retrospect, there were some pretty amazing and wonderful moments, which I never, ever would have predicted: being told by a complete stranger that she loved me; hearing a thirteen-year-old boy talk about feminism in the pulpit; taking in a Carnegie Hall-level performance of sacred music for free; laughing with a bunch of bodacious women who liked to repeat the word "shit" over and over; being told that I was part of the spirit that moved a woman minister to courageously address the concerns of her gender in the pulpit; being held in the quiet, loving presence of a circle of Mennonite women; sitting with a seventy-something crowd of Methodists and traveling back in time to Korea and World War II; meeting all sorts of people who just wanted to help me in whatever way they could.

There were also moments that weren't so pleasant: having to fill out study sheets; hearing the English language being mutilated to an unrecognizable form; seeing a minister begging his congregation for money to bail them out in a hurry; sitting amidst the weary survivors of shipwrecked churches; hearing words written over 2000 years ago being applied to our time with little regard for how we've grown and changed over those 2000 years; realizing that religion can breed a great deal of mental laziness.

It was always a total surprise each time I entered a new house of worship–like unwrapping a Christmas present each place I went. In one church the present might end up being a set of sterling silver candlesticks, in another, a Chia pet.

The only exception to the law of uniqueness was in the case of the Catholics. My husband explained that it was that way because everything was highly centralized and unidirectional: i.e., all roads came from Rome. I suppose that could be comforting for Catholics who like the ritual and want to have the same experience wherever they happened to worship. I found it uninspiring.

Another realization: church people are basically pretty gosh darn nice. As a satirist, I suppose I'm predisposed toward finding things to criticize about people, myself included. While it's true that I didn't hesitate to write about those people who seemed to be...unusual...I'd also like to think that I wrote about a lot of wonderful things I found in people. There was a lot that was wonderful to find. In fact, writing this book solidified my sense that basically, people, and in particular, church people, are really neat.

Oh sure, there are still the moments when you wonder about our species: like when you go to free ice-cream day at the baseball field and you see people pushing and shoving for their Nutty Buddies; or when you read about greedy white collar criminals who steal hundreds of millions and get ten months while a teenager with an ounce of pot gets five years; or when yet another victim of road rage is hugging your bumper as though they'd like to wipe you off the face of the earth. All in all though, going on my quest for the right house of worship made me realize that people have the potential for enormous good.

I was always amazed at the types of outreach activities being carried out in churches. People were volunteering their time for everything from being reading buddies to building houses. And then there is that whole category of "evangelism." In my smugness, I assumed that I was somehow better or less pushy than most of these people scrapping together eight hundred dollars to go to Haiti or Thailand to spread the "Good Word." Why did they have to go over there and foist a foreign ideology on these people? What made their God better than the God the people of the country already had?

But when I saw one woman, who had gone to Thailand, sharing the story of her trip with tears in her eyes and total respect for the cultural traditions of those she visited, I realized that "evangelism" doesn't have to be a bad word. Her goal was to go and offer help to young women who were at high risk for ending up as prostitutes. She helped run the center where they lived and learned skills; she took crochet needles and taught them all how to crochet; she enjoyed laughter and music with them–all in the safety of a center that had been built by those of the Christian faith. There were no conditions placed on the girls–they didn't have to say they were Christian to receive the help. The Christianity was simply the factor that had inspired her and others to devote their time, money and attention to helping these people in need. Done like that, it was a really beautiful thing to witness.

The very first people I met, and the very first words they said to me, seemed to epitomize how nice folks could be. It was the young couple at the Assembly of God church, who showed such an interest in me as a person, and then said, "you can come and sit with us if you'd like to." Complete strangers were asking me if I'd like to sit with them. They didn't want me to feel lonely.

Yes. People can be very sweet.

Here's another realization from my year of church-hopping: a lot of ministers aren't very good at giving sermons. Of the twenty-six churches I attended (five were different Catholic churches), two didn't have preaching: the Christian Scientists and the Quakers. The other twenty-three did. Of those twenty-three, at seven, or roughly one-third, I experienced what I would consider to be good preaching: a coherent message which had a definitive beginning, middle and end, delivered in an engaging and persuasive manner that showed respect for the listening audience. I may not have agreed with the basic premise of some of those sermons, but I would still concede that they were well thought-out within their frame of logic, and well-executed.

That leaves about 66% with speakers who were seriously lacking in one way or another. There were those who ranted or babbled, those who free associated (which is never good), the wannabe stand-up comics, those who appeared bored and those who were so stiff they looked as if they might snap in two.

Maybe there are pastors out there who can't speak well but still tend the herd in a very loving and giving way. My personal feeling is that the sermon is twenty to thirty minutes of the church experience. Add that up over 52 weeks and you've got close to 26 hours in a year spent listening to one person speak. If that person can't speak well, that's 26 hours of squirming, looking at your watch and running your grocery list through your mind. No matter how nice a person he or she is, for me, they've got to be able to give a good sermon.

Another aspect of the twenty-first century church experience that boggled my mind was how women are still relegated to the back of the bus. I've got to admit that it gives me the willies to think that in the year 2005, there are still religious institutions where women can't be the leaders or give sermons. Think about it. God was thought to be female for a long, long time before Judeo-Christian history. Women give birth, they are responsible for nurturing and developing the species, they're brains are anatomically compatible to those of men, they've proven themselves equal to men in every domain imaginable, including that of running nations. Margaret Thatcher, Corazon Aquino and Golda Meir would never have been told to hold their tongues or take their instructions from a man.

Yet in the realm of religion, people go from 2005 to 1005 simply by walking through a door once a week. What is going on here? I have to say that I think the traditional division of the sexes within religion occurs among groups that want to be taken care of–both the women and the men. They need to be told exactly how things are to be done, which relieves stress and makes them happy, I suppose. They like thinking that there is a big, powerful male God in the sky and his son, Jesus Christ, who is looking down on them and thinking of them as little children who need only to be instructed.

I suppose as long as we hold dear to this notion that God is male, women will never be able to feel as empowered as men. And what of the Bible? As a work of literature it's fascinating and often beautiful. But it's not my goal to be literally guided by a two to four thousand year-old document of unknown origins. And even within this seriously flawed work, there are many references to God which suggest that God is as much female as male. Consider the name for God, El Shaddai, which occurs 48 times in the Bible. The Hebrew word for shad is "breast" and ai is an old female ending. This suggests that God is "the breasted one." For those of us who are also breasted, it's a nice thought. It might be a nice thought even for those who don't have breasts. Women have made in-roads which would have never existed thirty years ago. In the churches I attended, ten had women in positions of significant leadership in the service. Seven had women pastors. Still, I only heard three women give sermons in twelve months of traveling from church to church. Hardly what you'd expect in a world where half of all graduates from medical school, humanities doctoral programs and law school are female.

One of the worst experiences in looking for the right place of worship was when I stumbled into the "needy" churches. It's such a bummer. Most of us come to church looking to be uplifted, inspired, refreshed, in other words, we come with needs of our own. When you walk into a place of worship you don't want to find that there is hardly anyone there and the ones who are there are grasping your hands begging you to come back. There are reasons that churches fail and if I may be so bold as to say it, some churches *should* fail.

If you, in your quest for the right place of worship, should happen upon a needy church that seems to be sucking you in, there's no reason for you to suffer needlessly. I recommend doing any one of the following:

    A. Mutter that you think you left your lights on. Leave, jump in your car and peel out.
    B. Ask where the bathroom is. Go in, lock the door and climb out the window.

C. Have it arranged ahead of time for someone to call you on your cell phone within five minutes of entering the church. If you need to escape, walk out, taking the call as though it is crucial.

If I can prevent even just one of you from spending an hour of your life in a dying, needy church, then it will have been worth the suffering I endured to give you this information. The needy church will never satisfy your needs: unless your need is to rescue failing religious institutions with decrepit buildings, poor leadership, no money and oh yeah, no congregation. If that's your thing–you'll have little difficulty finding your cause.

Here's another important conclusion: don't underestimate the value of being entertained in church. Let's face it–a lot of people probably don't go to church or synagogue because they find it boring. Who wants to sacrifice the luxury of sleeping in and the freedom the weekend brings by dragging themselves into a lackluster place week after week out of some sense of duty or obligation? Let me put it another way: do you think *God* wants you to be bored in your experience of worship? My God doesn't. My God wants me to have a wonderful, inspirational, meaningful time when I go to church.

Church should surprise and amaze you! The speakers, the music, the decorations! It should all delight you on a regular basis. In my mind, there should be nothing mediocre about church. Yes, after a time of being in one place, you may find that the community has come to mean so much to you that you can weather a change of minister or a new music director who isn't quite what you'd hoped for. But never ever forget that church is not only a place of comfort but also a place to enrich and hopefully ennoble your mind, body and spirit.

Whenever I felt that someone was merely going through the motions of their job–be it the woman who gave the "kids message," or the priest reciting a prayer, or even a bell-ringer in the choir, the energy of the Spirit seemed to be missing. But when someone did their part with *enthusiasm*, with *presence*, with *passion*, well then, God was at hand and you could feel it! There is nothing wrong with wanting to be engaged and inspired by your church experience–in fact, there is everything right about it. If you find that you're not, I say hit the highway and start looking again.

Another important aspect of the church experience: shared values. Research on married couples shows very clearly that those who are more alike will find the most happiness together. The old saying, "opposites attract," is a myth. Even if they do attract, they are likely to annoy each other over time. The same is probably true of your place of worship. Although it's important to look around and know what's out there, it's also important to know what things you value and look for a place that shares as many of those values as possible, or at least encourages tolerance of differences within the congregation.

Finally, I figure that if God exists, and I tend to think that God does, S/He is everywhere at all times. We have only to close our eyes and still ourselves to reconnect with our Source. Church is not necessary to find or experience God. But there really are significant merits to joining a church or synagogue. Not only will it create the time and space for you to connect with God through prayer, song and meditation, it will provide you with something just as precious: a community of caring people.

Even as an outsider looking in, it was obvious to me that the community aspect of nearly every church was a major, if not THE major source of satisfaction and comfort to those who were members. At the Mennonite church, members stood up one by one and shared intimate details about their physical conditions in front of a room full of people– knowing that their experiences and feelings would be held with care by the group. At the Assembly of God, people gasped and clapped for and laid hands on their fellow parishioners as a show of support and brotherhood. At the Jewish synagogue, they joyfully threw candy at a thirteen-year-old boy to wish him success and prosperity. The Methodists seniors shared their thoughts and ideas, challenging each other with the kind of respect and good-natured banter that only comes from years of being together in the same church. And even the obscenely rich Presbyterians were reaching out, happy to do whatever they could to help, particularly if it was convenient for them and fell within the 60 minutes they had allotted for "spiritual development" in their weekly planners.

So what church did I select? Well, based on my rating form, the Methodists received the highest overall score. I've already started going and have been there at least a half dozen times. I like it. Believe it or not, a part of me wants to keep looking. I don't think twelve months was enough! I know that there are more and more places to be discovered– places I can't even imagine.

And going from church to church over the course of a year has helped me figure out exactly what I want in a worship experience. It's got to be out there somewhere...I just have to keep looking.

It's like this: what I really want is a beautiful old church–not too large, not too small–made of stone and wood with gorgeous stained glass. The sun should stream through the windows in the mornings so that the colors from the glass fall on the laps of the people in the pews.

I want there to be two ministers leading the church–a man and a woman–who are equal in their roles and share all the duties. They should both be excellent speakers who give thought-provoking sermons that are so stimulating and meaningful that you never once want to look at the clock while they're speaking. They should love being on call for the members and happy to help us at any hour of the day or night. They need to believe fervently in God (preferably they've both had credible, direct encounters with God) so that I can tap into their confidence to avoid having to deal with any of my own uncertainty. God must be either genderless or a woman–just to balance out the mighty inequities of the past.

The members of the congregation should be varied in age, race and gender and tolerant to differences. In particular, there will be plenty of nice, wholesome and smart teenagers my daughter's exact age, who will provide her with life-long friendships of the most deep and lasting kind. Their parents will like to drive and insist that they take her to and from evening events at the church–particularly on cold or icy nights when I'm in my terry bathroom watching Law and Order or a documentary on PBS. I should make instant friendships with at least a half dozen very hip, funny and caring women who laugh at my jokes and think that I'm one of the most warm and delightful people they've ever known. My husband and I will receive regular dinner invitations, as well as invitations to other members' beach houses. The beach houses will all have the little outside showers for your feet.

The church should be extremely well-endowed and never once give us sermons about tithing or tell us that there are any financial difficulties. In fact, giving money will be optional and perfectly fine whichever way you choose to go.

And the music. The music must be a holy experience in and of itself–a veritable feast for the ears every single week! Music of the highest caliber–varied and just right for whatever mood I happen to be in on that particular day. The choir members will have been carefully screened and only selected if they sound like songbirds.

Selected parts of the Bible should be used as a guide for worship, but not solely. Other forms of wisdom from other religions should also be included in the services. There will be no big video screens or any other type of technology right in our faces. And *no study sheets* of any kind. There should be good old-fashioned ice cream socials, square dances and potluck suppers, and everyone should be very warm and friendly. Never once will I feel as though I am being judged or criticized by anyone.

Parking must be close–and actually, the church should be so close to my house that on a nice spring day I can just hop on my bike and pedal over.

Downhill both ways.

Give The Gift of

**How to Choose a Church or Synagogue:
A Twenty-One Pew Adventure**

To Your Family and Friends!
Order Here or go to www.sevenstarspress.com

_____ **YES,** I want _____ copies of ***How to Choose a Church or Synagogue: A Twenty-One Pew Adventure****,* for $14.95 each.

Include $2.95 shipping and handling for one book, and $1.95 for each additional book. Pennsylvania residents must include applicable sales tax. Canadian orders must include payment in US funds, with 7% GST added.

Payment must accompany orders. Allow 3 weeks for check clearance and delivery.

My check or money order for $_____ is enclosed.

Name_____

Organization_____

Address_____

City/State/Zip_____

Phone_____
E-mail_____
Questions? Call (610) 917-3021

Make your check payable and return to:
Seven Stars Press
P.O. Box 744
Kimberton, PA 19442